ALBERT SHAW LECTURES ON DIPLOMATIC HISTORY

1899. JOHN H. LATANÉ. The Diplomatic Relations of the United States and Spanish America. (Out of print.)

1900. JAMES MORTON CALLAHAN. The Diplomatic History of the Southern Confederacy. 1901. (Out of print.)

1906. JESSE SIDDALL REEVES. American Diplomacy under Tyler and Polk. 1907. $1.75.

1907. ELBERT JAY BENTON. International Law and Diplomacy of the Spanish-American War. 1908. $1.75.

1909. EPHRAIM DOUGLAS ADAMS. British Interests and Activities in Texas, 1838–1846. 1910. $1.75.

1911. CHARLES OSCAR PAULLIN. Diplomatic Negotiations of American Naval Officers, 1778–1883. 1912. $2.25.

1912. ISAAC J. COX. The West Florida Controversy. 1798–1813. 1918. $3.00.

1913. WILLIAM R. MANNING. Early Diplomatic Relations between the United States and Mexico. 1916. $2.50.

1914. FRANK A. UPDYKE. The Diplomacy of the War of 1812. 1915. $2.75.

1916. PAYSON JACKSON TREAT. The Early Diplomatic Relations between the United States and Japan, 1853–1865. 1917. $2.75.

1921. PERCY ALVIN MARTIN. Latin America and the War. 1925. $3.50.

1926. SAMUEL FLAGG BEMIS. Pinckney's Treaty. A Study of America's Advantage from Europe's Distress, 1780–1800. 1926. $3.00.

1927. BRUCE WILLIAMS. State Security and the League of Nations. 1927. $2.75.

State Security
AND
The League of Nations

THE ALBERT SHAW LECTURES ON DIPLOMATIC HISTORY

By the liberality of Albert Shaw, Ph.D., of New York City, the Johns Hopkins University has been enabled to provide an annual course of lectures on Diplomatic History. The courses are included in the regular work of the Department of History and are published under the direction of Professor John H. Latané.

**THE ALBERT SHAW LECTURES ON
DIPLOMATIC HISTORY, 1927**

State Security
AND
The League of Nations

BY
BRUCE WILLIAMS, Ph. D.
PROFESSOR OF POLITICAL SCIENCE IN THE
UNIVERSITY OF VIRGINIA

BALTIMORE
THE JOHNS HOPKINS PRESS
1927

Copyright 1927
By The Johns Hopkins Press

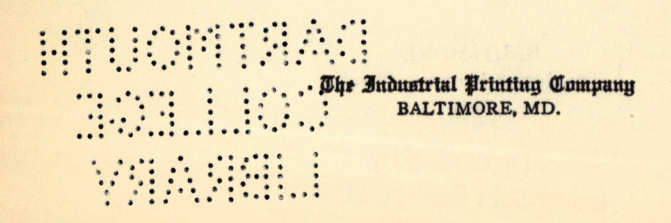

The Industrial Printing Company
BALTIMORE, MD.

TABLE OF CONTENTS

	PAGE
PREFACE	vii

CHAPTER I
INTRODUCTION 1

CHAPTER II
THE PRINCIPLE OF THE RIGHT OF THE STATE TO EXISTENCE .. 43

CHAPTER III
ARTICLE 10 OF THE COVENANT OF THE LEAGUE OF NATIONS .. 63

CHAPTER IV
ARTICLE 16 OF THE COVENANT 120

CHAPTER V
ATTEMPTS TO EXTEND CERTAIN PRINCIPLES OF THE COVENANT ... 151

   I. THE DRAFT TREATY OF MUTUAL ASSISTANCE 151

   II. THE PROTOCOL FOR THE PACIFIC SETTLEMENT OF INTERNATIONAL DISPUTES 182

CHAPTER VI
THE LOCARNO AGREEMENTS 206

CHAPTER VII
CONCLUSION 227

INDEX 341

LIST OF ANNEXES

		PAGE
I.	Selected Articles from the Covenant of the League of Nations	244
II.	Letter of President Wilson to Senator Gilbert M. Hitchcock with Reference to Article 10; March 8, 1920	249
III.	Extracts from the Replies of Certain Governments on the Proposal of Canada to Amend Article 10	253
IV.	Extracts from the Replies of Certain Governments on Resolution XIV of the Third Assembly	266
V.	Text of the Draft Treaty of Mutual Assistance Submitted by the Fourth Assembly to the Members of the League of Nations	277
VI.	Extracts from the Replies of Certain Governments on the Draft Treaty of Mutual Assistance	285
VII.	Text of the Protocol for the Pacific Settlement of International Disputes	295
VIII.	Extracts from the Observations of Certain Governments on the Protocol	306
IX.	Text of the Locarno Agreements	320

"To expect states to disarm, or even to limit armaments, in an atmosphere of distrust, is to expect the impossible. Disarmament, if it is to be more than a promise writ on wind and running water, must be, as it were, a fruit that has ripened to maturity under the influence of mutual trust and common security."

Ernest Barker, *A Confederation of Nations, Its Powers and Constitution.*

PREFACE

During the session of 1919-1920, at the Johns Hopkins University, the writer undertook an examination of certain fundamental principles of conduct which had long characterized the external relations of states. The inquiry centered around topics of the following order: the principle in international law that the state has a right to existence and self-preservation; the attitude of states towards the support or enforcement of the precepts of international law; the prevailing doctrine of neutrality; and the freedom of the state to initiate war at its own discretionary sovereign will. This study was carried forward and accepted in partial fulfillment of the University requirements for the degree of Doctor of Philosophy.

In 1920 the Covenant of the League of Nations had just been drawn and had incorporated a number of principles which had an intimate bearing on the topics enumerated above. The changes introduced by the Covenant in the juristic relations of the states signatory thereto, as contrasted with those which had prevailed under the general principles of international law, were in response to a seemingly widespread demand for a new legal and ethical order in the relations of states. In the Covenant of the League, the right of the Member-states to existence and security was recognized through the principle incorporated in Article 10, and, under this provision, the Members of the League assumed a general obligation to respect and preserve as against external aggression the territorial integrity and political independence of one another. The freedom to initiate war, exercised by the state as an attribute of sovereignty, was, for the Members of the League, limited by covenants to utilize certain processes for the pacific settlement of their disputes and to observe delay before an eventual resort to force. Provisions to enforce the observance of these agreements were embodied in Article 16, and the Members of the League agreed to apply the penalties set forth therein against a state which went to war in violation of its covenants. The provisions of Article 16, introducing as they did material sanctions and collective support to assure observance of the pacific methods embodied in the Covenant, constituted an important modification of the existing principles of neutrality.

In the form in which this investigation was presented as a doctoral thesis chief emphasis was placed upon an analysis of certain legal and ethical relations which existed between states prior to the organization of the League and upon the demands which were current at the time for a change in these relationships. A considerable amount of the material originally used is incorporated in the present study;[1] but as it is now pre-

---

[1] Another portion was used in an article by the writer on "State Morality in International Relations," published in *The American Political Science Review*, XVII, No. 1.

sented, emphasis has been shifted somewhat to the manner in which states have responded to the new system set up by the Covenant and to the efforts which have been made through the League to strengthen and expand that system. The essential purpose of the study, however, remains the same. It is an effort to review certain aspects of the movement within recent years for a more effective juridical order in the society of states and to indicate in some measure the strength and diffusion of the sentiment for international solidarity.

In the spring of 1927, through the generous invitation of Dr. John H. Latané, the author was invited to deliver the Albert Shaw Lectures on Diplomatic History at the Johns Hopkins University. These lectures are published here as chapters three to six inclusive and constitute, indeed, the central portion of the present volume. The inclusion of additional material has been permitted through the courtesy of Dr. Latané and those associated with him in the administration of the Albert Shaw Lectureship.

The publication of this volume enables the author to make some long deferred acknowledgments. Foremost among these, he would place his obligations to Dr. W. W. Willoughby of the Department of Political Science in the Johns Hopkins University. From this distinguished teacher, the author has received invaluable instruction, generous assistance and friendly counsel, and the example of profound and fruitful scholarship. In the same fashion, he would emphasize his indebtedness to Dr. John H. Latané of the Department of History. Dr. Latané has long perceived the necessity of advance in international organization, and his enlightened advocacy of the League of Nations has constantly stimulated the author's interest in that great enterprise. During some months of residence recently at Geneva, the author received uniform courtesy and valuable cooperation from various members of the Secretariat of the League of Nations. He is indebted also to Professor Arthur Kyle Davis, Jr., of the University of Virginia, for a careful and suggestive reading of the manuscript.

A feeling of gratitude to eminent teachers and helpful friends has prompted the above acknowledgments but the author would take care, himself, to assume complete responsibility for the shortcomings of this study.

B. W.

University of Virginia,
June, 1927.

CHAPTER I

INTRODUCTION

I

At the first session of the Institute of Politics held at Williamstown in the summer of 1921, the late Lord Bryce delivered a course of lectures on *International Relations* and in his opening address there occurs the following statement on the relations existing between modern states:

Some few words at the outset about a subject old but never yet exhausted, and not likely to be exhausted, viz.: Human Nature—by which I mean not merely the nature of Man, but Man as he was in a State of Nature. The significance of this point for the study of international relations is that although in civilized countries every individual man is now under law and not in a State of Nature towards his fellow men, every political community, whatever its form, be it republican or monarchical, is in a State of Nature towards every other community; that is to say, an independent community stands quite outside law, each community owning no control but its own, recognizing no legal rights to other communities and owing to them no legal duties. An independent community is, in fact, in that very condition in which savage men were before they were gathered together into communities legally organized.[1]

[1] *International Relations*, p. 3.

There was certainly nothing novel in this analogy between man in a state of nature and the position of independent states in the political system which now for some three centuries and more has been prevailing in world affairs. It was, on the contrary, an old[2] and recurring[3] comparison but is one which receives little support from those who accept the premise of an existing international society and who are sustained by a formula which likewise is old and often utilized, namely, *Ubi societas ibi jus est.* But the persistence of this viewpoint which regards the relations of states as essentially anarchic, and its expression, as in the present case, by a thoughtful and competent observer is, nevertheless, a sort of standing challenge to the assumptions of international jurisprudence. The above comment was made by Lord Bryce during the closing days of his active and varied career, almost on the eve, it may be noted, of the ter-centenary of Grotius, and two years after the signing of the Covenant of the

[2] "Since Nations are composed of men who are by nature free and independent, and who before the establishment of civil society lived together in the state of nature, such Nations or sovereign states must be regarded as so many free persons living together in the state of nature." Vattel, *Le Droit des Gens,* Introd. (1758 ed.).

[3] "Socially, economically and morally there may be a family of nations,—a *societas maxima,*—but, looked at from the point of view of the constitutional jurist, international life is atomistic, non-civic, individualistic. Thus regarded, nations are, as individuals, in that 'state of nature' in which Hobbes, Locke, Rousseau, and the other natural law writers placed primitive man." W. W. Willoughby, *The Fundamental Concepts of Public Law,* pp. 283-284.

INTRODUCTION

League of Nations. It was the sort of commentary which receives only a limited assent but it is worthy to record as a very definite and realistic viewpoint on the general topics with which we are here concerned.

It may properly be objected that the criterion of *law* implied by Lord Bryce in the statement quoted above is too narrow and uncompromising in its nature, but to dwell upon this point would be to rehearse an old controversy which grew out of diverse conceptions of law, and the respective sides of this debate have long since been adequately sustained. It will be well, however, at least to state one other conception of the relations of states, namely, the one which is accepted by those who speak of *international society* and *international law,* and to permit this statement to suffice here as warrant for the usage of those terms. In 1911, Professor Oppenheim wrote a brief but very thoughtful paper on *The Future of International Law* in the course of which he summarized in a clear and succinct manner the essential position of those who assume the existence of a society of nations and who claim a juristic basis for the relations of states:

He who cannot conceive of law apart from a superior power enforcing it on its subjects, may perhaps call the international society of states anarchic, but then he will also have to contest the existence of an international law, and, logically, he should also deny the possibility of the existence of an international society. He, however, who identifies law and order, and who, whenever he finds in any society rules making their appearance which are conceived as compulsory for the conduct of its members, speaks of law—in contrast to morality, the observance of which is left to the conscience of the members—will also be able to speak of law in a society where there is no relation of superior and subject, provided only that the relation between the members is regulated in an ordered manner.[4]

It is a premise of this study that certain of the relations between modern states are regulated in an ordered manner; that in the society of nations there exists a body of rules which are conceived of as compulsory for the members thereof and that these rules may properly be designated as laws.[5] Reference is commonly made to them as the positive law of nations, or as the accepted principles of international law, and they are said to be derived, in the main, from the uniform practices of states and from their conventional agreements. These rules are characterized by a certain precision of content, by a considerable uniformity of interpretation, by a general habitual obedience, and by a recognized justification for enforcement if they are not observed.

To the foregoing general statement, however, it is possible to add certain qualifications and yet retain the conception of a juristic international society. Admitting that the rules referred to above may properly be designated as legal, it is yet manifest that they are lacking in certain attributes common to other rules

[4] *The Future of International Law*, p. 9.

[5] "International rules or principles are entitled to be termed laws, even though they may not properly be spoken of as laws in the sense in which that term is employed in municipal jurisprudence." W. W. Willoughby, *op. cit.*, p. 298 (note).

which operate more effectively as forms of external compulsion. For example, a learned student of international jurisprudence has recently declared that "most important of all, international law still lacks an essential constituent element of real law, namely, effective means for enforcing respect for its commands and prohibitions."[6] Other defects of these rules, measured by the standards of "real law," are due in considerable measure to the lack of proper agencies to give them that definite and authoritative expression which municipal law receives through legislative and judicial declaration.

But apart from these obvious limitations of the rules which are designated as international law, there is another general condition which affects the strength and effectiveness of the juristic order of the society of states. Many of the vital issues in international relations have never been brought within the domain of international law at all but operate in what has been termed the "non-legal areas" of international life.[7]

---

[6] J. W. Garner, *Recent Developments in International Law*, p. 810. He adds: "It is believed that the only means by which this difficult task can be achieved is through international cooperation and organization under which the states of the world will agree to employ their joint power to restrain or punish those which violate their international obligations as they are defined by the law."

[7] "The occupation of these non-legal areas in international life by legal relationships, the change from a dynamic to a static situation, can come about only gradually and by the agreement of its members, gradually by tacit consent or through conscious agreement to reduce the dynamic to the static, reached in part by diplomatic adjustment, in part by law-making treaties, in

From this condition there results a clash of interests between states for which custom and usage afford no juridical basis for adjustment and concerning which conventional agreements are likewise wanting. Faced by situations of this order, states have necessarily acted independently of legal considerations, and, in consequence, many of the most vital and disturbing issues in international relations are not susceptible to settlement by law but are left to the hazards of political adjustment. In short, therefore, the contention that the present social order among states has produced a juristic society does not preclude the admission that the rules springing therefrom are deficient when judged by the standards of municipal or "real law" and that the juristic order itself is one of inadequate scope and imperfect organization.

It is something of a platitude to say that the past few years have been characterized by an almost unprecedented activity directed towards reconstructing and advancing the principles of international jurisprudence.[8] Some of these efforts represent attempts to expand and supplement the existing body of law in

---

part by the creation of an international judicial jurisdiction." J. S. Reeves, "International Society and International Law," *A. J. I. L.*, XV, p. 372.

[8] "Whether fairly or not, the world regards international law today as in need of rehabilitation; and even those who have a confident belief in its future will probably concede that the comparatively small part that it plays in the sphere of international relations as a whole is disappointing." J. L. Brierly, "The Shortcomings of International Law," *British Year Book of International Law*, 1924, p. 4.

order to bring under regularized control conduct which is now often left to the arbitrary will of the individual state.[9] There has been likewise a tendency to reexamine some of the fundamental concepts of the existing international law with respect to their conformity to changing standards of international right and justice. Many practices of states, based upon certain fundamental doctrines of the law, have been questioned from the standpoint of ethical validity and a demand has been put forward for a revision of these doctrines and for the acceptance by states of a new statement of their rights and obligations. Attention may be directed here in a brief and introductory fashion to some of the topics around which a good deal of this speculation and discussion has centered.

We may take in the first instance the matter of the claim of the individual members of international society to existence and security. Almost any standard treatise on the law of nations enumerates as one of the fundamental principles of international law, "the right of the state to existence."[10] In the statement of this doctrine, moreover, there was long the persistence of the dogma, drawn from the principles of natural law philosophy, that this right was an "absolute" or unlimited one and that the state concerned at a given time was the sole authoritative judge of the conduct necessary to protect and conserve its existence. From the

[9] Cf. the author's article, "Prospective Development of International Law," *Virginia Law Review*, XI, pp. 169-182.

[10] Various statements of the doctrine are given below, Chap. II.

actual conduct of states there has developed a considerable body of practices commonly treated by publicists under the title of the "rights of the state to self-preservation." For some of these practices warrant can be derived from the accepted principles of law; but others candidly transcend the law; they are frequently grouped under the formula of "acts of necessity" and justification for them, if sought at all, must usually be placed on a moral basis.

The early days of the World War witnessed an act which brought to the forefront of discussion the whole question of the type of conduct which a state may justifiably follow under the plea of protecting its existence. "We are in a state of legitimate defence, and necessity knows no law" said the German Chancellor in extenuation of the conduct of his Government for the invasion of Belgium. "Anyone in such grave danger as ourselves, and who is struggling for his supreme welfare, can only be concerned with the means of extricating himself."[11] The plea of the German Government was not without precedent in the previous conduct of states; excellent warrant could, in fact, be found for it in the precepts of certain writers on the law of nations, but it met with stern condemnation from large elements of the world opinion of the day. Two years later, the American Institute of International Law, with obvious reference to the matter, made the following declaration:

[11] J. B. Scott, *Diplomatic Documents Relating to the Outbreak of the European War*, I, p. 381.

Every nation has the right to exist, and to protect and to conserve its existence; but this right neither implies the right nor justifies the act of the state to protect itself or to conserve its existence by the commission of unlawful acts against innocent and unoffending states.[12]

During the same year, at the annual meeting of the American Society of International Law, Mr. Elihu Root took the above, and the other Declarations of the Institute on the "Fundamental Rights and Duties of Nations," as the subject of his Presidential address. In the following terms, he dwelt upon the consequences of the exercise of this right of self-preservation, in the manner invoked by Germany, upon the corresponding rights of other states and the effect upon the structure of international law if such practices continued to prevail:

The principles of action upon which the war was begun involve a repudiation of every element of fundamental right upon which the law of nations rests. The right of every nation to continued existence, to independence, to exclusive jurisdiction over its own territory, and equality with other nations, is denied. The right of any strong nation to destroy all those alleged rights of other nations in pursuit of what it deems to be useful for its own protection or preservation is asserted. Under this view what we have been accustomed to call fundamental rights would become mere privilege to be enjoyed upon sufferance according to the views of expediency held by the most powerful. If this view prevails the whole structure of modern international law will be without foundation.[13]

[12] For texts of the Declarations, see *A. J. I. L.* X, pp. 212-213.
[13] *A. J. I. L.* X, p. 215.

It was hardly adequate to the situation, however, merely to go on repeating that the state has a right to existence and to indulge in a condemnation of Germany, however justifiably made, for the application in her own behalf of a principle so universally held in esteem. The real basis of the problem lay in the order existing in international affairs which, in truth, was almost deserving of the term "anarchic." All states claimed the right to existence; it was a right universally proclaimed as one of the fundamental principles of the law of nations, but like all other "rights" under international law it was in the form merely of a "declared" and not a "protected" interest.[14] Each state under the existing order was, in the last analysis, the sole guardian of its own existence and the measures which states employed for self-protection were dictated by considerations of their own interests rather than by a regard for those which lay beyond their borders. States in general accepted the dictum of Hall on the matter and followed their own "conscientious judgment" as to the conduct which was essential to ward off a threatening danger:

In the last resort [said Hall] almost the whole of the duties of states are subordinated to the right of self-preservation. Where law affords inadequate pro-

[14] "The present methods of enforcing international rights partake almost wholly of the nature of 'self-help'. In so far, however, as a nation employing them correctly interprets its rights, it is enforcing international law and gives to it 'sanction'." A. J. Peaslee, "The Sanction of International Law," *A. J. I. L.* X, p. 328.

INTRODUCTION

tection to the individual he must be permitted, if his existence is in question, to protect himself by whatever means may be necessary; and it would be difficult to say that any act not inconsistent with the nature of a moral being is forbidden, so soon as it can be proved that by it, and it only, self-preservation can be secured.[15]

The invasion of Belgium, therefore, did something more than imperil the structure of international law. It revealed its grave inadequacy with respect to the protection of an interest which states regard as supremely important and raised the problem of a social protection of this interest if the prevailing and arbitrary methods of self-help were to be restrained.

The traditional attitude of states toward violations of international law was another subject of sharp reexamination during the course of the World War and the years which immediately followed. In theory, the law of nations admitted the right of states to protest against and to redress infractions of its provisions, but there had been little emphasis on an *obligation*[16] in this connection and states had generally refrained from

---

[15] *International Law*, p. 278. (7th ed.)

[16] "When a state grossly and patently violates international law in a matter of serious importance, it is competent to any state, or to the body of states, to hinder the wrong-doing from being accomplished, or to punish the wrong-doer. Liberty of action exists only within the law. . . . Whatever may be the action appropriate to the case, it is open to every state to take it. International law being unprovided with the support of an organized authority, the work of police must be done by such members of the community of nations as are able to perform it. It is however for them to choose whether they will perform it or not." Hall, *Ibid.*, p. 56.

action unless their own immediate interests were involved. The condition was not one which reflected great credit on the effectiveness and binding force of international law. Much indeed, had been written about its sanctions; they were said to exist in such forms as moral disapprobation, as economic and financial pressure, and ultimately in the form of intervention by force.[17] But these measures were lacking both in organization and in assured and appropriate application. The need of a change in theory and practice was manifest. We may be permitted, perhaps, to quote once more a statement of Mr. Root which represented the trend of large elements of opinion at a time when violations of international law were more conspicuous than its observance:

If the law of nations is to be binding, if the decisions of tribunals charged with the application of that law to international controversies are to be respected, there must be a change in theory, and violations of the law of such a character as to threaten the peace and order of the community of nations must be deemed to be a violation of the right of every civilized nation to have the law maintained and a legal injury to every nation. . . . International laws violated with impunity must soon cease to exist and every state has a direct interest in preventing those violations which if permitted to continue would destroy the law. Wherever in the world the laws which should protect the independence of nations, the inviolability of their territory, the lives and property of their citizens, are violated, all other

[17] R. F. Roxburgh, "The Sanction of International Law," *A. J. I. L.* XIV, pp. 26-37.

nations have a right to protest against the breaking down of the law.[18]

Subsequent opinion on the matter went much further than merely endorsing the right of nations "to protest against the breaking down of the law." It advocated the assumption of common obligations on the part of states to apply organized and effective penalties against a state which violated certain fundamental rules of conduct. The wide-spread scope and strength of this opinion was strikingly manifested in the various projects which at the time were springing up for a future "League of Nations." This movement, as it went forward during the World War, has been the subject of a comprehensive survey at the hands of M. Christian L. Lange, and it is instructive here to quote his comment on these antecedents of the League with respect to their endorsement of the principle of sanctions for the proposed international engagements:

Before the war the sanctions of international law were exclusively of a moral order and in general pacifists were convinced that the pressure of public opinion would be sufficient to enforce the observance of engagements between states. It is an historic fact that, without exception, arbitral awards have always been respected. Would it be the same for the basic engagements proposed for the Society of Nations, notably, the one for the observance of a delay before the actual opening of hostilities? Would moral sanctions suffice? Most authors who have drawn up programs express doubt concerning this. So far as I am aware, only "The World Court League" and "The Danish Peace Society" propose to maintain the pre-war condition. . . .

[18] "The Outlook for International Law," *A. J. I. L.* X, pp. 8-9.

It is evident that it was not without hesitation that other internationalists committed themselves to a new program—that of endorsing material sanctions to secure the fulfilment of international agreements. But they concluded that the exceptional magnitude of the evils which had been revealed by the outbreak of the Great War would demand a correspondingly exceptional remedy. In the first document of the "Bryce Group" which was circulated confidentially there were quoted the words of John Stuart Mill, namely that, "Small remedies for great evils do not produce small effects, they produce no effects." This was the sentiment which prevailed; a new departure was necessary even though it entailed some limitation on the sacred principle of "national sovereignty."[19]

It was manifest, of course, that the recognition by states of the obligation to support the general principles of international law, or even to guarantee the observance of specific covenants to which they were parties, would necessarily imply some departure from the traditional practice of neutrality. But the issues raised by the World War had provoked indeed some considerable doubt as to the ethical justification of this principle.[20] According to the prevailing theory and

[19] "Préparation de la Société des Nations pendant la guerre," in *Les Origines et L'Œuvre de la Société des Nations*, I, pp. 52-53.

[20] "The feeling has undoubtedly grown up that the intimate relations of the civilized world in modern times with its corresponding interdependence of nations in intercourse with each other and the more highly developed conscience of the world demand a fresh edition of neutrality, and there is a tendency to expect that states should assume a moral obligation to take positive action as regards the great issues of the struggle to enforce the canons of international law and to give effect to their sympathies with the cause of one belligerent group or the

practice, the neutral nation was enjoined to observe a strict impartiality toward the conflicting parties. The doctrine was certainly not without merit, given the circumstances under which a resort to war might be practiced in international relations. The presence or absence of just claims was not a conditioning factor; it rested with the discretionary judgment of each independent state to determine the circumstances under which it would institute war against another.[21] In the case of conflicts provoked by a clash of essentially selfish and particular interests, a doctrine could scarcely be condemned which sought to restrict the area of violence and to preserve the normal and peaceful relationships of states in general. On the other hand, was it consistent with the duty of nations to remain passive when some fundamental question of international right and wrong was in the balance? The late war and the problems of international organization which arose thereafter revived considerable interest in the precepts on neutrality which had been laid down by the natural

---

other by ranging themselves with it instead of standing out of a struggle which is deciding the future development of the world." G. G. Phillimore, "The Future Law of Neutrality," *Transactions of the Grotius Society*, IV, p. 44.

[21] "The right of a State initiating war with respect, either to the mode and extent of the pressure which it may bring to bear upon its enemy, or to the scope of its just claims upon and obligations towards neutral powers, is determined by principles of law which remain generally unaffected by the presence or absence of conditions to be regarded as justifying recourse to armed conflict." C. C. Hyde, *International Law Chiefly as Interpreted and Applied by the United States*, II, p. 190.

law writers on international law. The spirit of their teaching on the subject had been expressed in the writings of Westlake:

There is no general duty of maintaining the condition of neutrality. On the contrary, the general duty of every member of a society is to promote justice within it, and peace only on the footing of justice, such being the peace which alone is of much value or likely to be durable. . . . Neutrality is not morally justifiable unless intervention in the war is unlikely to promote justice, or could do so only at a ruinous cost to the neutral.[22]

But it was easier to admonish the promotion of justice in this abstract and general fashion than it was to determine, in the case of international wars, the side upon which the cause of justice lay. If nations were to abandon the practice of neutrality, there must first be established some criterion of a *just* or an *unjust* war; some definite principles and procedure which would warrant a departure by states from an attitude of abstention to one of the active support of justice. The problem was always raised as to the conditions

[22] *International Law*, II, pp. 161-162. (1907 ed.)

In 1917 Professor Nippold wrote the following: "It should not be forgotten today that Christian Wolff, in his *Jus Gentium*, 1749, took the view that every state was bound to render assistance to every other that conducted a *just* war, whereas no state dare support a state whose war was *unjust*. The right to remain neutral was, therefore, limited to those cases where the justness of a war was doubtful. Lammasch is right when he says that this is the most nearly perfect ethical conception of the rights and obligations of neutrals." *Development of International Law After the World War*, p. 46.

INTRODUCTION

under which one state might justifiably resort to war against another.

How, in fact, did the existing principles of international law meet this situation? Under these, war was recognized, said the authorities[23]; but with respect to the circumstances under which the state might justifiably redress its alleged wrongs by a resort to force, the law in general exercised no control. As an eminent constitutional jurist said:

Each independent state has full discretionary legal right to determine when, and under what circumstances, and for the attainment of what purposes, it will declare or threaten war against another state or take any other aggressive action toward it.

But note the consequences of this condition, and the remedy proposed. He continued:

Thus, at a stroke, all possibility of illegal acts upon its part is rendered impossible unless it be held that the exercise of a legal right by a state which is in violation of the fundamental principles of justice upon which international jurisprudence is itself founded is, regarded in the light of that jurisprudence, an illegal act, and, therefore, one that is voidable by those injured by it, if not void *ab initio*. Not to admit the foregoing conclusion destroys the foundation upon which international society rests.[24]

---

[23] "As international law is destitute of any judicial or administrative machinery, it leaves states, which think themselves aggrieved, and which have exhausted all peaceable methods of obtaining satisfaction, to exact redress for themselves by force. It thus recognizes war as a permitted mode of giving effect to its decisions." Hall, *op. cit.*, p. 61.

[24] W. W. Willoughby, "Principles of International Law and Justice Raised by China at the Washington Conference," *Proceedings, American Society of International Law*, 1922, pp. 21-22.

Thus it was proposed that war, conducted by a state in violation of fundamental principles of justice, be regarded as illegal in the light of international jurisprudence, or, in other words, that the exercise of the legal right to engage in war, assumed by the state in its sovereign capacity, and heretofore recognized by international law, should henceforth be subjected to restraint by international law itself.

That some sort of international juridical restraint on this legal competency of states should be developed has been an often reiterated demand in recent years. Even while the World War was in progress a publicist of distinction went so far as to assert that:

The entire world has, properly, a right to consider whether an alleged grievance is a justifiable and sufficient cause for making war. It has, further, a right to intervene when an alleged cause is unfounded, and to do its utmost to prevent the commencement of contemplated hostilities, or their continuance if they have already begun. . . . Nowadays the question whether war is to be held just or unjust is one that concerns not only the sphere of international ethics, involving the recognition of the moral conscience of humanity, with the inevitable distinction between good conduct and bad; it concerns also the domain of international law, involving the recognition of the juridical consciousness

---

"If the State is absolute, has no superior, and is subject to no law, then it is impossible to organize the world in a juristic sense; and there must ever remain as many ungoverned, ungovernable, and purely arbitrary entities as there are Sovereign States, thus ensuring perpetual anarchy in the realm of international relations." D. J. Hill, *World Organization and the Modern State*, pp. 21-22.

of mankind, with its inevitable distinction between right conduct and wrongful.[25]

There was, in fact, no shortcoming of international law more fundamental than its failure to restrict the arbitrary resort to war on the part of the members of the society of nations. We have noted the above statement of Hall[26] that international law recognized war as a permitted mode of giving effect to its decisions. But he added the following significant observation:

Theoretically therefore, as it professes to cover the whole field of the relations of states which can be brought within the scope of law, it ought to determine the causes for which war can be justly undertaken; in other words, it ought to mark out as plainly as municipal law what constitutes a wrong for which a remedy may be sought at law.[27]

That no such expansion of international law had come about was indeed at variance with the whole conception which had grown up respecting the proper mode of state action in the constitutional or municipal sphere. In the modern constitutional state, every act of the state was deemed to be in pursuance of some principle of law and in the municipal juristic order there did not exist those "non-legal areas" in which the state might act in an arbitrary and discretionary manner. Was it not a logical development that, in the international sphere as well, there should be juridical

---

[25] Coleman Phillipson, *International Law and the Great War*, pp. 1-2.

[26] See above, p. 17.

[27] Hall, *op. cit.*, p. 61.

rules, the product of an international jural consciousness, which would limit and prescribe the course of state action in the use of remedies for the redress of alleged wrongs?[28] "Never before in the history of mankind," one writer asserted shortly prior to 1914, "has it been so clearly perceived as at the present moment, that the whole of civilization is based upon the existence of guarantees that force shall not prevail until the voice of justice has been heard."[29]

"That force shall not prevail until the voice of justice has been heard," such was the substance of the claim which after July, 1914, was so widely expressed in the society of nations. And along with this demand there was necessarily associated the movement for a more comprehensive system for the pacific settlement of international disputes. There was, of course, considerable divergence of opinion as to the appropriate nature and scope of the projected system; in certain quarters it was advocated that the legal "right" of the individual state to resort to war be completely abolished and that a system of universal compulsory arbitration be established in its stead. In the opinion of

[28] "The solid ground for the justification of international guarantees based on juristic conceptions is found in the essentially juristic character of the Modern State. . . . Every modern nation aspires to the enjoyment of constitutional guarantees . . . . and it is difficult to see, how this general movement, following upon the lines of development throughout the world, can logically terminate in a refusal to recognize in international affairs the principles it has evoked and applied in national affairs." D. J. Hill, *op. cit.*, pp. 149-150.

[29] D. J. Hill, *op. cit.*, p. 150.

others, a less ambitious program was supported as being more expedient and more likely to be achieved.[30] Perhaps the general principle upon which there was the nearest approach to common accord was stated by President Wilson in his address on May 27, 1916, before the American League to Enforce Peace. Expressing on this occasion what he believed to be "the mind and wish" of the American people, he declared the support of the United States Government of "an universal association of nations. . . . to prevent any war begun either contrary to treaty covenants or without warning and full submission of the causes to the opinion of the world."

II

Enough has perhaps been said in the foregoing pages to indicate the nature of certain demands which have

[30] The various proposals for pacific procedure, advanced after the outbreak of the World War, either by individual writers or through unofficial programs for a League of Nations, are exhaustively reviewed by M. Lange in the article referred to above. The unofficial French programs advocated compulsory settlement for all disputes and the majority of pacifist organizations in the northern European neutral states supported this principle. The following comment of M. Lange is of interest, particularly in view of subsequent developments within the League of Nations: "The most remarkable fact of this discussion was the unanimity of the Anglo-Saxon authors who were content to recommend the more modest formula—that of an engagement to observe delay before the opening of hostilities. . . . It was not by chance that both English and American writers are in agreement. They know the burden of the proposed material sanctions will fall upon their own states; they must not, therefore, frighten their governments by excessive demands." *Op. cit.*, pp. 51-52.

been put forward during recent years for a strengthening of the juridical order of the society of states. These claims were urged on a basis of reason and morality; they emphasized the duties rather than the rights of states, and they were presented as principles of ethical import which, in the opinion of their proponents, should be incorporated into the law of nations. If the menace of exaggerated and unjustifiable measures of self-preservation on the part of states were to be eliminated, was it not essential that the law be expanded by creating adequate international guarantees of state existence and security? Should not the law itself be strengthened by adding to it that constituent of real law which would impel respect and obedience to its commands and precepts? And should not the existing practice of leaving international disputes to settlement by force, initiated at will by individual states, be superseded, at least in part, by obligatory processes of international justice? Such were some of the demands put forward for reconstructing and developing the system of international law which prevailed at the outbreak of the World War.

Within certain limits an effort was made to promote development along these lines through the Covenant of the League of Nations. But a word should be said at this point on the relation of the provisions of the Covenant to the general principles of international law. We are not assuming that the changes introduced by the Covenant in the legal relations of the Members of the League have been assimilated to, and have correspondingly modified, the general principles of the law of nations. The League Covenant is a treaty to which the vast majority, but not all, of the members of the international community are parties. As such, it has produced important changes in the legal relations of its Members; but, from a strictly legal viewpoint, it has left unchanged the general body of the law of nations.[31] Yet if we are seeking to trace the growth and strength of an international opinion which advocates changes in the international legal order, the most striking contemporary expression of this opinion was certainly manifested in the creation of the League, and the response of states to the system thus set up is of vast significance in any study of the trend of international legal institutions.

As has been said, the Covenant incorporated in some degree the principles which have been outlined above. Perhaps this statement should be briefly amplified. The principle that the state should have some external guarantee of its existence and security was recognized in Article 10 of the Covenant, through which the Members of the League undertook "to respect and preserve as against external aggression the territorial integrity

[31] Note, however, the tendency toward the development of penalties as discerned by Professor Hyde: "With or without the instrumentality of the League of Nations, or the processes developed in the Covenant thereof, the society of nations appears to be no longer disposed to leave merely to the mercies of an aggrieved State, whether strong or weak, and to the application of penalties of its own devising, the international law-breaker whose offense is deemed to have attained the character of an international felony." *International Law*, I, p. 11 (note).

and political independence of all the Members of the League." In substance, the "right of existence" of the Members of the League was advanced through this treaty agreement from the stage of an interest "recognized" or "declared" by the general principles of international law, to that of an interest "protected" by this international treaty. It is true that the measures for assuring this protection were stated in a somewhat vague and inexplicit form. In the case of external aggression, the Council of the League was merely to "advise upon" the means by which this obligation should be fulfilled. Without dwelling at this point on the various interpretations of Article 10 which have been put forward, the opinion may here be offered that under this Article, the Members of the League assumed, for the mutual protection of one another, international obligations of a legal character.[32]

Although the means for enforcing the provisions of Article 10 are not defined in the Covenant, in another connection the treaty more definitely embodied the principle of "sanctions." In Articles 12, 13, and 15 of the Covenant, the Members of the League agreed to observe, before a resort to war, certain processes designed to facilitate the peaceful settlement of their disputes. Article 16 outlines the penalties for the nonobservance of the procedure thus laid down. These sanctions, subject to the provisions of Article 17 of the Covenant, are applicable only in the cases specified in Article 16, but within these limits they record an effort

[32] See below, Chap. III.

to introduce into one branch of international law, namely, international treaties, the element of enforced compulsory obedience of its precepts. And "the fulfillment of their duties under Article 16", so the Second Assembly of the League declared, "is required from Members of the League by the express terms of the Covenant, and they cannot neglect them without a breach of their treaty obligations."[33]

The acceptance of the provisions of Article 16 signified in some measure a renunciation by the Members of the League of the status of neutrality which, under the general principles of international law, they were free to assume in the presence of international wars. Given the clearly established facts that a state has resorted to war in violation of the Covenant, the remaining Members of the League cannot, without a breach of their treaty obligations, assume an attitude of abstention and indifference toward the ensuing conflict. The extent to which the provisions of the Covenant have modified the principles of neutrality for League Members is intimately associated with the nature and scope of the obligations assumed by these states under Article 16, and this latter question is the subject of detailed treatment later.[34] But it may be noted here that there has been a tendency to over-estimate the scope of the changes introduced by the Covenant in the traditional doctrine of neutrality. The Covenant does not mark for the Members of the

[33] *Resolutions and Recommendations*, Second Assembly.
[34] See below, Chap. IV.

League a general abdication of the principle. There is still the possibility of "legal" war within the system set up by the League of Nations and so long as this exists the traditional practice of neutrality continues applicable to its Members.[35]

As to the restraint instituted by the Covenant on the pre-existing rights of its Members to initiate war, a brief reference only will here suffice. The covenant to observe delay before the eventual opening of hostilities is the significant principle in this connection. The League system adapted to its uses three long established methods for the adjustment of international controversies—arbitration, judicial settlement, and commission of inquiry. Any dispute between the contracting parties likely to lead to a rupture must be submitted to some one of these three methods of possible adjustment. And the Members of the League have agreed "in no case to resort to war until three months after the award of the arbitrators or the judicial decision, or the report by the Council."[36]

III

What has been the response of states to the principles thus embodied in the Covenant and what has been their attitude towards subsequent efforts made through

[35] The whole question is authoritatively discussed in an article by Georg Cohn, entitled, "Neutralité et Société des Nations," in *Les Origines et L'Œuvre de la Société des Nations*, II, pp. 153-204.

[36] Article 12 of the Covenant.

the League to broaden and expand these principles? The observation is sometimes made—and not without foundation—that the facts of international life and the actual practices of states do not accord with the theoretical assumptions of international law — that these facts are frequently given a "juristic or metaphysical cast to make them fit the theory."[37] It is important to avoid the recurrence of a similar disharmony between any theoretical assumptions regarding a "new law of nations" and the facts of international life which actually exist. It is the writer's belief that we are, indeed, in a period of development and change in the legal relations of states and that certain of the principles embodied in the Covenant of the League are becoming a part of the "juridical consciousness of mankind." But the degree and nature of this change should be the subject of constant measurement not only to preserve a consonance between fact and theory but to offer guidance as well for future constructive activity in the field of international jurisprudence.

The Covenant of the League of Nations, while not contemplating necessarily a membership embracing all states, was drafted on the principle that the new legal relationships set up should apply equally to all states

[37] "The seventeenth- and eighteenth-century theory of international law grew out of and was an interpretation of the facts, whereas the nineteenth- and twentieth-century applications of that theory to the facts of the political world since the middle of the nineteenth century do not interpret and grow out of the facts, but give the facts a juristic or metaphysical cast to make them fit the theory." Pound, "Philosophical Theory and International Law," *Bibliotheca Visseriana*, I, p. 75.

within the League. The evolution of the Covenant, however, has raised the question as to whether all of its principles are appropriate to a scheme of universal application and has prompted in certain quarters the belief that some must be utilized in a more restricted manner. What, for example, is the validity of the following conclusion of the Polish Government which occurs in its reply to the League on Resolution XIV, of the Third Assembly? "Inter-state military guarantees can be effective only within a radius of the direct common interests of individual states or groups of states. This community of interests is the foundation of all association, and constitutes a live and genuine guarantee."[38]

The general question may be illustrated by referring once more to Article 10. Here is a guarantee of territorial integrity and political independence participated in alike by all the Members of the League. But what is the strength and diffusion of the sentiment in the various states to sustain the obligations thus assumed? At the meeting of the First Assembly of the League, the Canadian Delegation proposed a motion that "Article 10 of the Covenant of the League of Nations be and is hereby struck out." Debate on the Canadian proposal went forward through the organs of the League over a period of four years and drew expressions which ranged from an assertion by a delegate of Canada that "if Article 10 were retained in the Covenant, a seed of dissolution would be retained which

[38] See below, Annex IV.

INTRODUCTION 29

would unfailingly destroy the League of Nations," to a declaration by a representative of France that "to deprive the League of Nations of Article 10 would be to sign its death warrant."[39] In the end, in deference to the Canadian Delegation, an interpretative resolution on the Article was presented to the Assembly; it received one dissenting vote and was accepted with obvious reluctance by a number of additional Members.[40] This resolution emphasizes the freedom of the constitutional authorities of each member of the League to decide, in what degree, it is bound to employ military forces in the execution of its obligations under the Article. An analysis of the attitude of the various states Members of the League on the Canadian proposal is an instructive means of determining both the strength of the demand for state security and the prospects of providing it through a principle of guarantee of universal application.[41]

The discussions which have centered around Article 16 of the Covenant afford likewise a means of measuring the manner in which states are responding to the new relationships. The Second Assembly of the League voted a series of amendments to Article 16 and adopted a body of resolutions for the guidance of the Member states pending the ratification of the proposed amend-

[39] See below, p. 104.

[40] Persia voted in the negative; Panama, Finland, Latvia, Esthonia, Lithuania, Poland, and Czechoslovakia were among the states which were absent or abstained from voting.

[41] Extracts from the replies of various Governments on the proposal are given in Annex III.

ments. None of these amendments have received the number of ratifications necessary to bring them into force and it seems unlikely that such approval will be forthcoming.[42] But the points of view expressed within the League on the proposed amendments throw an interesting light on the evolution of the principle of sanctions and on the importance attached by certain states to the principle of neutrality. The antecedents of the movement to amend Article 16 are of interest in this connection. When the Covenant was being drafted at Paris, the representatives of the Danish Government proposed to the League of Nations Commission that the Article on sanctions should incorporate provisions of the following order: first, that in designating states to participate in military and economic sanctions, account should be taken by the League of the special difficulties which participation in these measures might occasion for certain states by reason of their geographical or military position; second, that the states whose cooperation was desired in the application of these measures should be invited to take part in the deliberations and decisions respecting the use of such measures; and third, that the privilege of declaring permanent neutrality should be reserved to those states which by their history and pacific policy

[42] None were in force at the time of this writing, June 1, 1927. Cf. Manley O. Hudson, "Amendments of the Covenant of the League of Nations," *Harvard Law Review*, XXXVIII, No. 7, pp. 933-936.

could offer satisfactory guarantees of impartiality.[43] The second of the above provisions was met by Article 4 of the Covenant; the acceptance of the first was the object sought by the Scandinavian states in the amendments to Article 16 which they presented at the First Assembly of the League. These proposals, and the efforts of the League to prepare some organized scheme for the application of its economic weapon, resulted in the action on Article 16 by the Second Assembly to which reference has been made above. Among the resolutions adopted at that time for the guidance of Members of the League in connection with the application of Article 16, the following may be noted. It was declared, for example, that "it is the duty of each Member of the League to decide for itself whether a breach of the Covenant has been committed," and that "the unilateral action of the defaulting state cannot create a state of war: it merely entitles the other Members of the League to resort to acts of war or to declare themselves in a state of war with the Covenant-breaking state; but it is in accordance with the spirit of the Covenant that the League of Nations should attempt, at least at the outset, to avoid war, and to restore peace by economic pressure."[44]

At least one general deduction may be made as a result of the evolution to date of the principles embodied in Articles 10 and 16. Although they set up

[43] Cf. P. Munch, "Les États neutres et le Pacte de la Société des Nations," in *Les Origines et L'Œuvre de la Société des Nations*, I, pp. 173-178.

[44] *Resolutions and Recommendations*, Second Assembly.

general obligations of a legal nature, it is for the individual states, and not for an organ of the League, to decide when a *casus fœderis* has arisen, and furthermore, in accordance with the traditions of international law, the individual states are accorded the right to judge the scope of their obligations under these Articles. The point is of major importance in appraising the juristic character of the League.

IV

But such developments as these did not meet the requirements of the Members of the League who were chiefly concerned with the problem of state security. The assent of such states to a liberal construction of Articles 10 and 16 was given perhaps on the assumption that some supplementary system of security would be developed under the auspices of the League which would provide precise and adequate guarantees of national safety. It becomes necessary, therefore, at this point to direct attention to this phase of the League's activity.

It should be noted at once, however, that there was not, in these proposed supplementary systems, a renunciation of League principles of external guarantees, of sanctions, or of restraints on the use of force. On the contrary, these subsequent developments are attempts to expand these principles. And in the first effort, at least, an attempt was made to extend and apply certain of these principles within a more restricted geographical area than that which was contemplated by the Covenant.

INTRODUCTION

The whole question here becomes involved with the efforts of the League to promote a reduction of armaments. In July, 1922, Lord Robert Cecil presented to the Temporary Mixed Commission of the League that important group of resolutions which definitely associated the two questions of disarmament and security: "The majority of Governments would be unable to accept responsibility for a serious reduction of armaments unless they received in exchange a satisfactory guarantee of the safety of their countries."[45] The Third Assembly of the League accepted this principle in Resolution XIV, and the Fourth Assembly submitted to the Members of the League — and to other states as well—the Draft Treaty of Mutual Assistance which embodied the principles of that Resolution.

Mention need be made here of only one or two features of the system thus proposed. It was to be a scheme of mutual assistance "to facilitate the application of Articles 10 and 16 of the Covenant"; a general defensive agreement to provide immediate assistance in accordance with a pre-arranged plan, but the obligation to render assistance was to be limited in principle "to those countries situated in the same part of the globe." This general agreement was to be supplemented by a series of partial or regional treaties which the Members of the League were authorized to conclude between two or more of their number through

[45] See below, p. 155.

which they could determine in advance the assistance to be rendered in the event of any act of aggression.[46]

A certain connection had become apparent, the authors of the Draft explained, between the work of disarmament and certain Articles of the Covenant, such as Articles 10 and 16. The Treaty could be regarded as a prolongation of certain principles of the Covenant; the obligations and corresponding rights embodied in the Draft were narrower, and, at the same time, more definite, than these contained in the Covenant. In the Draft, the right to the guarantee in case of aggression was absolute, subject to reciprocity.[47] In this Treaty the Members of the League were virtually requested to renounce a part of their sovereignty to the Council, to pledge themselves to accept its decision both in the matter of determining whether or not there had been aggression and in deciding whether military forces should be contributed.[48]

But note the response of the British Government to a proposal of this order:

The Draft Treaty further appears to involve an undesirable extension of the functions of the Council of the League. Under Article 16 of the Covenant, the Council can only recommend action, while even under Article 10 it can only *advise*. By Article 5 of the Draft Treaty, the Council is authorized to decide to adopt various measures. Thus the Council would become an executive body with very large powers, instead of an

[46] The text of the Draft Treaty of Mutual Assistance is given as Annex V.

[47] *Report of the Third Committee*, Fourth Assembly (M. Benes, Rapporteur).

[48] Cf. Articles 4 and 5 of the Draft Treaty.

advisory body. In any event, the Council of the League is a most inappropriate body to be entrusted with the control of military forces in operation against any particular state or states.[49]

The same line of criticism was offered by the Canadian Government, and another aspect of the scheme was declared to be equally unacceptable. The proviso to limit the obligations of the Treaty to a continental basis was a meaningless exemption for the Members of the British Commonwealth. The latter under the Treaty would incur obligations in every region of the world, and, when the Commonwealth was at war, Canada would likewise be at war.[50] These objections were set forth in a memorandum on the Treaty from the Canadian Government to the League of Nations:

The position of Canada in the British Empire is such that, in spite of the fact that the application of the Treaty to the continent of North America is by its terms conditioned upon its ratification by the United States of America, the question of Canada's adherence to it has a more practical aspect than it would otherwise have. Apart from indications that the Government of the United States of America was likely to find the plan acceptable in principle, Canada has already indicated disapproval of the interpretation of the terms of Article 10 of the Covenant as implying an obligation upon her to intervene actively under that Article. The proposed Treaty creates an obligation wider in its extent and more precise in its implication than any which Article 10 could be interpreted as imposing, and it proposes, moreover, to transfer the right

[49] *Observations on the Draft Treaty*, see Annex VI.

[50] Cf. A. J. Toynbee's exposition of the reasons for the rejection of the Treaty by the British Commonwealth: *Survey of International Affairs*, 1924, pp. 27-36.

to decide upon the scope of the action Canada should take from the Canadian Parliament to the Council of the League of Nations ... Canada's position in the British Empire affects the protection afforded her by the continental limitation of which in any event the utility is uncertain since it appears doubtful if hostile action can widely or indeed safely be undertaken by any state upon the principle of limited liability.[51]

It is not necessary at this point to set forth in detail the various other features of the Draft Treaty which led to its decisive rejection by an important group of states within the League of Nations. The system of partial alliances; the emphasis on material guarantees; the enlarged powers of the Council; and the failure of the scheme to develop the juridical principles of the Covenant,—all of these were points of attack by various states which, for one reason or another, refused to endorse this first effort to "close the fissures of the Covenant." But the attempt itself was of first-rate importance and utility. It was, as so much of the League's activity along this general line has been, explorative in its nature rather than productive of immediate results. But it was an important test of sentiment and it gave a clarity to certain problems in international organization which hitherto had never been adequately perceived.

When the Fifth Assembly of the League convened in September, 1924, the effort to find some satisfactory basis for the reduction of national armaments was renewed. Experience with the Draft Treaty had dem-

[51] Annex VI.

onstrated the unwillingness of a large group of states to endorse a system which elaborated primarily the principles expressed in Articles 10 and 16 of the Covenant; the attempt to expand these principles for application within continental areas only had broken down by reason of the peculiar position of the British Commonwealth and the decisive refusal of its constituent members to assume additional obligations in the form of material guarantees. The work of the Fifth Assembly, therefore, was concentrated upon the elaboration of other principles of the Covenant, namely those which had introduced restraint on the freedom of states to resort to war and upon those which had set up processes for the peaceful settlement of disputes. The result of the Assembly's labors was the Protocol for the Pacific Settlement of International Disputes, and on October 2, the Assembly unanimously voted "to recommend to the earnest attention of all the Members of the League the acceptance of the said draft Protocol."

We may be permitted here to utilize a striking summary definition of the Geneva Protocol which has been given by Professor Rappard: "The Protocol may be defined in one sentence," he says, "as being an attempt to promote disarmament by creating security, to create security by outlawing war, to enforce the outlawry of war by uniting the world against the would-be aggressor, and to base this union of mutual protection upon the fundamental principle of universal compulsory arbitration."[52]

[52] *International Relations Viewed from Geneva*, p. 156.

It would prolong unduly the scope of this chapter to attempt an analysis at this point of the various provisions of the Protocol. Its basic principle of universal compulsory arbitration represents the point of emphasis in this second effort to expand the Covenant.[53] At a meeting of the Council of the League of Nations at Geneva on March 12, 1925, Mr. Austen Chamberlain reported the result of the deliberations of the British Government on the recently projected system. An elaborate body of criticism was proffered against the Protocol. The range and merit of this criticism need not be considered here, but it is interesting to note the tenor of this report on the subject of compulsory arbitration:

It was, of course, well known to the framers of the Covenant that international differences might conceivably take a form for which their peace-preserving machinery provided no specific remedy; nor could they have doubted that this defect, if defect it was, could in theory be cured by insisting that every dispute should, at some stage or other, be submitted to arbitration. If, therefore, they rejected this simple method of obtaining systematic completeness, it was presumably because they felt, as so many States Members of the League have felt since, that the objections to universal and compulsory arbitration might easily outweigh its theoretical advantages.

[53] "Our purpose was to make war impossible, to kill it, to annihilate it. To do this, we had to create a system for the pacific settlement of *all disputes* which might ever arise. In other words, it meant the creation of a system of arbitration from which no international dispute, whether juridical or political, could escape. The plan drawn up leaves no loophole; it prohibits wars of every description and lays down that all disputes shall be settled by pacific means." *Report of First and Third Committees*, Fifth Assembly.

INTRODUCTION 39

So far as the Court of International Justice is concerned, this view was taken in 1920 by the British Delegation, while the British Delegation of 1924 made a reservation in the same connection which, so far as Great Britain is concerned, greatly limits the universal application of the compulsory principle.[54]

Prior to the submission of the above report, the British Government had consulted the various Members of the Commonwealth on the advisability of adhering to the Protocol. The response of the Government of New Zealand to the proposal to accept as compulsory the jurisdiction of the Permanent Court of International Justice was expressed in the following terms:

So far Great Britain has never made a declaration under Article 36 of the Statute of the Court authorizing that Court to determine, without special submission, the matters defined in paragraphs A. B. C. D. of that Article, and New Zealand never will consent to such a declaration.[55]

The New Zealand Government found equally unacceptable the provision of the Protocol which vested the Court with authority to determine whether the subject-matter of a dispute came within the domestic jurisdiction of a state:

New Zealand's immigration laws are framed to preserve, as far as possible, British nationality in New Zealand. . . . Whatever the jurists at Geneva may think, the law advisers of the Crown in New Zealand believe that there is grave danger that the International Court of Justice at the Hague, consisting mainly

[54] Annex VIII.
[55] Annex VIII.

of foreigners, might hold that the New Zealand law is contrary to the comity of nations, and that the New Zealand system is not a question of merely domestic jurisdiction.

The foregoing statements have an important bearing on the prospects of developing in the society of nations a comprehensive system for the pacific settlement of all international disputes. They deserve, furthermore, the attention of those adherents of that attractive and simple formula, "the outlawry of war," some of whom are seemingly unaware that, concurrently with the elimination of force as a method of settling disputes, there must be created and accepted a comprehensive and obligatory system of international justice. But the excerpts quoted above are not to be taken as the sole, or indeed, the decisive reason for the rejection of the Geneva Protocol by the British Commonwealth:

As all the world is aware (the Report observed) the League of Nations, in its present shape, is not the League designed by the framers of the Covenant. They no doubt contemplated. . . .the difficulties that might arise from the non-inclusion of a certain number of states within the circle of League membership. But they never supposed that, among these states, would be found so many of the most powerful nations in the world; least of all did they foresee that one of them would be the United States of America. . . . Surely it is most unwise to add to the liabilities already incurred without taking stock of the degree to which the machinery of the Covenant has been already weakened by the non-membership of certain great states. For in truth the change, especially as regards the "economic sanctions," amounts to a transformation. . . .

INTRODUCTION 41

If the particular case of aggressors who are outside the League be considered, is not the weakness of the Protocol even more manifest. . . . How does the Protocol deal with them? It requires them to treat the situation as if they were members of the League, to accept its methods and conform to its decisions. If they refuse, they are counted as aggressors, they become the common enemy, and every signatory state is bound to go to war with them. They may be in the right and have nothing to fear from impartial judges. Yet national pride, in some cases perhaps the sense of power, dislike of compulsory arbitration, distrust of the League (to which presumably they have already refused to belong)—all these motives, or any of them, may harden their objections to outside interference. If so, the Protocol, designed to ensure universal peace, may only extend the area of war—a possibility which, if realized, will not improve the chances of general disarmament.[56]

In the essay by Professor Oppenheim from which quotation was made at the opening of this chapter there occurs another passage, appropriate in this instance to the conclusion of these introductory remarks:

The growth and final shaping of the international organization will go hand in hand with the progress of the law of nations. Now the progress of the law of nations is conditioned by the growth of the international community in mental strength, and this growth in mental strength in its turn is conditioned by the growth in strength and in bulk, the broadening and the deepening, of private and public international interests, and of private and public morale. In the nature of the case this progress can mature only very slowly. . . . Much, if not all, depends on whether the *international* interests of individual states become stronger than

[56] Annex VIII.

their *national* interests, for no state puts its hand to the task of international organization save when, and so far as, its international interests urge it more or less irresistibly so to do.[57]

Thus with an almost prophetic insight, he foresaw those factors which have in the main determined the attitude of states to the system of international organization instituted by the Covenant of the League of Nations.

[57] *Future of International Law*, pp. 16-17.

CHAPTER II

STATE EXISTENCE AND SECURITY

I

We have spoken in the preceding chapter of the doctrine, commonly stated as a fundamental principle of international law, that the state has a right to existence and self-preservation. It was pointed out, however, that in the present stage of the development of international law, the effective enjoyment of this so-called right is, in the last analysis, dependent upon such measures of self-help as the state may be able to employ in its own behalf.[1] The observation was also made that in the application of these measures of self-help, states have on occasions gone beyond the scope of legal conduct permitted in the interest of self-preservation, and have resorted to extra-legal measures for which justification has often been sought under the "doctrine of necessity." It is proposed in the present chapter to subject this condition to some further analysis. We shall not attempt a comprehensive review of the historical development of the principle of the right of the state to existence but will seek rather

[1] "It must be said, therefore, that while the right of existence is possessed in principle equally by all states, its actual enjoyment is largely conditioned upon the physical power of the individual state." C. G. Fenwick, *International Law*, p. 143.

to outline the form in which the doctrine has recently been stated.

This has long been a subject for treatment by publicists, and comment has ranged from a consideration of the duties which a state owes to its individual members to maintain its corporate existence[2] to the discussion of measures of state protection which are obviously within the limits of legitimate self-defense. The doctrine is usually discussed under the title of "self-preservation," and, accepting the governing principle that the state has a right to existence and self-preservation, the authorities proceed to examine the various practices which states have followed under the plea of conserving and protecting their existence. Indeed, much of the modern practice of intervention, through which states at times exercise a dictatorial interference in the affairs of other states, is based on this general principle of self-preservation.

There has been, however, wide variation in the manner in which writers have interpreted the nature and scope of this so-called fundamental right. Recent studies have emphasized the influence exerted by the law of nature philosophy in the formulation of the existing concepts of international law[3] and nowhere is

[2] Cf. for example, Vattel, *Le Droit des Gens*, Chap. II (1758 ed.).

[3] E. D. Dickinson, "The Analogy Between Natural Persons and International Persons in the Law of Nations," *Yale Law Journal*, XXVI, pp. 565-591; Cf. likewise, the same author's volume on *The Equality of States in International Law*; Roscoe Pound, "Philosophical Theory and International Law," *Bibliotheca Visseriana*, I, pp. 73-90.

this influence more strikingly portrayed than in the statements concerning the right of the state to existence as they have come from the hands of certain writers. The result, in these instances, has been the formulation of the doctrine in terms of an inherent and absolute right which could be exercised, if need be, with all the latitude which such a concept implies. We may quote one or two nineteenth century writers who reveal this influence and who are representative of a certain tendency in the interpretation of the principle. In the discussion of the subject by Wheaton, whose influence both in the United States and in England was considerable, we find the following statement:

Of the absolute international rights of states, one of the most essential and important, and that which lies at the foundation of all the rest, is the right of self-preservation. It is not only a right with respect to other states, but a duty with respect to its own members, and the most solemn and important duty which the state owes to them. The right necessarily involves all other incidental rights, which are essential as means to give effect to the principal end.[4]

An even more extreme assertion of the doctrine is that given by Rivier:

When a conflict arises between the right of self-preservation of a state and the duty of that state to respect the right of another, the right of self-preservation overrides the duty. *Primum vivere.* A man may be free to sacrifice himself. It is never permitted to a government to sacrifice the state of which the destinies are confided to it. The government is then authorized, and even in certain circumstances bound, to violate the

[4] Phillipson's *Wheaton*, p. 87.

right of another country for the safety (*salut*) of its own. This is an excuse of necessity, an application of the reason of state. It is a legitimate excuse.[5]

The question is considered by T. J. Lawrence under the title of "interventions to ward off imminent dangers to the intervening state," and, utilizing an analogy drawn from municipal jurisprudence, he makes the following declaration:

The right of self-preservation is even more sacred than the duty of respecting the independence of others. If the two clash, a state naturally acts on the former. Nor is the doctrine that self-preservation overrides ordinary rules, peculiar to the law of nations. In every civilized state a woman who slays a man in defence of her honor is accounted blameless, and during invasion the military authorities are allowed to destroy property, if such destruction is necessary for the performance of warlike operations against the enemy. By parity of reasoning we obtain the rule that intervention to ward off imminent danger to the intervening power is justifiable. But we should note carefully that the danger must be direct and immediate, not contingent and remote, and, moreover, it must be sufficiently important in itself to justify the expenditure of blood and treasure in order to repel it.[6]

---

[5] *Principes du Droit des Gens*, t. i., p. 227. Quoted by Westlake, *International Law*, I, p. 296. (1904 ed.)

[6] *Principles of International Law*, p. 125. (7th ed.)

Professor Hershey places the right of self-preservation in a category apart from other rules of international conduct. Thus he states: "Authorities have always differed widely on what constitutes *legal* or *justifiable* grounds for intervention, or, indeed, as to whether any such right exists. The only approach to unanimity is in respect to intervention for the sake of self-preservation, which, be it observed, is not, properly speaking, a right or law in the ordinary sense of these terms as applied to

The Right of the State to Existence

What influence such precepts as these exerted on the minds of statemen and correspondingly on the policies of states during the period of their currency in the law of nations is, of course, a matter of conjecture, but under the guidance of such theories there could be little restraint in the way of law in the path of a nation which chooses to set out upon an aggressive crusade of self-preservation.

But it cannot properly be said that the doctrine in the form stated above received the general endorsement of writers on international law up to the outbreak of the World War. Analysis of the nature and source of legal rights and duties had long before shown that they could not logically be expressed in the form of absolutes.[7] To accord to states an absolute right of self-preservation was to annul for other states a whole category of rights which it was equally the purpose of the law to protect.

The fallacy of the doctrine of absolute rights was very ably analyzed by Westlake:

The doctrine of absolute rights threatens to lead to no practical results for states, as it would lead to none

---

positive rules and regulations, but a fundamental right or principle which underlies and takes precedence of all systems of positive law and custom." *Essentials of International Public Law*, p. 149.

[7] "Rights spring from the legal recognition of definitely determined interests. Any other kind of alleged right belongs to the sphere of morals and has no place in a science of law." P. M. Brown, "The Rights of States Under International Law," *Yale Law Journal*, XXVI, pp. 85-86.

for men if there was not the law of the land over them to measure their rights in all ordinary cases. Wolff, to whom more than to anyone else international law is indebted for that doctrine, taught that states have a right to those things by means of which they may avert their destruction and what tends to it, or without which they cannot perfect themselves or avoid what tends to their imperfection. But what two states deem that they require in order to avert their destruction or to promote their perfection may be incompatible, and then the doctrine gives only a clashing of equal rights. . . .

Even then, although as a general rule we must admit the truth of Wolff's principle, that a state ought to preserve and protect itself as an association of its citizens in order to promote their common good, patriotism should not allow us to forget that even our own good, and still less that of the world, does not always and imperatively require the maintenance of our state, still less its maintenance in its actual limits and with undiminished resources. The first interest of a society, national or international, is justice; and justice is violated when any state which has not failed in its duty is subjected to aggression intended for the preservation or protection of another.[8]

Oppenheim, likewise, rejected the idea of the state possessing an absolute and inherent right to existence and he sought to define the rights of self-preservation within limits that would preserve respect for the common rights of all states under the law of nations. He wrote as follows:

Although, as a rule, all states have mutually to respect one another's personality, and are therefore bound not to violate one another, as an exception, cer-

[8] *International Law*, I, pp. 294 and 299. (1904 ed.)

tain violations of another state committed by a state for the purpose of self-preservation are not prohibited by the law of nations. Thus, self-preservation is a factor of great importance for the position of the states within the family of nations, and most writers maintain that every state has a fundamental right of self-preservation. But nothing of the kind is actually the case, if the real facts of the law are taken into consideration. If every state really had a *right* of self-preservation, all the states would have the duty to admit, suffer, and endure every violation done to one another in self-preservation. But such duty does not exist.[9]

Oppenheim's treatment of the subject, however, does not lead far toward determining the actual legal scope of the rights derived from the principle of self-preservation. He continues with the following statement:

On the contrary, although self-preservation is in certain cases an excuse recognized by international law, no state is obliged patiently to submit to violations done to it by such other state as acts in self-preservation, but can repulse them. It is a fact that in certain cases violations committed in self-preservation are not prohibited by the law of nations. But, nevertheless, they remain violations, may therefore be repulsed, and indemnities may be demanded for damage done. Self-preservation is consequently an excuse, because violations of other states are in certain exceptional cases not prohibited when they are committed for the purpose, and in the interest, of self-preservation, although they need not be patiently suffered and endured by the states concerned.

It is not, however, consistent to speak, as Oppenheim does, of conduct in the interest of self-preservation as being "excused" and not "prohibited" by the law of

[9] *International Law*, I, p. 214. (3rd ed.)

nations and at the same time to designate it as a "violation" of the state at whose expense it is carried out. If it is really a "violation," is it not prohibited by the law of nations? Oppenheim notes that "it becomes more and more recognized that violations of other states in the interest of self-preservation are excused in cases of necessity only,"[10] and, he proceeds to discuss certain instances of intervention by states within the jurisdiction of others under the doctrine of self-preservation. It would seem that in so far as these interventions have a juristic basis it must necessarily be found in the failure of the state subjected to the intervention to fulfil some legal obligation towards the intervening state.[11] Otherwise the conduct is a "violation" and certainly is not "excused" by international law. What, indeed, do publicists mean when they speak of conduct being "excused" by international law? Apparently the term is used in extenuation of conduct for which a legal basis is wanting but for which ethical justification may be claimed. But the fact is, as Professor Fenwick points out in discussing circumstances of this order, "the conflict of rights thus resulting is governed by a few general principles of law, which are, however, so vague as to leave it an open question in many cases whether the right of one has justified a breach of the right of the other."[12]

[10] *Ibid.*, pp. 214-215.
[11] Says Fenwick: "The fact that the invaded state in such a case recognizes no *duty* to acquiesce does not limit or qualify the legal right, provided the public opinion of the international community gives it approval." *Op. cit.*, p. 143 (note).
[12] *Ibid.*, pp. 142-143.

II

However, this attempt to define the actual legal scope of the rights of the state under the principle of self-preservation is only one of the problems connected with state existence and security. It was well enough to discard the conception of absolute right in this connection, and in the interest of clear thinking to draw clearly the distinction between what the state may claim as a matter of ethical right and that which is actually allowed under the existing rules of law. But we are dealing, it must be remembered, with claims which are indeed fundamental to the state itself, irrespective of the manner in which the society of nations may view the claim of any given state to existence and security. The author has endeavored elsewhere to present this aspect of the problem and from this previous comment an extract may here be quoted:

What principle, however, in the ethics and politics of the modern state is given a higher position than its right to existence? The exercise of political authority within the state may be assailed and may be the occasion of criticism, or of revolution, but its actual right to existence, as a separate political entity, is ordinarily, within the state itself, accepted and proclaimed as absolute. Indeed it may be said that there is no doctrine relating to their mass organization more deeply intrenched in the conscience of mankind than the principle of the ethical right to existence of the political state organized on the basis of nationality. Existence and security, therefore, from the view point of the state itself, become matters of fundamental ethical importance irrespective of the manner in which the existence of a particular state may be regarded by an external judgment.[13]

The bearing of this condition upon the question of the right of the state to existence would seem to be apparent. International law indeed recognizes the claim and declares the right of the state to existence; it has not, however, made adequate provision for the protection of the right thus acknowledged and declared. It is evident that here is presented an additional aspect of the problem of state existence and security—the inadequacy of the law to protect the legal interest which is regarded as supreme by the subjects of the law itself. The condition is, in fact, taken by Hall as the point of departure in his examination of the whole question of state existence and self-preservation. He wrote as follows:

In the last resort almost the whole of the duties of states are subordinated to the right of self-preservation. Where law affords inadequate protection to the individual he must be permitted, if his existence is in question, to protect himself by whatever means may be necessary; and it would be difficult to say that any act not inconsistent with the nature of a moral being is forbidden, so soon as it can be proved that by it, and it only, self-preservation can be secured. But the right in this form is rather a governing condition, subject to which all rights and duties exist, than a source of specific rules, and properly perhaps it cannot operate in the latter capacity at all. It works by suspending the obligation to act in obedience to other principles. If such suspension is necessary for existence, the gen-

[13] "State Morality in International Relations," *The American Political Science Review*, XVII, No. 1, p. 24.

The Right of the State to Existence 53

eral right is enough; if it is not strictly necessary, the occasion is hardly one of self-preservation.[14]

Without accepting with all its implications the analogy drawn by Hall between the position of the individual and that of the state, it must, nevertheless, be admitted that the inadequate protection to state existence afforded by the existing law is a basis for self-help of far-reaching consequence. We may conceive of a state threatened and imperiled—genuinely or merely in its own belief—by the expansion or aggression of an ambitious neighbor. The state which thus regards itself endangered is aware that no guarantee of its protection is forthcoming other than its own individual efforts and it proceeds to defensive measures which may involve a violation of the rights of innocent and unoffending states. The plea is set forth that law which does not afford security has no moral claim to obedience when protection which violates no ethical principle can be had outside the realm of law. The question, however, of what constitutes a violation of an ethical principle or what conduct is "not consistent with the nature of a moral being" is still undetermined. That the judgment of the state thus acting is not necessarily acceptable to international society; that the plea put forth may be, in fact, a specious one, presented to excuse aggressive conduct, may readily be admitted. But until the security of the state has become sufficiently assured to remove the occasion for this type of action, its recurrence must be expected and

[14] *International Law*, p. 278. (7th ed.)

the question of moral justification thrown into the realm of controversy after the act has been accomplished. This condition admits of no answer other than that offered by Westlake some years ago:

> We take it to be pointed out by justice that the true international right of self-preservation is merely that of self-defence.... The conscientious judgment of the state acting on the right thus allowed must necessarily stand in the place of authoritative sanction, so long as the present imperfect organization of the world continues.[15]

It is customary for many publicists to treat under the heading of self-preservation various instances, often of a minor character, of interference by one state within the jurisdiction of another for which there may (or may not) have been legal justification by reason of the failure of the state subjected to such action to fulfil its international obligations. It is rarely true in such cases that the actual existence of the state taking such action has been appreciably threatened—its territory may have been subjected to hostile incursions, and the lives of its citizens temporarily endangered, but its actual position in the society of nations is not thereby involved. Its measures of self-help, moreover, are directed against the state which is presumed to be responsible for the offense—or often against individuals within the state—and these measures do not involve the interests of states not parties to the controversy.[16]

---

[15] *International Law*, I, pp. 299-300. (1904 ed.)

[16] Occurrences of this order frequently cited are, *The Case of The Caroline*, 1837; *The Virginius*, 1873; and more recently, the

The plea of self-preservation is occasionally invoked, however, in extenuation of conduct more drastic and far-reaching than that mentioned above. On occasion, usually under the threat or stress of war, states have professed to see their existence so vitally endangered that action involving the interests of third states has been deemed essential to their own self-preservation.[17] Thus there has developed the so-called "doctrine of necessity," a principle which supports conduct of such extraordinary nature that it is sometimes candidly admitted to have no semblance of legality. The explanation frequently offered under such circumstances is the inability of small neutral states to protect their territory and resources from utilization by some powerful enemy, and the state which professes to see its safety thus endangered proceeds to anticipate the plans of its enemy by itself bringing under its own control the territory or resources of the weaker state. A pretext of this sort has, of course, an element of plausibility. Westlake, who is extremely cautious in stating the rights which flow from the doctrine of self-

---

American Punitive Expedition into Mexico, 1916; The Occupation of Juarez, 1919. See Oppenheim, I, Chap. V; Hall, Chap. VII.

[17] Says Hall: "The right of self-preservation in some cases justifies the commission of acts of violence against a friendly or neutral state, when from its position and resources it is capable of being made use of to dangerous effect by an enemy, when there is a known intention on his part so to make use of it, and when, if he is not forestalled, it is almost certain he will succeed, either through the helplessness of the country or by means of intrigues with a party within it." *Op. cit.*, p. 281.

preservation, finds here a defense for the seizure of the Danish fleet by England in 1807. Writing in justification of this act he says:

The principle that the legal rights of a state are not to be violated without its own fault is not really infringed, for when a state is unable of itself to prevent a hostile use being made of its territory or its resources, it ought to allow proper measures of self-protection to be taken by the state against which the hostile use is impending, or else must be deemed to intend that use as the necessary consequence of refusing the permission. It is a principle of jurisprudence that every one is presumed to intend the necessary consequences of his actions. We cannot therefore subscribe to the condemnation which many continental writers have pronounced on the conduct of England in 1807.[18]

The line of conduct followed by states under circumstances of this order can be illustrated by citing a few major instances of the application of the doctrine of necessity which have drawn neutral states into the area of conflict of their more powerful neighbors. Without raising here the question of justification in these various cases, they are recalled merely to indicate the type of explanation offered by Governments on occasions when recourse has been made to this exceptional course of action.

An early nineteenth century example of such action was that referred to above, namely, the seizure of the Danish fleet by England in 1807 upon information of secret provisions in the Treaty of Tilsit which provided for the forcible utilization by France of the

[18] *International Law*, I, pp. 302-303. (1904 ed.)

Danish navy in the war with England. The action by England was preceded by the explanation to Denmark that:

We ask deposit—we have not looked for capture; so far from it, the most solemn pledge has been offered to your government, and it is hereby renewed, that, if our demand be acceded to, every ship of the navy of Denmark shall, at the conclusion of the general peace, be restored to her in the same condition and state of equipment as when received under the protection of the British flag.[19]

It is interesting at this point to contrast with the above statement the declaration made by the German Government to Belgium, on August 2, 1914:

Germany has in view no act of hostility against Belgium. In the event of Belgium being prepared in the coming war to maintain an attitude of friendly neutrality towards Germany, the German Government bind themselves, at the conclusion of peace, to guarantee the possessions and independence of the Belgian Kingdom in full.

Germany undertakes, under the above-mentioned conditions, to evacuate Belgium territory on the conclusion of peace. If Belgium adopts a friendly attitude, Germany is prepared, in cooperation with the Bel-

[19] Quoted by Hall, *op. cit.*, p. 283. "The emergency," says Hall, "was one which gave good reason for the general line of conduct of the English Government. The specific demands of the latter were also kept within due limits. Unfortunately Denmark, in the exercise of an indubitable right, chose to look upon its action as hostile, and war ensued, the occurrence of which is a proper subject for extreme regret, but offers no justification for the harsh judgments which have been frequently passed upon the measures which led to it." Cf. also, Westlake, *Collected Papers*, p. 121.

gian authorities, to purchase all necessaries for her troops against a cash payment, and to pay an indemnity for any damage that may have been caused by German troops.[20]

The doctrine of necessity was invoked likewise by Japan in justification of the violation of Korean neutrality in the war with Russia in 1904. The defense offered by Japan was based on the grounds that one of the main objects of the war was the maintenance of the territorial integrity and independence of Korea which was menaced by Russian aggression. Commenting on this conduct of Japan, Professor Hershey says:

There can be no doubt but that, according to the strict letter of the law, Japan was guilty of a violation of one of the most fundamental rules of international law,—viz., the right of an independent state to remain neutral during the war between other members of the family of nations, and to have its neutrality and territorial sovereignty respected by the belligerent states. On the other hand, as the Japanese Government was careful to point out in its official reply to the Russian note, "the maintenance of the independence and territorial integrity of Korea is one of the objects of the war, and, therefore, the dispatch of troops to the menaced territory was a matter of right and necessity, which had the distinct consent of the Korean Government."[21]

The German invasion of Belgium in 1914 was preceded by an explanation to the Belgian Government which was in singular accord with the above traditions:

[20] J. B. Scott, *Documents Relating to the Outbreak of the European War*, I, p. 372.

[21] *International Law and Diplomacy of the Russo-Japanese War*, pp. 71-72.

THE RIGHT OF THE STATE TO EXISTENCE 59

The Imperial Government are in possession of trustworthy information regarding the proposed drawing up of French forces on the Meuse, on section Givet-Namur. This information permits of no doubt that the French intend to advance against Germany through Belgian territory. The Imperial Government fear that Belgium, even with the best of intentions, will not be able, without assistance, to ward off a French approach with so great a chance of success as to furnish a sufficient guarantee against the threatened danger to Germany. It is the postulate of self-preservation that Germany should anticipate the hostile attack. The German Government would therefore much regret if Belgium should consider it an act of hostility towards herself that Germany, through the design of her adversaries, in her own defence is compelled in turn to enter Belgian territory.[22]

But the Belgian Government, "in the exercise of an indubitable right"— to apply here the comment of Hall on the action of Denmark in 1807—"chose to look upon the action as hostile, and war ensued," and, in justification of events which followed, the German Chancellor offered the following apology in the Reichstag on August 4, 1914:

We are in a state of legitimate defence, and necessity knows no law. Our troops have occupied Luxemburg and have perhaps already entered Belgium. This is contrary to the dictates of international law. France has, it is true, declared at Brussels that she was prepared to respect the neutrality of Belgium so long as it was respected by her adversary. But we knew that France was ready to invade Belgium. France could wait; we could not. A French attack upon our flank in the region of the Lower Rhine might have

[22] Scott, *op. cit.*, II, p. 813.

been fatal. We were, therefore, compelled to ride rough-shod over the legitimate protests of the Governments of Luxemburg and Belgium. For the wrong which we are thus doing, we will make reparation as soon as our military object is attained. Anyone in such grave danger as ourselves, and who is struggling for his supreme welfare, can only be concerned with the means of extricating himself; we stand side by side with Austria.[23]

In the foregoing pages we have sought to point out a fundamental weakness of international law in connection with the principle of the right of the state to existence. The mere declaration of this right has not sufficed to provide security to the state, and measures of self-help have persisted in the absence of collective protection of this interest by the community of nations. The prospects of developing this protection by the advancement of international law along various lines will be considered in succeeding chapters.[24]

[23] *Ibid.*, I, p. 381.

Note Mr. Roosevelt's appraisal of the conduct of Germany: "Whatever we may think of the morality of this plea, it is certain that almost all great nations have in time past again and again acted in accordance with it. England's conduct toward Denmark in the Napoleonic wars, and the conduct of both England and France toward us during those same wars, admits only of this species of justification; and with less excuse the same is true of our conduct toward Spain in Florida nearly a century ago." *America and the World War*, pp. 20-21.

[24] The principle in international law that "the state has a right to existence" might profitably be examined from a number of additional standpoints. What criteria, for example, should the law set up for determining the validity of the claim of a state to existence and what principles should govern the recognition of this claim as a legal interest? The topic is the subject of an

interesting comment by Professor Krabbe. He writes as follows: "The value of this interest [i. e. the interest which a nation has in creating a state] is no more unconditional than that of any other interest; and hence it falls to international law to determine its legal value. In order that this may be done, however, it must be made clear to the outside world that the nation really has a right to be a state or independent legal community. This is shown by the existence of an organization proceeding from its own national law, either written or unwritten, competent to enforce this law. In order that the real importance of this national interest may stand above question, there must exist a legal order providing for legislation, for the administration of justice, and for the machinery needed to enforce the law. It is only after the interest of a nation in leading its own legal life has been sanctioned by national law that this interest can receive legal sanction from the international community, thus determining the right of the nation to form a state. . . .

"A nation's character as a state, therefore, is rooted in a law which is international in scope. A nation has no natural right to lead an independent legal life. If the legal value of the interests of the international community is not furthered by such an independent legal life, the claims of a nation to regulate its own communal life according to its legal standards are invalid. And the sense of right of the international community expresses itself with reference to these claims when a nation is recognized in any manner as a state by other states, though it is not necessary that this recognition shall proceed from *all* states." *The Modern Idea of the State*, pp. 238-239.

Under what conditions, furthermore, does a state forfeit its right to continue existence as a member of the international community? This problem is likewise regulated by law which is international in scope. Thus declares Professor Hyde: "The continuance of the right of a state to membership for all purposes in the family of nations may be said to depend in a strict sense upon the effect of its conduct upon the international society. The welfare of that society may not require the maintenance of a particular state; its very extinction as such may be for the general good. When the acts of a state have caused the family of nations, or those members of it which unite to express the will of all, to reach such a conclusion, it forfeits the right to retain its place therein or to continue existence as a full-fledged member thereof. Various considerations may be productive of this result. These may be commonly assigned to the failure of a state either through incompetency or political aggressiveness, to respond generally to its primary obligations to the outside world." *International Law*, I, p. 83.

CHAPTER III

ARTICLE 10 OF THE COVENANT OF THE LEAGUE OF NATIONS

I

The foregoing review of the principle of the right of the state to existence and self-preservation has indicated the status of the doctrine in the law of nations at the outbreak of the World War. The situation may be summarized in a single sentence. By the principles of international law, the claim of the members of the community of nations to existence was recognized as a legal right but for the enjoyment of this right no assured protection was provided, and, consequently, the state, in the exercise of self-help, not only frequently transcended the law, but at times embarked upon conduct extremely grave and of questionable ethical validity.

We have taken occasion already to review in some measure the currents of thought on the relations of states set in motion by the World War, and it has been said that concrete expression was given to these ideas in the form of a Covenant of a League of Nations. While all of this movement had as its general objective the prevention or decrease of future wars, there was naturally wide diversity in the means proposed for the attainment of the end in view. At the very outset of the War, however, the invasion of Belgium focused attention upon the fundamental question of state existence and security. Amidst all the contention which then existed respecting the origins and responsibility of the War, the fate of Belgium stood out with indubitable clarity. The rights of a small neutral nation under the general principles of international law, and, under treaty agreements as well, were violated on the plea that the use of its territory was essential to the self-preservation of a powerful neighboring state.

Much was written during the early days of the War in condemnation of this line of conduct of the German Government. To most of this criticism one could subscribe and yet realize that events of this order were the inevitable outcome of the existing conditions in international affairs. It is appropriate to refer to it here once more because the invasion of Belgium really marked the beginning of all the recent consideration of the problem of state security, the various aspects of which are gradually being unfolded. The problem which was thus so clearly set forth was immediately perceived as one for which provision must be made in any comprehensive scheme of international organization.[1] The duty which the United States should as-

[1] In Temperley, *History of the Peace Conference*, the invasion of Belgium is given as one of the three practical causes of the desire for a League: "The violation of Belgium demonstrated the need for a more comprehensive guarantee of the safety of small nations than could be furnished by incidental treaties between a group of powers. . . . This second (consideration) found expression in Article 10, with its guarantee of territorial integrity

sume in this connection was expressed at this time, not by the head of the Government, but by a distinguished private citizen:

It should ever be our honorable effort [Mr. Roosevelt declared in January, 1915] to serve one of the world's most vital needs by doing all in our power to bring about conditions which will give some effective protection to weak or small nations which themselves keep order and act with justice toward the rest of mankind. There can be no higher international duty than to safeguard the existence and independence of industrious, orderly states, with a high personal and national standard of conduct, but without the military force of the great powers; states, for instance, such as Belgium, Holland, Switzerland, the Scandinavian countries, Uruguay, and others. A peace which left Belgium's wrongs unredressed and which did not provide against the recurrence of such wrongs as those from which she has suffered would not be a real peace.[2]

All of the topics treated in this study are related to this central problem of state security and much attention is devoted herein to the various efforts for its adjustment which have been made in connection with the League of Nations. At this point, however, it is proposed to direct attention to one only of the methods through which it has been approached, namely through the principle of a collective guarantee of territorial integrity and political independence which is contained in Article 10 of the Covenant of the League.

---

and political independence, and secondly, in Article 16, with the obligation it imposes on all Members of the League to enforce the maintenance of peace." II, pp. 22-23.

[2] *America and the World War*, p. 15.

"Two methods of guarantee," says Ray Stannard Baker, "were much discussed in connection with the League—and a third was mentioned."

1. A guaranteed process of arbitration such as that recommended in the Phillimore Report. This was finally incorporated in Articles XII to XVI of the Covenant.

2. A simple guarantee of rights and possessions against invasion was supported by President Wilson, and became Article X of the Covenant.

The direct guarantee had been discarded by British writers on the League. All content themselves with the guarantees surrounding the arbitration agreements as sufficient to insure safety of the members. It is found in none of the significant plans of later years except Wilson's. . . . Here again, in this method of direct guarantee, he drew his inspiration straight from the fundamental American documents, as the Articles of Confederation in which (Article III) the colonists bind themselves "to assist each other against all force offered to, or attacks made upon them, or any of them" and as in the Constitution (Article IV, Section 4) "the United States shall guarantee to every State in this Union a republican form of government, and shall protect each of them against invasion.[3]

Although the history of the origins of Article 10 of the Covenant has been in many places the subject of review,[4] it may be well here to recall in something

---

[3] *Woodrow Wilson and World Settlement*, I, pp. 219-221.

[4] Notably in the following works: Titus Komarnicki, *La question de l'intégrité territoriale dans le Pacte de la Société des Nations: L'Article X du Pacte* (Les Presses Universitaires de France, Paris, 1923); Temperley, *History of the Peace Conference at Paris*, VI, pp. 444-446; R. S. Baker, *Woodrow Wilson and World Settlement*, I, Chap. XIII; Philip Baker, *The Making of the Covenant from the British Point of View*, in *Les Origines et L'Œuvre de la Société des Nations* (Copenhagen, 1924); Robert Lansing, *The Peace Negotiations*, Chaps. V and X.

more than summary fashion the story of its adoption. With regard to President Wilson's part in framing the Covenant as a whole, Mr. Baker has observed that practically none of its provisions were original with the President, and that he contented himself with selecting principles proposed by others and erecting them into a fabric for the future organization of the society of nations.[5] Such was indeed, in the main, the procedure of the President, but for the inclusion of Article 10 in the Covenant he was primarily responsible and the Article itself is properly regarded as being essentially American in its origin. It embodied, furthermore, at least in the mind of Mr. Wilson, the very essence of the American creed—a renunciation of imperialistic policies and acceptance of the doctrine that "governments derive all their just powers from the consent of the governed."[6] Rarely did he fail in his

[5] R. S. Baker, *op. cit.*, I, p. 214.

[6] "He had read and re-read with a student's care and an evangelist's ardour the writings and the speeches of the great men who formed the Republic and built up the splendid fabric of her political philosophy. . . . In European eyes the peculiarity was that he conceived all his principles of public policy upon American lines, but believed these contained all the doctrines necessary to the salvation of the world as a whole. The Virginia Bill of Rights supplied him with the cogent doctrine that 'a people has a right to do anything they please with their own country and their own government'. . . . This was the creed of freemen on which the Constitution, the independence, and the existence of the United States was based. It was associated with a principle of equal importance; the United States held that all their citizens were equal and therefore could not contemplate annexation or the permanent control of subject races." Temperley, *op. cit.*, I, pp. 174-175.

steadfast defense of this favorite Article to insist that the principles and policies which he was seeking to project into the international sphere were essentially American. In one of the final and most powerful pleas which he made in its behalf he reiterated this contention in a singularly eloquent and forceful manner. "The choice is between two ideals," he wrote Senator Hitchcock on March 8, 1920, "on the one hand, the ideal of democracy, which represents the rights of free peoples everywhere to govern themselves, and on the other hand, the ideal of imperialism which seeks to dominate by force and unjust power.... Every imperialistic influence in Europe was hostile to the embodiment of Article X in the Covenant of the League of Nations, and its defeat now would mark the complete consummation of their efforts to nullify the Treaty. I hold the doctrine of Article X to be the essence of Americanism. We cannot repudiate it or weaken it without at the same time repudiating our own principles.... The enemies of a League of Nations have by every true instinct centered their efforts against Article X, for it is undoubtedly the foundation of the whole structure. It is the bulwark, and the only bulwark, of the rising democracy of the world against the forces of imperialism and reaction."[7]

In his often quoted address before the Second Pan-American Scientific Congress in Washington on January 6, 1916, Mr. Wilson first definitely associated the ideas of a guarantee of territorial integrity and politi-

[7] The text of this letter is given as Annex II.

cal independence—urging on this occasion the application of the principle to the states of the Western Hemisphere:

> The states of America [he said] have not been certain what the United States would do with her power. That doubt must be removed. . . . If America is to come into her own, into her legitimate own, in a world of peace and order, she must establish the foundations of amity so that no one will hereafter doubt them. I hope and I believe that this can be accomplished. . . . It will be accomplished in the first place by the States of America uniting in guaranteeing to each other absolutely political independence and territorial integrity.[8]

Some four months later, the President stated his con-

[8] The rôle attributed to Colonel House in suggesting the above proposal to the President should be noted. As early as December, 1914, the Colonel made a special visit to the President to urge him to "inaugurate a policy that would weld the Western Hemisphere together." The following is the Colonel's account of the interview:

"It was my idea to formulate a plan, to be agreed upon by the republics of the two continents, which in itself would serve as a model for the European nations when peace is at last brought about. I could see that this excited his enthusiasm. My idea was that the republics of the two continents should agree to guarantee each other's territorial integrity and that they should also agree to government ownership of munitions of war. I suggested that he take a pencil and write the points to be covered.

"He took a pencil, and this is what he wrote:

1st. Mutual guaranties of political independence under republican form of government and mutual guaranties of territorial integrity.

2nd. Mutual agreements that the Government of each of the contracting parties acquire complete control within its jurisdiction of the manufacture and sale of munitions of war." *Intimate Papers of Colonel House*, I, pp. 209-210.

viction that the time had arrived when the United States should actively cooperate in an organization for maintaining the peace of the world. He set forth a declaration of American political ideals and expanded his proposal for mutual guarantee to a world-wide application:

We believe these fundamental things: First, that every people has a right to choose the sovereignty under which they shall live. . . . Second, that the small states of the world have a right to enjoy the same respect for their sovereignty and for their territorial integrity that great and powerful nations expect and insist upon. And, third, that the world has a right to be free from every disturbance of its peace that has its origins in aggression and disregard of the rights of peoples and nations. . . .

If it should ever be our privilege to suggest or initiate a movement for peace among the nations now at war, I am sure that the people of the United States would wish their Government to move along these lines. . . . An universal association of the nations to maintain the inviolate security of the highway of the seas for the common and unhindered use of all the nations of the world, and to prevent any war begun either contrary to treaty covenants or without warning and full submission of the causes to the opinion of the world,—a virtual guarantee of territorial integrity and political independence.[9]

Subsequent addresses, declaring the war aims of America, and outlining conditions for peace, carried forward these ideas. Before the Senate of the United States, on January 22, 1917, he spoke as follows:

[9] Address before the American League to Enforce Peace, May 27, 1916.

No peace can last, or ought to last, which does not recognize and accept the principle that governments derive all their just powers from the consent of the governed, and that no right anywhere exists to hand peoples about from sovereignty to sovereignty as if they were property. . . .

I am proposing, as it were, that the nations should with one accord adopt the doctrine of President Monroe as the doctrine of the world: that no nation should seek to extend its polity over any other nation or people, but that every people should be left free to determine its own polity, its own way of development, unhindered, unthreatened, unafraid, the little along with the great and powerful. . . . I am proposing government by the consent of the governed.

And finally in the address containing the famous Fourteen Points, he declared that:

A general association of nations must be formed under specific covenants for the purpose of affording mutual guarantees of political independence and territorial integrity to great and small states alike.

In the early summer of 1918, President Wilson received from the British Government the Phillimore Report on a League of Nations which had been presented to the British Cabinet in the preceding March. He discussed the project with Colonel House and requested the latter to draw up a new draft of the proposed Covenant in collaboration with the experts of the Inquiry Commission. "By far the most important of the new elements in the House draft," says Baker, "was the article of direct guarantee of the 'territorial integrity and political independence' of the Members of the League."[10]

[10] *Woodrow Wilson and World Settlement*, I, p. 219.

From the House report, the President made, during the summer of 1918, his own first draft of a Covenant which he later took to the Paris Conference. This draft contained as Article III the provision for a direct and affirmative guarantee which in modified form was later to become Article 10 of the League Covenant. While at Paris, the President drew up two subsequent drafts in which he embodied various suggestions offered at Paris respecting the provisions of the Covenant; and his own draft and that of Lord Robert Cecil of January 20,—the British draft—were used as a basis in preparing the Hurst-Miller compromise draft which was in turn accepted as a basis for discussion before the League of Nations Commissions on February 3rd.

Both President Wilson's draft of the Covenant and the draft presented by Lord Robert Cecil on January 20th contained, as a portion of the article on territorial guarantee, extensive provisions for affecting future territorial readjustments. The text of the article submitted by President Wilson ran as follows:

The Contracting Powers unite in guaranteeing to each other political independence and territorial integrity as against external aggression; but it is understood between them that such territorial readjustments, if any, as may in the future become necessary by reasons of changes in present racial conditions and aspirations or present social and political relationships, pursuant to the principle of self-determination, and also such territorial readjustments as may in the judgment of three-fourths of the Delegates be demanded by the welfare and manifest interest of the people concerned,

ARTICLE 10 OF THE COVENANT

may be effected if agreeable to those peoples and to the States from which the territory is separated or to which it is added; and that territorial changes may in equity involve material compensation. The Contracting Powers accept without reservation the principle that the peace of the world is superior in importance to every question of political jurisdiction or boundary.[11]

No such qualifying clause as the above for effecting future boundary readjustments survived in the Hurst-Miller draft. Respecting its omission, Mr. Lansing has stated:

It was generally believed that the elimination of the modifying clause from the President's original form of guaranty was chiefly due to the opposition of the statesmen who represented the British Empire in contradistinction to those who represented the self-governing British Dominions. It was also believed that this opposition was caused by an unwillingness on their part to recognize or to apply as a right the principle of 'self-determination' in arranging possible future changes of sovereignty over territory.[12]

It may, however, be noted that the clause in question

---

[11] Baker, *Ibid.*, III, p. 119. The qualifying clause in the Cecil draft provided that: "If at any time it should appear that the boundaries of any state guaranteed . . . . do not conform to the requirements of the situation, the League shall take the matter under consideration and may recommend to the parties affected any modifications which it may think necessary. If such recommendation is rejected by the parties affected, the states members of the League shall, so far as the territory in question is concerned, cease to be under the obligation to protect the territory in question from forcible aggression by other states, imposed upon them by the above provision." Baker, *Ibid.*, III, p. 132.

[12] *The Peace Negotiations*, pp. 94-95.

was also opposed by Mr. David Hunter Miller,[13] and a British commentator has suggested that President Wilson himself, in the interval between the submission of his own draft and the preparation of the Hurst-Miller draft, "had definitely changed his opinion and. . . . had come to regard the last words of his reservation— 'the peace of the world is superior in importance to every question of political jurisdiction or boundary'— as embodying the essential object which it was desirable to attain."[14] At all events, the President permitted no change in the text of this clause after its introduction in the Hurst-Miller draft and in his opposition to modification he "was supported throughout by all the representatives of continental countries, and particularly of the new states being established under the peace settlement, and of the other states which thereby acquired large new territories."[15]

In his report on the "Peace Negotiations," Mr. Lansing has recorded the difference of opinion between President Wilson and the other Members of the American Commission at Paris concerning the form which a territorial guarantee should take. The Miller-Auchincloss memorandum on the President's text of the Covenant criticised the proposed affirmative guarantee and proposed as a substitute the following "self-denying covenant":

[13] House and Seymour, *What Really Happened at Paris*, p. 411.
[14] Philip Baker, *Les Origines et L'Œuvre de la Société des Nations*, II, p. 59.
[15] Philip Baker, *Ibid.*, p. 60.

Each contracting power severally covenants and guarantees that it will not violate the territorial integrity or impair the political independence of any other contracting power.[16]

The insistence of the President for the affirmative form, despite this counsel of his advisers, led Mr. Lansing to state that while the President's advisers "were practically unanimous in the opinion that policy, as well as principle, demanded a change in the guaranty, he clung tenaciously to the affirmative form. The result was that which was feared and predicted by his colleagues. The President, and the President alone, must bear the responsibility for the result."

Upon his return to the United States in the summer of 1919, the President held, on August 19th at the White House, a conference with the members of the Foreign Relations Committee of the Senate for a discussion of the Treaty and the Covenant contained therein. His exposition of Article 10 on this occasion may properly be regarded as the most carefully considered utterance made by Mr. Wilson concerning the nature and scope of the obligations assumed by the

---

[16] *The Peace Negotiations*, p. 123.

On December 23, 1918, Mr. Lansing submitted to the President his "Suggested Draft of Articles for Discussion" which contained the self-denying covenant in the following form: "Each power signatory or adherent hereto severally covenants and guarantees that it will not violate the territorial integrity or impair the political independence of any other power signatory or adherent to this convention except when authorized so to do by a decree of the arbitral tribunal hereinafter referred to or by a three-fourths vote of the International Council of the League of Nations created by this Convention." *Ibid.*, p. 53.

Members of the League under this provision. In advance of the conference he had prepared a statement on some of the chief controversial issues involved in the Treaty, and with reference to Article 10, he spoke as follows:

Article 10 is in no respect of doubtful meaning when read in the light of the Covenant as a whole. The Council of the League can only "advise upon" the means by which the obligations of that great Article are to be given effect to. Unless the United States is a party to the policy or action in question, her own affirmative vote in the Council is necessary before any advice can be given, for a unanimous vote of the Council is required. If she is a party, the trouble is hers anyhow. And the unanimous vote of the Council is only advice in any case. Each Government is free to reject it if it pleases.

Nothing could have been made more clear to the Conference than the right of our Congress under our Constitution to exercise its independent judgment in all matters of peace and war. No attempt was made to question or limit that right. The United States will, indeed, undertake under Article 10 to "respect and preserve as against external aggression the territorial integrity and existing political independence of all members of the League," and that engagement constitutes a very grave and solemn moral obligation. But it is a moral, not a legal, obligation, and leaves our Congress absolutely free to put its own interpretation upon it in all cases that call for action. It is binding in conscience only, not in law.

Article 10 seems to me to constitute the very backbone of the whole Covenant. Without it the League would be hardly more than an influential debating society.[17]

[17] *Senate Document No. 76*, 66th Congress, 1st Session.

In the course of the subsequent discussions, the following dialogue ensued between the President and Senator Borah:

Senator Borah.—Mr. President, with reference to Article 10 . . . in listening to the reading of your statement I got the impression that your view was that the first obligation of Article 10, to wit: The members of the League undertake to respect and preserve as against external aggression the territorial integrity and existing political independence of all members of the League, was simply a moral obligation.

The President.—Yes, sir; inasmuch as there is no sanction in the Treaty.

Senator Borah.—But that would be a legal obligation as far as the United States was concerned if it should enter into it, would it not?

The President.—I would not interpret it in that way, Senator, because there is involved the element of judgment as to whether the territorial integrity or existing political independence is invaded or impaired. In other words, it is an attitude of comradeship and protection among the members of the League, which in its very nature is moral and not legal.

Senator Borah.—If, however, the actual fact of invasion were beyond dispute, then the legal obligation, it seems to me, would immediately arise.

The President.—The legal obligation to apply the automatic punishments of the Covenant, undoubtedly; but not the legal obligation to go to arms and actually to make war. Not the legal obligation. There might be a very strong moral obligation.

Despite these asurances of the President, the opposition to Article 10 developed in the United States Senate in radical and uncompromising form. On September 10, 1919, the Committee on Foreign Relations reported the Treaty to the Senate with recommendations in the majority report for a number of amendments and reservations. With respect to Article 10, it was proposed that the following reservation be made a part of the resolution of ratification:

The United States declines to assume, under the provisions of Article 10, or under any other Article, any obligation to preserve the territorial integrity or political independence of any other country or to interfere in controversies between other nations, Members of the League or not, or to employ the military or naval forces of the United States in such controversies, or to adopt economic measures for the protection of any other country, whether a Member of the League or not, against external aggression or for the purpose of coercing any other country, or for the purpose of intervention in the internal conflicts or other controversies which may arise in any other country, and no mandate shall be accepted by the United States under Article 22, Part I, of the Treaty of Peace with Germany, except by action of the Congress of the United States.[18]

This Article, which the President regarded as the "very backbone of the whole Covenant" was designated in the Committee Report as "the most vital objection to the League Covenant as it stands." In an accompanying explanatory note, the Committee outlined these objections:

This reservation is intended to meet the most vital objection to the League Covenant as it stands. Under no circumstances must there be any legal or moral obligation upon the United States to enter into war or to send its army and navy abroad or without the unfet-

[18] *Senate Report, No. 176*, 66th Congress, 1st Session, Part I.

tered action of Congress to impose economic boycotts on other countries. Under the Constitution of the United States the Congress alone has the power to declare war, and all bills to raise revenue or affecting the revenue in any way must originate in the House of Representatives, be passed by the Senate, and receive the signature of the President. These constitutional rights of Congress must not be impaired by any agreements such as are presented in this treaty, nor can any opportunity of charging the United States with bad faith be permitted. No American soldiers or sailors must be sent to fight in other lands at the bidding of the League of Nations. American lives must not be sacrificed except by the will and command of the American people acting through their constitutional representatives in Congress.[18]

In the meanwhile the President, confronted with the insistent demand of certain elements in the Senate for "interpretative reservations" or amendments to the Treaty, had undertaken a direct appeal to the people of the country, seeking through a series of addresses to bring sufficient pressure to bear upon the Senate to obtain ratification of the Treaty in the form which he deemed acceptable. The substance of the proposed reservation to Article 10 reached him while on his Western tour and in an address at Salt Lake City on September 23, 1919, he stated his unequivocal opposition to the change proposed. He read the text of the reservation to his audience and then declared:

That is a rejection of the Covenant. That is an absolute refusal to carry any part of the same responsibility that the other Members of the League carry.

[18] *Senate Report, No. 176*, 66th Congress, 1st Session, Part I.

Does the United States want to be in on that special footing.... Article 10 is an engagement on the part of all the great fighting nations of the world, because all the great fighting nations are going to be Members of the League, that they will respect and preserve as against external aggression the territorial integrity and the existing political independence of the other Members of the League. That is cutting at the heart of all wars. Every war of any consequence that you can cite originated in an attempt to seize the territory or interfere with the political independence of some other nation.... This is the heart of the Covenant, and what are these gentlemen afraid of? Nothing can be done under that article of the Treaty without the consent of the United States. I challenge them to draw any other deduction from the provisions of the Covenant itself. In every case where the League takes action the unanimous vote of the Council of the League is necessary; the United States is a permanent Member of the Council of the League, and its affirmative vote is in every case necessary for every affirmative, or for that matter every negative, action.[19]

During the succeeding months, while the Treaty of Versailles was before the Senate, that body on two occasions voted affirmatively for reservations to Article 10. The first reservation was voted on November 13, 1919, by 46 yeas to 33 nays, all of the Republican Senators and five Democrats voting or being paired in favor of the reservation. The text thus approved on that date was as follows:

The United States assumes no obligation to preserve the territorial integrity or political independence of any other country or to interfere in controversies be-

[19] *Addresses of President Wilson on His Western Tour, Senate Document, No. 120*, 66th Congress, 1st Session, pp. 323-324.

tween nations—whether Members of the League or not—under the provisions of Article 10, or to employ the military or naval forces of the United States under any article of the treaty for any purpose, unless in any particular case the Congress, which, under the Constitution, has the sole power to declare war or authorize the employment of the military or naval forces of the United States, shall by act or joint resolution so provide.[20]

On the same date the Senate rejected by a vote of 32 yeas to 44 nays the following substitute reservation offered by Senator Hitchcock:

That the advice mentioned in Article X of the Covenant of the League which the Council may give to the member nations as to the employment of their naval and military forces is merely advice which each member nation is free to accept or reject, according to the conscience and judgment of its then existing Government, and in the United States this advice can only be accepted by action of the Congress, at the time in being, Congress alone under the Constitution of the United States having the power to declare war.

On November 19, a resolution of ratification of the Treaty containing the so-called "Lodge Reservations" failed of adoption by a vote of 41 yeas to 51 nays; on the same day a resolution of unconditional ratification presented by Senator Underwood was rejected by a vote of 38 yeas to 53 nays. Formal action on the Treaty was not resumed until the following February

[20] *Congressional Record*, November 13, 1919, 66th Congress, 1st Session. Cf. the survey by George A. Finch, *The Treaty of Peace With Germany in the United States Senate*, International Conciliation Bulletin, No. 153.

9, but during the last two weeks of January an unofficial Bi-Partisan Conference, consisting of nine Senators—five Democrats and four Republicans—met in Washington to consider changes in the reservations which might be recommended to the other Members of the Senate.[21] Although tentative agreement was reached on certain reservations, the Conference was unable to arrive at accord on Article 10. Senator Lodge refused his consent to any modification of the reservation which he had submitted. "I had made up my mind at the beginning," he later recorded, "that if the Conference was to break up without an agreement it should be on Article 10, which was the crucial point throughout the contest over the Covenant of the League of Nations."[22]

In a letter to Senator Hitchcock on January 26, 1920, President Wilson accepted the reservations proposed by Mr. Hitchcock to take the place of those proposed by Mr. Lodge. The Hitchcock Reservations embodied the one on Article 10 which Senator Hitchcock had submitted and which had been rejected by the Senate on November 13. "Any reservation or resolution," the President wrote Senator Hitchcock at this time, "stating that 'the United States assumes no obligation under such and such an Article unless or except' would, I am sure, chill our relationship with the nations with which we expect to be associated in the

[21] *Senate Document, No. 193*, 66th Congress, 2d Session.
[22] *The Senate and the League of Nations*, p. 194.

great enterprise of maintaining the world's peace."[23] The Hitchcock reservation on Article 10, submitted now by Senator King, was rejected a second time by the Senate on March 15, and on this date a second reservation, proposed by Senator Lodge, was adopted by a vote of 56 yeas to 26 nays. The text of this reservation is given below:

The United States assumes no obligation to preserve the territorial integrity or political independence of any other country by the employment of its military or naval forces, its resources, or any form of economic discriminations, or to interfere in any way in controversies between nations, including all controversies relating to territorial integrity or political independence, whether members of the League or not, under the provisions of Article 10, or to employ the military or naval forces of the United States under any article of the Treaty for any purpose, unless in any particular case, the Congress, which, under the Constitution, has the sole power to declare war or authorize the employment of the military or naval forces of the United States, shall, in the exercise of full liberty of action, by act or joint resolution so provide."[24]

II

Upon all of this controversy between the President and the Senate over Article 10—which thus far has been treated in a purely factual manner—one or two observations may here be made. President Wilson recognized—and always took care to point out—that

[23] *Congressional Record*, February 9, 1920, 66th Congress, 2d Session, p. 2622.

[24] *Congressional Record*, 66th Congress, 2d Session, p. 4333.

Article 10 involved for the Members of the League of Nations international obligations of far-reaching significance. At the White House Conference in August, 1919, he said to Senator Borah that under Article 10 there might be a very strong moral obligation to go to arms and actually to make war.[25] Speaking at St. Louis on September 5, he told his audience that "the solemn thing about Article 10 is the first sentence, not the second. ... When you read Article 10, therefore, you will see that it is nothing but the inevitable, logical center of the whole system of the Covenant of the League of Nations, and I stand for it absolutely." And again, in writing to Senator Hitchcock on March 8, 1920, he reiterated this position. "There is no escaping the moral obligations which are expressed in positive terms in this Article of the Covenant."[26]

On the other hand, Senator Lodge and his associates were unalterably opposed to the assumption of these obligations by the United States. The reservation on Article 10 which Senator Lodge presented and which he refused to modify was clearly, as Mr. Wilson said, a fundamental modification of the principle expressed in that Article. Whether Mr. Wilson or Mr. Lodge was supporting the proper principle of politics need not at this point be discussed. Each clearly perceived that the Article entailed obligations; these obligations were supported by the one and rejected by the other and both refused to compromise on the positions thus defi-

[25] See above, p. 77.
[26] See Annex II.

nitely assumed. Throughout the Peace Conference and the Senate controversy, Mr. Wilson was intent upon having incorporated in the public law of nations the principle expressed in Article 10. He saw with perfect clarity the essential need in the society of nations of some effective system of state security. Under the prevailing conditions, he maintained, no power was obliged to respect territorial integrity or the political independence of another if it possessed the force necessary to disregard it. "Article 10," he said, "cuts at **the very heart, and is the only instrument that will cut** to the very heart, of the old system."[27] In this choice of instruments, the President may have been wrong but in his conviction that some remedy was needed he was undeniably right.

It will have been noted that in construing the obligations incurred by the Members of the League under Article 10, Mr. Wilson maintained that these obligations are of a moral and not of a legal character. In so doing, it is the writer's opinion that Mr. Wilson was in error and that his interpretation was not in accord with the principles of international jurisprudence. To the general obligation expressed in the first sentence of Article 10 there attaches every element of legality which may be ascribed to any international treaty or to any of the customary rules of international law. To assert, as Mr. Wilson did, that no legal obligation was created because "there is no sanction in the Treaty" is to set up a criterion of legality which

[27] St. Louis Address, September 5, 1919.

would deny the quality of law to practically the whole body of customary and conventional rules which govern the relations of states.[28] Under the first sentence of Article 10, "the Members of the League *undertake to respect and preserve* as against external aggression the territorial integrity and existing political independence of all Members of the League." The juristic relations thus established among the Members of the League are merely in the stage of declaration but in this respect their status is in nowise different from that of practically all other relations between states which by the standards of international law are commonly designated as legal. And the second sentence

[28] By the term "sanction," Mr. Wilson evidently referred to the absence of any provision in the Treaty for the application of penalties in case the obligations in question were not fulfilled. In his recent work on the *Fundamental Concepts of Public Law*, Professor Willoughby rejects the idea that even for positive law the term sanction connotes "penalty," or evil threatened to be inflicted by political superiors upon political inferiors for disobedience to commands. The essential fact connoted by the term sanction, he says, is the "official imprimatur of the state," and, "the true sanction of a positive law consists, then, in the fact that the authority issuing it claims to be politically superior to the persons to whom it is directed; or, looking at the law from the point of view of the ones commanded, that they recognize the law-issuing authority as having a legal right to regulate their conduct in the premises." (Pp. 147-148.)

The above statement appears to recognize a closer approximation of international law to the nature of positive law than is commonly admitted. Could it not as logically be said that the essential fact connoted by the term "sanction" in international law is not the element of penalty for its violation but the fact that the rule has been declared in the manner recognized by the subjects of international law as the valid mode of enunciation?

of Article 10—"in case of such aggression, etc. . . . the Council shall advise upon the means by which this obligation shall be fulfilled"—introduces no modification on the legal relations expressed in positive terms in the preceding sentence. On the contrary, it tends to advance these relations beyond the mere stage of declaration by indicating the means through which their effective enjoyment may be assured.

To say, however, that Article 10 sets up a general obligation of a legal nature is by no means a complete analysis of the matter. Other questions arise. Who, for example, is to determine when a *casus fœderis* has arisen, and, who is to determine the nature and scope of the means through which the obligations shall be fulfilled? To each of these questions President Wilson offered a reply. He insisted that the constitutional authorities of each Member state would be free to decide whether the circumstances called for action, and, that the unanimous vote of the Council would be only advice which each Government would be free to reject if it pleases.[29] To what degree have these interpretations been sustained by the subsequent evolution of Article 10?

The most authoritative evidence on the question can be obtained by a survey of the discussions on the Article which have gone forward through the organs of the League of Nations. The process began at the First Assembly with the introduction by Canada of a motion to strike the Article from the Covenant, and

[29] See above, p. 76.

produced certain concrete results in 1923 when the Fourth Assembly voted upon an interpretative resolution. We shall turn now to a consideration of these discussions in order to illuminate the problems mentioned above and to note the attitude of various states towards Article 10 as expressed by their representatives at Geneva.

III

We have quoted Mr. Wilson as saying that every imperialistic influence in Europe was hostile to Article 10.[30] Granting that this was true, opposition to the Article came, nevertheless, from another source, and this hostility was prompted by motives which can scarcely be designated as imperialistic.

During the Peace Conference, the two representatives of Canada at Paris, Sir Robert Borden and Mr. C. J. Doherty, submitted memoranda advocating the alteration or suppression of Article 10.[31] These papers set forth arguments of a general nature against the principle expressed in the Article and raised, in the name of Canada, specific objections which were, it was contended, equally important to other states in an analogous position. Both of the Canadian delegates questioned the right and the competence of the Peace Conference to make a declaration concerning the legiti-

[30] See above, p. 68.

[31] The texts of the memoranda are reprinted in *Bibliotheca Visseriana*, I, as annexes to an article by A. A. H. Struycken on "La Société des Nations et l'intégrité territoriale."

macy and justice of existing territorial distribution among the nations of the world. Such an undertaking, it was pointed out, ought to be preceded by a careful re-examination of all the territorial possessions of the proposed signatories of the Covenant and ought to afford opportunity for a hearing to all states or peoples who held a grievance under existing arrangements. Even if this program were practicable, the Canadians declared, the decisions taken would not satisfy all existing claims nor arrest the course of future aspirations.[32] The Covenant envisaged the possibility of

[32] Cf. the similar criticism by Mr. Elihu Root. In a letter to Mr. Will H. Hays on March 29, 1919, he wrote:

"The fourth point upon which I think there should be an amendment is Article X. . . . Looking at this Article as a part of a perpetual league for the preservation of peace, my first impression was that the whole Article ought to be stricken out. If perpetual, it would be an attempt to preserve for all time unchanged the distribution of power and territory made in accordance with the views and exigencies of the Allies in this present juncture of affairs. It would necessarily be futile. . . .

"I think, however, that this Article must be considered not merely with reference to the future, but with reference to the present situation in Europe. . . . Order must be restored. The Allied nations in their council must determine the lines of reconstruction. Their determinations must be enforced. . . . . Under these conditions the United States cannot quit. It must go on to the performance of its duty and the immediate aspect of Article 10 is an agreement to do that. I think, therefore, that Article 10 should be amended so that it shall hold for a limited time and thereafter any member may withdraw from it. Add to Article 10 the following:

"After the expiration of five years from the signing of this convention any party may terminate its obligation under this article by giving one year's notice in writing to the Secretary-General of the League." *Senate Document, No. 41*, 66th Congress, 1st Session.

future wars. Suppose, Sir Robert Borden asked, a nation attacked occupies and proposes to annex (possibly with the consent of the majority of the population) a portion of the territory of the aggressor nation—what shall be the operation of the Article?

The memorandum of Mr. Doherty elaborated the distinction between Powers of general interests and those of limited or particular interest. Canada and many other states were in the latter class. The Great Powers at the Conference were arrogating to themselves authority to determine territorial changes and allotments. Was it fair that the smaller Powers be required to assume responsibility for the maintenance of these decisions? The burden of a reciprocal guarantee would, moreover, in the case of Canada and of other states, be well out of proportion to any advantage which might be derived from the proposed arrangement. If there were to be a principle of guarantee, Mr. Doherty argued, let it apply only to the states created by the Conference and to those whose territory was altered by its decisions. And the burden of this guarantee should be assumed by the states responsible for the Treaty and, if it were judged appropriate, by the states which have benefited thereby.

The obligation under Article 10, Mr. Doherty asserted, was direct and absolute; it allowed no conditions; it imperiously called for military action. It vested the Council of the League with the function of advising upon the means by which the obligations under the Article should be fulfilled, and, following this advice, each nation would be called upon to participate in the guarantee with all the forces at its disposal. He was convinced that the people of Canada would strongly resent their representatives subscribing to an engagement of this character.

In September, 1919, however, in presenting the Covenant to the Canadian Parliament, Mr. Doherty gave a different construction to the Article. It stated a principle, he maintained, but imposed upon Canada no obligation to go to war without the approval of the constitutional authorities of the Dominion.[33]

Twelve months later before the First Assembly of the League of Nations the whole question was reopened. At the Fourteenth Plenary Session of the Assembly, Mr. Doherty presented in the name of Canada the following motion:

That Article 10 of the Covenant of the League of Nations be and is hereby struck out.

This motion, he said, "represents the view which Canada entertained at the time the Covenant was under discussion, and which she endeavored to cause to prevail."[34]

Prior to the introduction of the Canadian motion, the Assembly had decided that action on amendments to the Covenant should be deferred until the meeting of the Second Assembly and that in the meanwhile proposed amendments should be subjected to investigation and report by a committee to be appointed by the

[33] Temperley, VI, p. 350.
[34] *Plenary Meetings*, First Assembly, p. 281.

Council. It applied, therefore, this procedure to the motion offered by Mr. Doherty.

The Committee on Amendments to the Covenant was set by the Council at a meeting in Paris, February, 1921, and received the Canadian proposal along with others which had been submitted for the modification of the Covenant. With respect, however, to the proposed amendment to Article 10, a somewhat special procedure was followed. At the above mentioned meeting in Paris, the Council had appointed a body known subsequently as the Committee of Jurists[35] for the purpose of giving an opinion on the legal scope of Article 18 of the Covenant. The Committee on Amendments was of opinion that Article 10 also was in need of such interpretation and decided to avail itself of the services of the Committee of Jurists for obtaining the interpretation.

The Committee on Amendments requested the Committee of Jurists to consider the following question:

What obligations does Article 10 impose on Members of the League, in addition to and apart from, the obligations contained in the other Articles of the Covenant?

The Report of the Commission of Jurists on Article 10 and that of the Committee on Amendments was submitted to the Council at the Geneva meeting in September, 1921, and both Reports were transmitted in turn by the Council to the Second Assembly. Certain

[35] The Committee was composed of M. Scialoja (Chairman), M. Bourquin, Sir Cecil Hurst, M. Struycken, and M. Gout.

extracts from the Report of each of these Committees are given below:[36]

EXTRACTS FROM THE REPORT OF THE COMMISSION OF JURISTS

The fundamental idea of Article 10 is as follows: no change can henceforth be made, by means of aggression, in the territorial integrity and political independence of states, which are essential elements of their international status; such changes can only be made as a result of peaceful negotiation and by the helpful mediation of the League of Nations.

This involves for all Members of the League the twofold obligation of mutually respecting each other's territorial integrity and existing political independence, and of maintaining these against all external aggression, either on the part of other Members of the League or on the part of states which are not Members.

This legal conception constitutes one of the guiding principles of the League of Nations. In view of the fact that war almost always has for its object some change in the territorial integrity or political independence of other states, the new rule of law expressed in Article 10 makes the League of Nations an organization for the maintenance of peace, which is called upon to safeguard the principle that no changes can be made in the territorial limits and political independence of states except as the result of peaceful negotiation and friendly mediation.

We cannot, however, interpret Article 10 as unreservedly confirming the territorial *status quo* as it has been established by the last treaties of peace, and as future treaties will perhaps establish it.

The League of Nations neither could, nor should, assume responsibility for such a confirmation; but the League of Nations can, and indeed should, if it desires

[36] The text of each Report is given in League Document, A.24 (1) 1921. V. [A. C. 40 (a)].

to become a peaceful organization of peoples and to contribute to the maintenance of world peace, adopt as its own the thesis that a state can no longer endeavour to establish by violence, that is to say by war, its claims to any territorial change whatsoever, however justifiable these claims may appear to be. . . .

Article 10 contains the governing principle to which all Members of the League subscribe, the methods of application and the legal means of enforcement thereof being laid down in the succeeding Articles.

A State Member of the League which infringes the legal principle formulated in Article 10 and violates the teritorial integrity and the political independence of one of its fellow-Members will find itself confronted by all the other Members of the League, who will have to fulfil their duty of maintaining the *status quo* against the wrongful act of violence. Article 16 lays down in detail the obligations which rest upon the Members of the League in such a case. . . . If the aggressor is not a State Member of the League, Article 17 of the Covenant, by refering to Article 16, provides for the manner in which the Members of the League shall fulfil their duties. . . .

The Members are not obliged to take part in any military action. It is true that Article 16 alludes to joint military action to be organized, on the recommendation of the Council, by the several Governments concerned; but, in general, the Members are not legally bound to take part in such action. . . .

The Committee considers that the Article applies to all cases of actual violation of the territorial integrity and political independence of a Member, even if the ultimate purpose of such violation is not the definite annexation of the territory or diminution of the political independence of the Member. . . .

The Committee wishes to point out that there can be no doubt that the Council, under the terms of this Article, can only advise as to the means to be employed; it cannot impose them. . . .

Finally, if it be asked whether the considerations set forth above do not lead to the conclusion that Article 10 duplicates Articles 16 and 17 of the Covenant, the answer is in the negative. Although Article 10 lays down no general rules of procedure, and contains no obligation which cannot be found elsewhere in the Covenant, it nevertheless possesses a certain value of its own. It enunciates one of the legal principles upon which the League of Nations is based, namely, the principles of mutual respect for, and preservation of, the territorial integrity and existing political independence of all Members of the League. This is a governing principle to be observed, not only by the Members in their relations with one another, but also by the organs of the League, whenever they are called upon to exert their influence or authority in any way for the settlement of disputes or for the maintenance or restoration of the peace of the world.

Extract From the Report of the Committee on Amendments

The Committee has had referred to it the proposal, presented by the Canadian Delegation at the First Assembly, that Article 10 of the Covenant be struck out. The very able Memoranda of the Right Honorable Charles J. Doherty and of Sir Robert Borden, in support of this proposal, have been based principally upon the premise that Article 10 implies a recognition of the rightfulness of the existing territorial settlement and an obligation for all the Members of the League to guarantee its continuance perpetually.

The Committee considers that this interpretation does not take into account sufficiently the peaceful procedures set out in the Covenant for modifying the existing *status quo,* if its modification appears to be just and in the interest of peace. Indeed, the Canadian interpretation is closely connected with a tendency, only too general, to exaggerate the scope of the obligations of Article 10.

From this same tendency there results the view, which has been held in certain countries, that the States Members of the League have contracted, as a result of their adhesion to the Covenant, an absolute obligation to put their forces at the disposal of the Council, which may use them in any part of the world where aggression occurs.

The provisions of the Covenant, in fact, are confined to conferring on the Council the power to make simple recommendations. Political and geographical considerations will influence the nature of the recommendation addressed to each Member.

The Committee has decided unanimously in favor of the maintenance of the principle set out in Article 10. The exclusion of acts of aggression as a means of modifying the territorial integrity and the political independence of States is the very essence of the League of Nations. On the other hand, Article 10 has its application and its own value, and it cannot be said to be a duplication of any other Article whatever of the Covenant. It enunciates as a general principle the maintenance of political independence and territorial integrity against violence. The Articles which follow it (Articles 12 to 17) provide in detail the procedure to be followed for cases of actual aggression....

The Committee received a very able report from the Committee of Jurists, and then found itself confronted with two possible solutions: (1) the adoption of an amendment of the text of Article 10; (2) the adoption by the Assembly of a declaration interpreting the present wording of Article 10. After considering the advantages and the inconvenience of each method, the Committee has decided in favor of the maintenance of the present text of the Article, for the following reasons:—

Article 10 is one of the fundamental Articles in the system established by the Covenant. Only with the greatest prudence can it be touched, and then only if clear and pressing reasons justify such modification.

The great political importance of the Article also necessitates this caution. Many States regard the Article as embodying the best protection of their integrity and of their independence, and as the counterpart of the program of the reduction of armaments.

A limitation of the present scope of the Article would be calculated to alarm public opinion, perhaps even to cause embarrassment to Governments.

Finally, the League of Nations is still incomplete; it awaits the entrance of new Members. It would appear, therefore, premature to wish to undertake the revision of Article 10.

It is impossible, however, not to recognize the gravity of the divergence between the different interpretations of the present text, which interpretations present the common characteristic of enlarging unduly the scope of the obligations of Article 10, to the point of making the Article appear unacceptable. It has seemed to the Committee that the adoption by the Assembly of a declaration establishing the meaning to be attached to Article 10 would be the most appropriate procedure to follow in the present circumstances. It would furnish an adequate response to unjustified criticisms, without sacrificing any of the strength of the essential principle. Sanctioned by the vote of the Assembly, this declaration will have all the moral force of an authentic interpretation.

The Committee has unanimously approved, and has the honor to submit to the Assembly, the following text of such a declaration:—

Proposed Interpretative Resolution

With a view to indicating more precisely the scope and intention of Article 10 of the Covenant, the Assembly adopts the following Resolution:—

Article 10 was not intended to perpetuate the territorial and political organization as established and as existing at the time of the recent treaties of peace.

Changes may be effected in that organization by various legitimate means. The Covenant admits of this possibility.

The intention of Article 10 is to enunciate the principle that hereafter the civilized world cannot tolerate acts of aggression as a means of modifying the territorial *status quo* and the political independence of the States.

To this end, the Members of the League have pledged themselves, first, to respect the territorial integrity and the existing political independence of all the States Members of the League, and, secondly, to maintain this integrity and this independence against any external aggression, whether on the part of a State Member or a State not Member of the League. With a view to assuring the fulfilment of this second obligation, the Council shall advise upon the means; it must do so not merely in the case of actual aggression, but also in the case of any danger or threat of such aggression. The Council will perform this function by addressing to the Members such recommendations as are deemed proper in regard thereto, taking into account Articles 11, 12, 13, 15, 16, 17 and 19 of the Covenant.

IV

When the Second Assembly convened, the foregoing Reports, together with the original Canadian proposal, were referred by the Assembly to its First Committee.[37] The latter appointed a Sub-Committee to prepare a report, M. Struycken (Netherlands), serving as Rapporteur. This Sub-Committee prepared a draft report, the substance of which was a summary of the conclusions of the Commission of Jurists and of the Committee on Amendments. The report of the Sub-

[37] The Committee on Constitutional Questions.

ARTICLE 10 OF THE COVENANT

Committee contained, however, one important modification of the conclusions of the Committee on Amendments. The report of the latter had stated:

The purpose of Article 10 was not to perpetuate the territorial and political organization as established and existing at the time of the conclusions of the recent treaties of peace. Changes may be effected in that organization by various legitimate means. . . .

The Sub-Committee had added:

and even by war, provided that the peaceful measures laid down in the Covenant have been exhausted.

The proposed change was the subject of immediate dissent in the discussions which followed in the main Committee:[38]

M. Freire d'Andrade (Portugal) believed that the League of Nations was still too young for the Covenant to be amended so drastically. . . . Neither could he accept the draft resolution which was at the end of the report, which was, moreover, only an interpretation of the Covenant. . . . Unless his Government should expressly instruct him to do otherwise, he would vote against the resolution proposed in the report. He wished to draw the attention of the Committee to the fact that the report admitted war as a means to modify the actual *status quo* of states.

M. Rolin (Belgium) spoke of the importance attached by Belgium to Article 10 since her neutrality was no longer guaranteed by the various Powers:

As regards the object of the guarantee [he said], the interpretation of Article 10 could not be that of the

[38] The discussions are reported in the *Minutes, First Committee*, Second Assembly, pp. 107-114.

Sub-Committee. Article 10 guaranteed "as against external aggression." This was very clear, and the interpretation which it was desired to give to it would have the effect of restricting the application of this Article only to the case of war being declared before the means to safeguard peace, provided by the Covenant, had been exhausted. Even if this procedure under the Covenant had been exhausted, the speaker thought that in any case, in the present state of the League, the result of a war could not be any modification of territory. The text was explicit. . . .

As regards the exercise of the guarantee, recourse might be had to the interpretative resolution proposed by the Sub-Committee.

If they stopped at the first sentence of Article 10, they could obviously find there a mutual engagement of the Members of the League towards each other; but every one agreed to consider that two important limitations must be applied to this engagement:

1. The League had not received the power to decree, through its organs, that any kind of military intervention could be imposed upon its Members;

2. The Members of the League had the right to say that they had all agreed to assure the political independence and territorial integrity of each state, and that this obligation must be interpreted in good faith to mean, that, as Mr. Doherty had said himself, every state was bound to the extent of its forces, and according to its political or geographical situation.

Mr. Doherty (Canada) was of the opinion that the old version of Article 10 was perfectly clear, but that it had been explained and interpreted to such an extent that it had become incomprehensible. He dissented from the opinion of the Commission of Jurists that the execution of the obligations of the Article was provided for in Article 16. Article 16 dealt only with the obligations arising from Articles 12, 13 and 15. It was obvious that the authors of the Covenant had in mind the conception embodied in Article 10 as something absolutely distinct from the obligation of Article 12:

> Article 10 was unfair not only in principle but also in its application.... Even if certain reasons appeared to justify the maintenance of the territorial integrity of various nations, it was impossible to justify an Article which imposed such an obligation on all the nations of the world alike.... The attack made by the Canadian Delegation was not upon the League but upon the Covenant, which was only an instrument of the League.... If Article 10 were retained in the Covenant, a seed of dissolution would be retained which would unfailingly destroy the League of Nations.

M. Urrutia (Columbia) proposed that the matter of an interpretative resolution be postponed until the following Assembly. At a subsequent meeting of the Committee, with the assent of Mr. Doherty, a resolution to this effect was adopted by the Committee and later approved by the Assembly in the following form:

> Whereas a motion has been submitted by the Canadian Delegation for the striking out of Article 10 of the Covenant;
> Whereas widely different opinions have been expressed with regard to the legal bearing of this Article and its relationship to the other Articles of the Covenant, especially as to Articles 12 to 17;
> And whereas the legal and political arguments made both in favor of and against the striking out of Article 10 are of great weight:
> The Assembly postpones the continuation of the examination of the proposal and the decision until its next Session, and recommends that this proposal be decided before any other amendment.[39]

[39] *Resolutions*, Second Assembly.

In the course of the Assembly debates on this resolution, Mr. Doherty declared:

> Rightly or wrongly, we think we perceive a dangerous principle in Article 10. By its wording it seems to lay down the principle that possession can take precedence over justice. I think we all agree that, if this opinion is justified, Article 10 must disappear.[40]

V

At the Third Assembly of the League, Canada gave up the proposal for a deletion of Article 10. Speaking before the First Committee—which once more had the proposal on its agenda—Mr. Lapointe (Canada) stated that he recognized the impossibility of the elimination of the Article. He conceded that strong arguments had been adduced for its retention. But there existed, nevertheless, misunderstandings and uncertainty as to its present scope despite the efforts thus made for its clarification. Moreover, the maintenance of Article 10 prevented several states from adhering to the League of Nations. Since it was not possible entirely to eliminate the Article, Canada must once again insist upon an amendment which would obviate the uncertainty of its scope. He proposed, therefore, that the Committee should affirm its approval of the principle recognized by the First Committee and by the Committee on Amendments last year, by adding at the end of Article 10 the following words:

> Taking into account the political and geographical circumstances of each state.

[40] *Plenary Meetings*, Second Assembly, p. 834.

Further, in order to give due weight to the sovereign authority of Parliaments in the various states Members of the League of Nations, the Canadian Delegation proposed the following amendment:

The opinion given by the Council in such cases shall be regarded as a matter of the highest importance, and shall be taken into consideration by all the Members of the League, which shall use their utmost endeavors to conform to the conclusions of the Council; but no Member shall be under the obligation to engage in any act of war without the consent of its Parliament, Legislature or other representative body.

The First Committee proceeded to a discussion of this new proposal.[41]

M. Dissesco (Roumania) considered that there was no need for an amendment . . . the text of no law was so clear and precise as to be free from the possibility of divergent interpretation. . . . Of the three "sanctions" provided in the Covenant — diplomatic, economic and military—the last-named had unfortunately been suppressed, in spite of a French proposal which took account of the lessons to be drawn from history. Were they then to abandon the two sanctions which still remained in the Covenant?

M. Barthélemy (France) had been instructed by his Government to resist the [original] Canadian proposal; but the fresh situation created by the new proposal . . . permitted his association with it. The French view was that Article 10 was merely a principle, the organization and practical scope of which were contained in Articles 16 and 17 of the Covenant. . . . The Article was a statement of a new and essentially democratic international law. . . . They did not desire to

[41] *Minutes, First Committee*, Third Assembly, pp. 23-27 and pp. 36-37.

arrest the course of history, but merely by directing its movement, to insure that the justification for territorial changes should not reside in force. ... To deprive the League of Nations of Article 10 would be to sign its death warrant.

M. Babinski (Poland) said the Polish Government attached special importance to Article 10. He proposed that the Article should be maintained as it stood and that the question should not be referred to a Committee.

M. Alvarez (Chile) regarded the Canadian proposal as an occasion for discussing the new idea of continental guarantee of territorial integrity. It was in reality an old idea; President Wilson's first idea. It had been realized in the A. B. C. Agreement and was the underlying principle of Article 10. In 1915, the United States had proposed to all the American states a territorial guarantee in constitutional republican form; and it had again been proposed in 1916 in a report which he (Alvarez) had submitted to the American Institute of International Law. The object should not be absolutely to prevent any territorial changes, but to guarantee that such changes should not be determined by force.

M. Rolin (Belgium) stated that the Belgian delegation would not oppose the reference of the Canadian proposal to a Sub-Committee. ...

He was ready to vote at once for the amendment proposed by the Canadian delegation; the Covenant must be interpreted in good faith. A system of continental guarantees seemed capable both of allaying the uneasiness of the American states and of satisfying the desire for security of certain European states. He suggested that the question should be examined by the Mixed Commission on Armaments.

M. Motta (Switzerland) considered that, by rejecting the Canadian proposal, they would leave the point in obscurity. . . . In spite of the great importance which his country attached to Article 10, he would be prepared to sacrifice it in order to obtain the adhesion of the United States to the League of Nations, but only on that condition. He proposed that the Committee should refer the Canadian proposal to the Assembly.

The Committee adjourned without reaching a decision on the question. At a subsequent meeting M. Struycken (Netherlands) presented a draft report for submission to the Assembly. It said in part:

The First Committee has not thought it advisable to discuss during the present session of the Assembly the substance of the above new proposals. It is necessary that the Governments should be placed in a position to consider them, and they should be carefully examined before a decision is taken.

The following draft resolution was proposed in the report and adopted by the First Committee and later by the Assembly:

The Assembly decides that the Canadian proposal with regard to Article 10 of the Covenant shall be adjourned until the Fourth Assembly, in order that the subject may be considered in all its bearings. The Assembly leaves it to the Council to decide as to the steps to be taken to provide for a detailed study of the Canadian proposal before the meeting of the Fourth Assembly.[42]

[42] *Resolutions*, Third Assembly.

VI

At a meeting of the Council of the League on January 29, 1923, decision was taken to invite the Members of the League to communicate their respective views on the new proposals of the Canadian Government. In the course of the succeeding months some twenty-five Governments responded to this request. Some extracts from these replies are given in Annex III.

When the Fourth Assembly convened, the above mentioned replies were referred to the First Committee for a further consideration of the Canadian proposal. Sir Lomer Gouin, the Canadian representative on the Committee, continued the advocacy of the Amendment. He recalled the origin of this important question. As early as 1919, Sir Robert Borden and Mr. Doherty drew up and presented to the Peace Conference two memoranda recommending the deletion of Article 10. Canada considered that the Article ought never to have been inserted. When the Treaty containing the Covenant was before the Canadian Parliament, the Opposition had submitted a motion to the effect that Canada, in giving its assent to the Treaty, in nowise accepted that the autonomy of the Dominion was thereby diminished and that the country could be drawn into war without the authorization of Parliament. The Government had replied that the situation could not be otherwise; that the Council of the League could not pretend to have any power over the Canadian Government. The Treaty was ratified without the motion offered by the Opposition but the motion itself was an exact reflection of the opinion of the country.

The speaker went on to review the efforts of Canada before the League of Nations for the deletion or the amendment of the Article. He summarized the replies of the Governments to the Canadian proposals which the Committee had before it. Twenty-five states had replied to the invitation of the Council; the majority had expressed themselves as against the amendment; six were in favor of it; and four or five were content with the *status quo*.

The principal argument invoked against the Canadian proposal was that Article 10 was perfectly clear and already contained everything which the amendment proposed to add. The majority of the Members had expressed the opinion that, under the terms of Article 10, the Council could do no more, if the case arose, than address recommendations which did not in any way bind the various Parliaments. Such, however, was not the view held by Albania, Greece, Poland, and Finland. These states considered, on the contrary, that the various Parliaments were bound by the ratification of the Covenant. Under these circumstances, it was important to define exactly the scope of the Article. Canada did not now ask for the elimination of Article 10 but she insisted upon the amendments proposed last year by Mr. Lapointe.[43]

The consensus of the Committee appeared to be in

[43] *Minutes, First Committee*, Fourth Assembly, pp. 11-18; and pp. 24-28.

favor of an interpretative resolution rather than an amendment, especially in view of the fact that the amendments[44] to Article 26 of the Covenant were not yet in force. On the Chairman's suggestion, a Sub-Committee was appointed to draw up an interpretative resolution. At the following meeting, the Sub-Committee brought forward the following proposal presented by M. Rolin as Rapporteur:

The Assembly, desirous of defining the scope of Article 10 of the Covenant, adopts the following resolution:

It is in conformity with the spirit of Article 10, that, in the event of the Council considering it to be its duty to recommend the application of military measures in consequence of an aggression or danger or threat of aggression, the Council shall be bound to take account more particularly of the geographical situation and of the special conditions of each state.

The opinion expressed by the Council shall be regarded as an invitation of the utmost weight which all the Members of the League shall take into consideration in the sincere desire of executing in all good faith their engagements.

It is for the constitutional authorities of each Member to decide whether the circumstances do give rise to the obligation of preserving the independence and the integrity of the territory of Members, and in what degree the Member is bound to assure the execution of this obligation by the employment of its military forces.

The Rapporteur explained these paragraphs in detail. He pointed out that the Sub-Committee had been careful to indicate, by the form which it gave to the first

[44] Amendments respecting the procedure on Amendments to the Covenant.

paragraph, that the guarantee afforded by Article 10 did not necessarily imply military action. With further reference to the first paragraph—as the French Government in its comment on the Canadian proposal had pointed out—the Council should not confine itself exclusively to taking account of the geographical situation and the special conditions of each state, but should also take account of other factors as well; but to avoid making an exhaustive list, the phrase "more particularly" had been used.

With reference to the second and third paragraphs, M. Rolin continued:

It was stated in Article 10: "The Members of the League *undertake* . . .," and a little further on: "In case of any such aggression or in case of any threat or danger of such aggression, the Council shall advise upon the means by which this *obligation* shall be fulfilled." Article 10 thus implied both undertakings and international obligations.

The text submitted by the Sub-Committee emphasized the legal nature of these international obligations.

On the other hand, it had been repeated many times that the League of Nations was not a super-State, and that its Members had not surrendered their sovereignty. It followed, therefore, that the Members of the League who had, in virtue of the Covenant, contracted various engagements were, in accordance with the tradition of international law, the proper judges of those engagements. . . .

In drafting the last paragraph, the Sub-Committee had been guided by the recommendation of the Institute of International Law. . . . The two principles embodied in the last paragraph were an almost literal reproduction of the Institute's recommendation.

In this last paragraph the Sub-Committee had brought into prominence the two questions which the Governments Members of the League of Nations would have to decide when called upon to fulfil the guarantee obligation contained in Article 10.

The first question was whether the guarantee came into play and whether the circumstances constituted a *casus fœderis;* the second question was whether the action to be taken should assume a military form.

It was generally admitted that if a Parliament, when consulted by its Government, recognized the force of the guarantee obligation, it could not refuse to fulfil the guarantee provided in Article 16, at least in its minimum form (economic blockade and severance of all trade or financial relations); but with regard to active intervention by military or naval forces, the Sub-Committee had recognized that, in estimating the force of its obligations, every Member had as much right as the Council to take account of the geographical situation and the special circumstances of each state.

Two obligations were therefore involved—a general obligation, which should be discharged so soon as good grounds were recognized for bringing the guarantee into operation; and a potential obligation to give military assistance, which would fall upon particular states according to circumstances not defined in the Covenant, which each state was bound, as was the Council, to interpret in good faith.

Each Member of the League was therefore pledged to fulfil its obligations, which existed independently of the deliberations of any Parliament; but, just as the various Parliaments were free to decide whether the *casus fœderis* had arisen and whether the guarantee came into action, the Members of the League of Nations were free to determine the limits and the conditions of their obligations and the manner in which these were to be carried out.[45]

[45] Cf. The article by M. Rolin on "L'Article 10 du Pacte de la Société des Nations," in *Les Origines et L'Œuvre de la Société des Nations*, II, pp. 453-488.

There were seductions in the foregoing interpretations of Article 10, M. Barthélemy (France) warned the Committee:

According to the spirit of the Covenant, it was for the Council to declare whether there was a legal necessity for the states to intervene, whereas, according to the proposed interpretation, the Parliaments were to judge whether the Council had been mistaken or not. That constituted a kind of sovereign right of the Parliament to determine the scope of the obligations involved—a dangerous conception, in view of the fact that the Covenant laid down that the Council should give an authoritative opinion, against which there could be no appeal.

Other members of the Committee associated themselves with the viewpoint of the French representative:

To adopt the text of the Sub-Committee, declared M. Manolesco-Ramniceano (Roumania), would be to destroy the authority of Article 10 by transforming an obligation into merely facultative action; it was, however, contrary to all principles of law to make the legality of an obligation depend upon the appreciation of the party on whom the obligation lay.

M. Erich (Finland) likewise, said that paragraph three was inadmissible:

It suggested the possibility of conflict between the Council and a state Member of the League and, in such case placed the authority of the individual state above that of the Council.... The Council had no power to impose its will upon the Members of the League. It was most undesirable, however, that the ineffectiveness of an invitation from the Council should be emphasized. In his opinion it would be well to refrain from amending or interpreting Article 10, which was the corner-stone of the guarantee provided by the Covenant.

Prince Arfa-ed-Dovleh (Persia) agreed:

His Government would accept no amendment or interpretation of Article 10, which constituted one of the most important guarantees of the Covenant.

The Rapporteur, in reply to the point raised by M. Barthélemy, called the attention of the Committee to the action taken by the Second Assembly in the interpretation of Article 16:

It had voted a resolution with regard to Article 16 which was more precise than Article 10 of the Covenant. In a case where it was a question of measures to be taken automatically, the Second Assembly had unanimously decided that it was for the various Members of the League to say whether there had been a breach of the Covenant or not. If they could admit, in connection with Article 16, that it was for the various Members of the League to decide whether there had been a breach of the Covenant, *a fortiori* they were bound to recognize that it was for the various Members of the League to judge whether the Council had been right in deciding that the conditions of the guarantee were realized.

The discussion wandered from the point at issue. M. Alvarez (Chile) asked permission to say a few words concerning the scope of Article 10 as interpreted by the Canadian proposal, and the efficacy of the Monroe Doctrine. He concluded that the latter doctrine furnished a more ample guarantee of the territorial integrity of American states than was supplied by Article 10. It followed that the American states did not need Article 10 to give them a guarantee of territorial integrity. It was the desire of America to extend the advantages of the Monroe Doctrine to the whole world.

The Chairman (M. Motta, Switzerland) observed that the Monroe Doctrine was not under discussion at the moment.

M. Scialoja (Italy) suggested that the discussion be adjourned to an indefinite date. The interpretation of Article 10, he said, had always given rise to insurmountable difficulties, the chief of which arose in connection with the word "aggression." The real value, he believed, of Article 10 was due to the fact that the principles which it expressed would in the future form part of the conscience of nations. These principles would then have something more than a mere legal value because moral conscience was worth more than law. Moreover, the Third Committee was then examining a guarantee scheme (The Draft Treaty of Mutual Assistance) and there were, therefore, sound reasons for postponing the present discussion until the latter scheme had been elaborated in detail.

The Committee agreed to an adjournment in order that the members might have the opportunity to consult their respective Delegations.

When the Committee resumed its discussions some days later, an amendment was offered by the British representative to replace Paragraph 3 of the resolution originally presented by the Sub-Committee. It was proposed that the third paragraph of the interpretative resolution should read as follows:

It is for the constitutional organs of each Member to decide, in reference to the obligation of preserving the independence and the integrity of the territory of

Members, in what degree the Member is bound to assure the execution of this obligation by employment of its military forces.

This resolution was framed obviously to meet the objections previously raised in the Committee to the paragraph proposed by the Sub-Committee which read as follows:

It is for the constitutional authorities of each Member to decide *whether* the circumstances do give rise to the obligation of preserving the independence and the integrity of the territory of Members.

Commenting on his substitute proposal, Sir Willoughby Dickinson (British Empire) said:

The Committee must avoid very carefully any interpretation which left it open for a state to say that, when another state became the aggressor against another state's territory, it was free to maintain the *status quo* and to initiate a discussion on the rights and wrongs of the principal act of aggression. . . . It was very important that it should be clearly understood that no soldier could be called out at the word of the League, but, nevertheless, it was the duty of every state to lose no time in taking whatever action was necessary in order to fulfil the moral obligation that lay upon it to prevent aggression by one state against another.

M. Barthélemy, likewise, expressed his assent:

He had been formally instructed to support the British proposal. . . . Hitherto France had opposed any amendment or interpretation of Article 10, but the French Delegation was now faced with a new fact—the insistence of Canada. . . . The present amendment did not weaken the force of Article 10; it merely adjusted law to facts. Moreover, if apprehensions were felt by any countries, they must assuredly be dispelled by the fact that the Third Committee was now preparing a treaty of mutual assistance, to which nations which felt any anxiety were invited to adhere. In this draft treaty it was laid down that it was for the Council to judge of any *casus fœderis,* and to inform each nation of the strength of the forces which it wished each assisting nation to supply.

M. Winiarski (Poland) pointed out that he had not declared himself in favor of the interpretative resolution and had reserved the right to propose certain amendments:

Sir Lomer Gouin had quoted the words of President Wilson, who had been weak enough to declare that Article 10 created, not a legal but a moral obligation for states. It would be desirable to amend the text of the resolution submitted in order that it might receive the adhesion of certain delegations who considered it inopportune.

He felt that it would be advisable to set the following preamble to the resolution:

The Assembly, realizing the legal nature of the obligation assumed by the Members of the League of Nations by virtue of Article 10 of the Covenant, and being desirous of defining the scope of that Article more accurately, adopts, etc. . . .

Furthermore, he was of opinion that an important modification would be required in paragraph 2. The "opinion" expressed by the Council should be considered as a "recommendation"—not an "invitation."

The compromise resolution was not entirely acceptable in other quarters as well—but for different reasons. M. Marks von Wuertemberg (Sweden) observed that:

Articles 10 and 16 both applied to breaches of the Covenant. Article 16 could not be interpreted as meaning that the advice of the Council was binding on the Members of the League; on the contrary, it had been stated, and stated with reason, in a resolution of the Second Assembly that it was for the different Members of the League to decide whether a breach of the Covenant had taken place.... For the moment he could not support the amended text, although he would have willingly supported the original text of the Sub-Committee.

Dr. Limburg (Netherlands) shared the apprehensions of the delegate of Sweden:

He preferred the original text.... He noted, however, that the amendment of the British Delegate in no way infringed the full liberty of each state to judge for itself whether the case contemplated by Article 10 had arisen. This question remained, as hitherto, an open question.

M. Rolin proposed to the Polish Delegate the following wording for the preamble:

The Assembly, desirous of defining the scope of the obligations contained in Article 10, etc....

The formula was accepted by M. Winiarski. The delegate of Sweden, in view of the interpretation given by Dr. Limburg, was prepared to support the resolution. The representatives of Persia and Finland respectively regretted that they could not support the interpretative clauses. The delegate of Czechoslovakia would refrain from voting. The completed resolution was adopted by a vote of 26 to 4 in the form which follows:

The Assembly, desirous of defining the scope of the obligations contained in Article 10 of the Covenant so far as regards the points raised by the Canadian Delegation, adopts the following resolution:

1. It is in conformity with the spirit of Article 10 that, in the event of the Council considering it to be its duty to recommend the application of military measures in consequence of an aggression, or danger or threat of aggression, the Council shall be bound to take account, more particularly, of the geographical situation and of the special conditions of each state.

2. It is for the constitutional authorities of each Member to decide, in reference to the obligation of preserving the independence and the integrity of the territory of Members, in what degree the Member is bound to assure the execution of this obligation by employment of its military forces.

3. The recommendation made by the Council shall be regarded as being of the highest importance and shall be taken into consideration by all the Members of the League with the desire to execute their engagements in good faith.

The resolution adopted in this form by the First Committee was presented to the Twelfth Plenary meeting of the Fourth Assembly. The debates[46] which followed reflected, in general, the viewpoints already expressed in the Committee discussions. For instance, M. Barthélemy, although supporting the resolution, said:

[46] *Plenary Meetings*, Fourth Assembly, pp. 75-87.

Speaking quite frankly, France would have preferred that there should have been neither amendment nor interpretative resolution. If today she accepts an interpretation, it is because certain new facts have arisen of which I propose to give you an account.

The opposition of Persia remained unalterable. The Persian delegate declared:

It is absolutely imperative for Persia to insist upon the retention of Article 10 intact with its full force unimpaired. ... The Persian Delegation interprets Article 10 of the Covenant to mean that the recommendation made by the Council, in case of necessity, is binding upon the Members of the League; whereas, under the proposed interpretation, the action to be taken in pursuance of the recommendation made by the Council in case of necessity depends upon its ratification by the Parliaments of the countries Members of the League.

The delegate of Panama shared his viewpoint:

In accordance with the definite instructions which I have received, I must declare that the Government of the Republic of Panama is opposed to any attempt to restrict the scope of Article 10, whether by means of amendment or by an interpretative resolution.

A reservation was noted by the delegate of Netherlands:

The question whether each state is free to determine whether the circumstances are such as to enforce an obligation to preserve the independence and territorial integrity of Members is left undecided by the interpretative resolution proposed by the Comimttee. Subject to this reservation, the Netherlands delegation is able to accept the proposed resolution.

In the final voting, Persia voted in the negative;

ARTICLE 10 OF THE COVENANT

Panama abstained from voting. The following states voted for the resolution:

Australia, Austria, Belgium, Brazil, British Empire, Bulgaria, Canada, Chile, China, Cuba, Denmark, France, Greece, Hungary, India, Ireland, Italy, Japan, Luxemburg, Netherlands, New Zealand, Norway, Portugal, Salvador, South Africa, Spain, Sweden, Switzerland, Uruguay (29).

The following states were absent or abstained from voting:

Albania, Argentine, Bolivia, Colombia, Costa-Rica, Czechoslovakia, Esthonia, Finland, Guatemala, Haiti, Honduras, Latvia, Liberia, Lithuania, Nicaragua, Panama, Paraguay, Peru, Poland, Jugo-Slavia, Siam, Venezuela (22).

The Chairman, in accordance with a precedent, declared the motion neither adopted nor rejected. He proposed that the results be communicated to the Council.[47]

[47] *Plenary Meetings*, Fourth Assembly, p. 87.

CHAPTER IV

Article 16 of the Covenant

I

Perhaps it would be well to state once more the major purpose of this study. We are attempting, it will be recalled, to review the attitude of states towards some of the juristic relations set up by the Covenant of the League of Nations. It is believed that this inquiry will throw some light on the future development of the international legal order. The Covenant has here been regarded as the medium through which certain fundamental changes were made in the juristic relations of the Member states and we have said that the evolution of this new order would probably influence the legal relations of the members of the international community as a whole.

From among the principles embodied in the Covenant, a limited number have been examined by reason of their special bearing on certain existing postulates of international law. It was said, for example, of Article 10 that, broadly viewed, it could be regarded as an attempt to provide League Members with an effective guarantee of their claim to existence. The foregoing chapter has reviewed the evolution of this Article and indicated its utility as a means of providing state security.

We have spoken also of the limitation introduced by the Covenant upon the discretionary legal right of Member states to resort to war, and of the methods embodied in the Covenant for the peaceful settlement of international disputes. The vital principle of restraint was said to be the provision for a period of delay pending the possible adjustment of controversies by some one of the pacific processes set up by the Covenant. Upon the nature of these various methods —arbitration, judicial settlement, and inquiry—it has not been deemed necessary to dwell, because they are but the continued application through the Covenant of procedure already substantially developed by international usage. Along with these provisions of the Covenant there is associated the principle of penalties, applicable to a state which resorts to war in violation of its engagements to utilize the accepted methods of peaceful settlement and to observe the specified period of delay. It is now proposed to review the evolution of this principle of sanctions which was embodied in Article 16 of the Covenant.

II

Reference has been made above to the widespread endorsement of the principle of sanctions in the unofficial projects for a League of Nations.[1] In his survey of these proposals, M. Lange notes agreement on a general principle, but on the question of the organiza-

[1] See above, p. 13.

tion of sanctions, he records a significant divergence of opinion among the various authors. "All are in accord," he says, "in demanding the institution of diplomatic and economic sanctions, directed and controlled by a common authority; there was agreement also that it would be necessary to support the application of these sanctions by the force of arms. But the question was raised whether this implied the creation of an international force or merely the cooperation of contingents from the various states. All of the French proposals supported the former view."[2]

The observation is significant because it indicates the point of view which was later put forward in the official French program for the League of Nations. It has been remarked of this program that its chief interest lay in the development of military sanctions.[3] But it ought to be noted as well that, like the unofficial French proposals, the general provisions of the official plan indicate acceptance of the principle of compulsory settlement of all disputes, although on procedural methods for reaching decisions, the scheme is singularly inadequate. On the other hand the provisions for sanctions in this plan are comprehensive and explicit. The proposed League was to be represented by an international body, composed of the responsible heads of Governments or their delegates. Among the powers of this international body the following were enumerated:

[2] *Les Origines et L'Œuvre de la Société des Nations*, I, p. 53.
[3] R. S. Baker, *Woodrow Wilson and World Settlement*, I, p. 281.

It shall enforce the execution of its decisions and those of the International Tribunal; at its demand every nation shall be bound, in agreement with the other nations, to exert its economic, naval, and military power against any recalcitrant nation.

Every nation shall likewise be bound, at the demand of the International Body, to exert, in common accord with the other nations, its economic, naval, and military power against any nation which, not having become a member of the League of Nations, shall attempt, by any means whatsoever, to impose its will on another nation.[4]

The scheme goes forward with elaborate provisions for diplomatic, legal, economic, and military sanctions. The organization and execution of the military sanctions were outlined as follows:

The execution of the military sanctions on land or at sea shall be entrusted either to an international force, or to one or more Powers members of the League of Nations, to whom a mandate in that behalf shall have been given.

The International Body shall have at its disposal a military force supplied by the various member states of sufficient strength:
1. to secure the execution of its decisions and those of the International Tribunal
2. to overcome, in case of need, any forces which may be opposed to the League of Nations in the event of armed conflict.

The International Body shall determine the strength of the international force and fix the contingents which must be held at its disposal.

Each of the member states shall be free to settle as it deems best the conditions under which its contingents shall be recruited. . . .

[4] The text of the French plan is given in Baker, III, pp. 152-162.

A permanent international staff shall investigate all military questions affecting the League of Nations. Each state shall appoint the officer or officers who shall represent it, in a proportion to be determined later. . . .

When circumstances shall so require, the International Body shall appoint, for the duration of the operations to be undertaken, a Commander-in-chief of the international forces.

Upon his appointment, the Commander-in-chief shall nominate his Chief of General Staff and the officers who are to assist him.

The foregoing program went far beyond the British and American proposals for enforcing the provisions of the Covenant, and when presented to the League Commission at Paris it raised the chief point of difference with which the authors of the Covenant had to contend.[5] The plan proposed a series of rigid and far-reaching agreements contrary to British instinct and tradition and set up demands on national compliance well beyond the possibility of realization. President Wilson was able to base his opposition to the scheme of international military control upon a practical consideration which was conclusive:

[5] "The real divergence lay between the adherents of the rigid, the definite, the logical, in other words the juridical point of view, and those who preferred the flexible, the indefinite, the experimental, the diplomatic; between those who feared human nature and wished to bind the future, and those who believed in human nature and were content to trust the future; between those who desired written guarantees, and those who desired moral obligations only; to be cynical, between those who expected to receive under the Covenant, and those who expected to give; in a word, between the Continental point of view and the Anglo-Saxon." *Temperley*, VI, p. 441.

No nation [he said] will consent to control. As for us Americans, we cannot consent to control because of our Constitution. We must do everything that is possible to ensure the safety of the world. ... I know how France has suffered, and I know that she wishes to obtain the best guarantees possible before she enters the League, and everything that we can do in this direction we shall do, but we cannot accept proposals which are in direct contradiction to our Constitution. ... The only method by which we can achieve this end lies in our having confidence in the good faith of the nations who belong to the League. There must be between them a cordial agreement and good will.[6]

In the end, the provisions for sanctions finally embodied in the Covenant were substantially those contained in the British draft of January 20 and, subject to the provisions of Article 17, they were limited in application to the agreements not to resort to war laid down in Articles 12 to 15.

But even these limited provisions for the collective application of sanctions by all Members of the League were received with apprehension in certain quarters. On March 20, the League of Nations Commission held at the Hotel Crillon in Paris a conference with the representatives of the states neutral during the War and received from them a number of recommendations respecting the provisions of the future Covenant. On this occasion, the representative of Denmark proposed, with the support of the other Scandinavian delegations, a modification of Article 16 which foreshadowed the subsequent attitude of an important group of

---

[6] Baker, *Woodrow Wilson and World Settlement*, I, p. 368.

states on the question of applying sanctions when this matter later came up for consideration within the League. In substance the Danish proposals were as follows. In designating states to participate in economic and military measures, the League should take account of the special difficulties which participation in these measures would occasion for certain states by reason of their military and geographical situation. It was desirable, moreover, that assurance be given that states invited to cooperate in measures of an economic and military nature should have a voice in the decisions reached in this regard. If decision to employ such measures could be taken by the League without the unanimity rule, the states which did not vote for the application of sanctions should be exempted from the obligation to apply them. It was also requested that states which, by their history and pacific policy, could offer guarantees of impartiality, should have the privilege of declaring their permanent neutrality.

In making these proposals the Danish representative observed that participation in military sanctions might quickly exhaust the resources of a small country and endanger its existence; that if the small country were an immediate neighbor of a powerful covenant-breaking state it would not be to the interest of the League that the weaker state should take action which would probably lead to its occupation by the more powerful country. It was urged, therefore, that a Member of the League which could give the necessary guarantees should have the privilege of declaring its permanent neutrality and, having so declared, would not be compelled to participate in military sanctions nor permit the passage of the military forces of the League through its territory.[7]

In reply to these observations, Lord Robert Cecil pointed out that provision for the convocation of states whose cooperation was desired was already made in the Covenant through Article 3 (which later became Article 4). If a state declared that it did not wish to take part in military action, the League would have no right to demand its participation; but it was otherwise with the economic sanctions and the obligation to give free passage to the military forces of the League; these obligations were absolute. In the final conference with the Neutral States held on April 29, it was expressly

[7] Cf. P. Munch, "Les états neutres et le Pacte de la Société des Nations," in *Les Origines et L'Œuvre de la Société des Nations*, I, pp. 173-178.

Says Munch: "The common desire of the Neutral States was to give a more juridicial character to the new organization. If they had been able to obtain such a change, they would have willingly accepted greater restrictions on the sovereignty of the member states. But the Great Powers were of the opinion that it was necessary to maintain the political character of the organization. In this situation, the Neutral States believed it was necessary to accentuate the sovereignty of the members and to define as much as possible the limits of the powers of the League. . . . The Neutral States desired the prohibition absolutely of legal wars and real guarantees of a substantial reduction of armaments, but not realizing this idea, they sought to avoid the obligations in the Covenant of such character that would increase their risk of becoming involved in the conflicts of the Great Powers. This is why the majority of the Neutral States were concerned in limiting the legal obligations to take part in sanctions." (Pp. 184-185.)

pointed out that the provisions of Article 4 of the Covenant giving each member state the right to sit on the Council when matters concerning it were before the Council implied its right to vote on equality with other states and should allay all fears with respect to compulsion under Article 16.[8]

III

One of the first tasks undertaken by the League was that of working out some concrete plan for the application of the sanctions which the Covenant provided. At a meeting on August 3, 1920, at San Sebastian, the Council had before it a Memorandum from the Secretary-General of the League respecting the preparatory measures necessary for the prompt and effective application of Article 16. The document called attention to a number of reasons why this matter should receive immediate consideration: the financial and economic weapon of the League could not effectively be applied without great loss of time and efficiency unless there had been considerable preparation in advance of the time at which action might be required. While the Article contemplated that responsibility for enforcing economic pressure be decentralized, there was, nevertheless, a clear need for some coordinating authority. Furthermore, cooperative action was required in order that the Members of the League might, as the Covenant provided, "mutually support one another in the financial and economic measures which are to be taken

[8] *Ibid.*, I, p. 182.

in order to minimize the loss and inconvenience resulting from the blockade." It was suggested that "general uniformity in the legislative and administrative provisions of the different states would be of great assistance to each particular Government in defending its action to its own commercial interests which are affected." The Memorandum summarized the circumstances arising under the Covenant which would seem to call for the application of the economic weapon and recommended that, as a preparatory measure, "an International Blockade Committee should be appointed under the authority of the First Assembly for the purpose of studying the problem and settling the general plan of action, the organization of the more permanent machinery required and the principles on which it should work."[9]

The matter was presented to the Council in a report by M. Tittoni, the representative of Italy. He concurred in the recommendation of the Secretary-General respecting the need of working out some pre-arranged plan of action, for as soon as the League had decided, in principle, to have recourse to the application of Article 16, the various measures should be taken immediately by all states. The question, he believed, was one of a series of similar measures to be taken simultaneously rather than one of collective and united action. It was important, moreover, to give exact meaning, in accordance with the principles of international law, to the provisions of the Covenant which

[9] *Minutes, Sixth Committee*, First Assembly, pp. 334-336.

contemplated the prevention of trade between states not Members of the League and states which had defied the Covenant. "In my view," he said, "it should be clear that the states Members of the League of Nations who declare the blockade have the right to render it effective against all states, including those who are not Members of the League, but they have no right to force the states who do not form part of the League to declare the blockade themselves."[10]

The Council decided to place the matter on the agenda of the First Assembly and to recommend to that body the creation of an International Blockade Committee for the general purpose outlined in the memorandum of the Secretary-General.

The question in this stage was brought before the First Assembly which referred the recommendation of the Council, the report of M. Tittoni, and the Memorandum of the Secretary-General, to its Sixth Committee.[11] During the early discussions in this Committee a question arose which was destined to be fundamental in the interpretation and application of Article 16, namely; "Who was to decide whether a breach of the Covenant had taken place and whether the provisions of Article 16 should be applied?" The following excerpts from the minutes of the discussion indicate the viewpoints expressed at this time:[12]

[10] *Ibid.*, pp. 332-333.

[11] *The Committee on Mandates, Armaments, the Economic Weapon.*

[12] *Minutes, Sixth Committee*, First Assembly, pp. 261-263.

M. Fock (Netherlands) insisted that every state should have the right to decide for itself whether the facts were really such as to justify the Council in instituting economic measures, and to refuse to take part in such measures if they appeared to be unjustifiable.

Lord Robert Cecil (South Africa) said that it was the business of the Council to decide in the first instance whether the occasion for the exercise of economic pressure had in fact arisen, and to call the attention of the Members of the League to the obligation. They could then, however, decide for themselves—as M. Fock had maintained—as to whether they were morally justified in obeying the Council.

Mr. Fisher (British Empire) thought the Council would decide whether the Covenant had been violated and whether action was necessary. It would then communicate with those members of the League whose assistance it desired in order to bring pressure on recalcitrant members. Although it was true that the obligation rested on all Members of the League, he did not think it would be necessary as a rule for every Member to be called upon to fulfill that obligation.

M. Schanzer (Italy) thought there was some danger in allowing each state to decide for itself whether or not to carry out the blockade, when ordered by the Council to do so.

A Sub-Committee was appointed to study the various problems which had arisen in the discussion and the broader question of the advisability of recommending to the Assembly the creation of an International Blockade Committee. This Sub-Committee reported at the following meeting of the main Committee, Lord Robert Cecil acting as Rapporteur. The Sub-Committee's report recommended the establishment of a Blockade Committee and submitted, in addition, a number of proposals for recommendation to the Assembly, in order immediately to render as effective as possible the economic weapon of the League. The proposals which are of interest in the present connection were as follows:

1. It shall be the duty of the Secretary-General to call the attention of the Council to any facts which in his opinion show that a Member of the League has become a Covenant-breaking state within the meaning of Article 16.
2. Upon receiving such an intimation, the Council shall hold a meeting with the least possible delay to consider it, and shall inform the Members of the League of the results of their deliberations, whether they are unanimous or not.
3. As soon as a Member of the League is satisfied, whether in consequence of the communication of the proceedings of the Council or otherwise, that a breach of the Covenant within Article 16 has occurred, it is its duty to take measures for the purpose of carrying out the first paragraph of Article 16.[13]

The Rapporteur reminded the Committee that it was left to each Member of the League to determine for itself whether a breach of the Covenant had occurred but once they decided that this was the case, they were bound to act.

M. Benes (Czechoslovakia) likewise drew the attention of the Committee to this point:

He thought that it would be extremely dangerous if each Member of the League were left to decide for itself whether to institute a blockade. The Council alone had the right to decide whether a breach of the Covenant had taken place, and to order the Members of the League to resort to a blockade.[14]

[13] *Ibid.*, p. 337.
[14] *Ibid.*, p. 266.

His misgivings were shared by M. Negulesco (Roumania) who pointed out that:

According to Article 16 it was clearly the duty of the Council to take the decision for the exercise of economic pressure. Article 4 (of the report), in view of Lord Robert Cecil's opinion that blockade was an act of war, also corroborated this contention. It was inadmissible therefore to leave the responsibility to the various Members of the League.[15]

M. Schanzer (Italy) believed there was danger in leaving too much liberty to each individual state, lest the corporate will of the League should be impaired.[16]

M. Fock (Netherlands) supported the view that the Members of the League should be free to judge for themselves whether a violation of the Covenant had taken place. He considered, however, that it was perhaps premature to lay down a definite method of procedure, and thought that the Blockade Commission should be invited to examine the matter more closely.[17]

This view was supported by Mr. Fisher (British Empire) who suggested that this portion of the report should be adopted *provisionally,* subject to review at the next meeting of the Assembly when the report of the International Blockade Committee would have been prepared. This suggestion was adopted by the Committee, and the First Assembly subsequently adopted this section of the report in the following form:

After quoting the first paragraph of Article 16 of the Covenant, the resolution declared:

That is a duty which now actually rests upon every

[15] *Ibid.*, p. 268.
[16] *Ibid.*, p. 266.
[17] *Ibid.*, p. 267.

Member of the League, but there are two difficulties in the way of its performance. In the first place, it may easily be uncertain whether a state has actually resorted to war in violation of the Covenant, and no machinery has been provided for ascertaining the facts. In the second place, there are considerable difficulties which were pointed out in the discussion before the Committee on a previous occasion in carrying out to the full what may be, for shortness, described as the blockading operations contemplated by the article.

To obviate these difficulties we propose *provisionally* and subject to review at the next Assembly on the report of the International Blockade Commission:

(a) It shall be the duty of the Secretary-General to call the attention of the Council to any facts which in his opinion show that a Member of the League has become a Covenant-breaking state within the meaning of Article 16.

(b) Upon receiving such an intimation, the Council shall, on the request of any of its Members, hold a meeting with the least possible delay to consider it, and shall send a copy of the procès-verbal of the meeting to all the other Members of the League.

(c) As soon as a Member of the League is satisfied, in consequence of the communication of the procès-verbal of the Council, that a breach of the Covenant within Article 16 has occurred, it is its duty to take measures for the purpose of carrying out the first paragraph of Article 16. . . .

It is also desirable (for the International Blockade Commission) to consider, in accordance with the proposals made by Denmark, Norway and Sweden, what measures, if any, should be taken in the case of Members of the League, which, from smallness of their resources and their geographical position, might be in serious danger if they carried out to the full their obligations under the first paragraph of Article 16 against a powerful Covenant-breaking state. This is a matter which may have to be considered at any moment from a practical point of view if the necessity for coercion of a Covenant-breaking state should arise. In that case the Council would have to take whatever measures it thought suitable for the emergency.[18]

The proposals of the Scandinavian states to which the above paragraph of the report referred was a proposed amendment to the Covenant, submitted at the First Assembly in identical form by the Governments of Norway, Sweden, and Denmark. The amendment proposed the following:

To add to the first paragraph of Article 16:

At the request of a Member for whom the application of the above provisions might entail serious danger, the Council may authorize this Member to maintain intercourse, in such measure as the Council shall decide, with the Covenant-breaking state.[19]

The Swedish Government supported the proposal with the following comment:

The economic blockade, which by virtue of this Article threatens a state which violates the Covenants of the League, constitutes the most effective coercive weapon of the League; and it is clearly of the utmost importance that the blockade should be enforced in the most rapid and effective fashion possible. In the view of the Swedish Government, however, the fact should not be ignored that, for certain states of secondary importance—whose situation, owing to the vicinity of other and more important states, is especially exposed —a complete rupture of economic relations with such powerful neighbors would present grave dangers.

It can, indeed, be imagined that in such a case the Great Power in question might be tempted to occupy

[18] *Plenary Meetings*, First Assembly, pp. 408-409.
[19] *Minutes, First Committee*, First Assembly, p. 68.

the territory of the smaller Power, so as to protect the very important economic interests which, as a result of the blockade, would be at stake. For this reason the Swedish Government is of opinion that it would be desirable in cases of this nature to leave to the Council the option of modifying in some measure the obligation upon a Member of the League to take part in the blockade.[20]

The First Assembly decided not to give the above proposal immediate consideration but to refer it to the Committee on Amendments to be instituted by the Council. In view, however, of the work subsequently undertaken by the International Blockade Commission, the Scandinavian proposals were not considered by the Committee on Amendments but were re-drafted by the Blockade Commission in a form which will be referred to later.[21]

IV

The International Blockade Commission was instituted by the Council at a meeting in Paris, February 22, 1921. The Commission assembled at Geneva during the following August and concluded a Report for submission to the Council at the September meeting.[22]

The Commission based its program of work on the following questionnaire:

1. Under what conditions should sanctions be applied?

[20] *Ibid.*, p. 72.
[21] See below p. 144.
[22] The Report was published as League Document A. 28, 1921, V. (C. 288, 1921, V.).

2. Whose duty is it to decide that the necessity for sanctions has arisen?
3. At what moment and by whom should these measures be applied?
4. How should they be applied?

The Report of the Blockade Commission was transmitted by the Council to the Second Assembly and was subsequently referred by the Assembly to its Third Committee. This Committee proceeded to draw up a new reading of Article 16, using the Report of the Blockade Commission as the basis of its work. The Third Committee, in collaboration with the First Committee, drafted as amendments to Article 16 three proposals which were recommended to the Assembly by a majority of the Third Committee. The Third Committee submitted also concerning Article 16 a number of interpretative declarations which it did not consider essential to embody in the form of amendments. In reporting its work to the Assembly, the Third Committee outlined the general considerations which had guided it and the Blockade Commission in drafting the changes proposed:

The starting point of the argument and of the conclusions arrived at by the Blockade Committee has been as follows: The authors of the Covenant had considered the League of Nations as an organization embracing all or nearly all states, and capable of prompt action in the event of breach of the Covenant. In the view of the International Blockade Committee, the application of Article 16, even had the League been universal, might have formidable consequences either for the League of Nations in general or for some of its

Members. But the aforementioned Committee was of the opinion that as the League of Nations had not yet attained a world-wide or nearly world-wide character, a very rigid application of Article 16 would not only meet with very great obstacles, but might also place the states Members of the League in very difficult situations. That is why the International Blockade Committee has seen fit to recommend solutions which, in the present stage of the League of Nations, will, so far as possible, make allowance for the facts as they are.[23]

The Report continued with extensive comments on the amendments and interpretative resolutions proposed and certain extracts from these observations will be given below. It will, however, be convenient to have stated at this point the final texts of the amendments to Article 16 adopted by the Second Assembly on October 4, 1921. On that date the Assembly adopted the following resolutions, being amendments to Article 16 of the Covenant:[24]

1. The latter part of the first paragraph of Article 16 of the Covenant shall read as follows:

" . . . which hereby undertake immediately to subject it to the severance of all trade or financial relations, the prohibition of all intercourse between persons residing in their territory and persons residing in the

[23] *Minutes, Third Committee*, Second Assembly, p. 381.

[24] *Resolutions, Second Assembly*, p. 14. The introductory statements attached to Amendments 2, 3, and 4 may give the erroneous impression that the new texts were intended as substitutions for paragraphs two, three, and four of the original text of Article 16. But it was the clear intent of the Assembly to insert the new texts after the first paragraph of the Article, and the proposed Amendments would not affect, therefore, the original texts of the second, third, and fourth paragraphs of the Article.

territory of the Covenant-breaking state, and the prevention of all financial, commercial or personal intercourse between persons residing in the territory of the Covenant-breaking state and persons residing in the territory of any other state, whether a Member of the League or not."

2. The second paragraph of Article 16 shall read as follows:

"It is for the Council to give an opinion whether or not a breach of the Covenant has taken place. In deliberations on this question in the Council, the votes of Members of the League alleged to have resorted to war and of Members against whom such action was directed shall not be counted."

3. The third paragraph of Article 16 shall read as follows:

"The Council will notify to all Members of the League the date which it recommends for the application of the economic pressure under this Article."

4. The fourth paragraph of Article 16 shall read as follows:

"Nevertheless, the Council may, in the case of particular Members, postpone the coming into force of any of these measures for a specified period where it is satisfied that such a postponement will facilitate the attainment of the object of the measures referred to in the preceding paragraph, or that it is necessary in order to minimize the loss and inconvenience which will be caused to such Members."

To return now to the Report of the Third Committee, it will be noted that the change proposed by Amendment 1 is the substitution of the words "persons residing in their territory" for the words "nationals" wherever the latter appears in the original text of the Article. The Third Committee's Report outlined in the following terms the considerations which appeared to render this change desirable:

As regards the most essential parts of the sanctions of Article 16, that is to say, the severance of all trade and financial relations, and the prohibition of all financial, commercial or personal intercourse between the people of the blockaded state and of other states, the word "nationals" used in this Article has raised serious problems. Last year, it was held in the Assembly that the word "nationals" should be interpreted as a synonym for "inhabitants" in the sense that a Member of the League shall not be obliged to prohibit, in its own territory, the intercourse of its own nationals with the nationals of the defaulting state. The prohibition of intercourse, according to this interpretation, should apply from country to country, i. e., between states, and not within states. It has been observed that any contrary interpretation might create extremely difficult situations, especially in countries the population of which comprises a large proportion of foreigners.

The International Blockade Committee has held that the word "nationals" should be understood in the sense of "residents," but that this interpretation of the word "nationals" was not an obvious one, so that it was necessary to amend Article 16 in this respect. Your Committee shares this view, and consequently submits to you a proposed amendment to the second portion of the first paragraph of Article 16.[25]

During the course of the Assembly debates on this proposal, M. Reynald (France) offered a substitute amendment which provided that, for the severance of

[25] *Minutes, Third Committee*, Second Assembly, p. 390.

relations between persons belonging to the Covenant-breaking state and persons belonging to other states Members of the League, the test should be both *residence* and *nationality*. In support of his proposal, M. Reynald declared:

> The word "nationals" exists in the Covenant. This word was included because it appeared to constitute a necessary guarantee. The legal discussions taking place today had already been considered in the course of the war. Legal theories were put forward among the Allies, and certain jurists maintained that territory alone should be considered and that consequently the word "nationals" should not have been inserted and should be replaced by the word "residents." But the war taught us many hard lessons. . . . Experience and logic both require that the word "nationals" should be preserved.[26]

At the Fourth Assembly, France declared that she could not approve the first amendment to Article 16 adopted by the Second Assembly. In 1924, the Fifth Assembly, noting that the amendment proposed by the Second Assembly "appears to be open to objections which seem to render its entry into force impossible," adopted in place thereof the following:

> The latter part of the first paragraph of Article 16 of the Covenant shall read as follows:
> Which hereby undertake immediately to subject it to the severance of all trade or financial relations and to prohibit all intercourse at least between persons resident within their territories and persons resident within the territory of the Covenant-breaking state and, if they deem it expedient, also between their nationals

[26] *Plenary Meetings*, Second Assembly, p. 419.

and the nationals of the Covenant-breaking state, and to prevent all financial, commercial or personal intercourse at least between persons resident within the territory of that state and persons resident within the territory of any other state, whether a Member of the League or not, and, if they deem it expedient, also between the nationals of that state and the nationals of any other state whether a Member of the League or not.[27]

A protocol embodying this amendment was opened for signature on September 27, 1924.

The principles embodied in Amendments 2 and 3 above were discussed in the Report of the Third Committee under the titles of, "The nature and limitations of the powers of the Council," and, "At what moment should the sanctions be applied?" The Committee endorsed the principle expressed in Amendment 2 but the text which it presented was altered before final adoption by the Assembly. The principle of Amendment 3 was proposed by the Committee to take the form of an interpretative resolution but was adopted by the Assembly as an amendment. In connection with its exposition of the functions and powers of the Council, the Committee dwelt also upon what was termed "the liberty and independence of the states in the determination of a breach of the Covenant." It proposed on this point an interpretative resolution which was adopted by the Assembly without modification.[28] On the general problem of reconciling the freedom of the Members of the League with an effec-

[27] *Resolutions*, Fifth Assembly.
[28] See below, p. 148.

tive program for the application of the provisions of Article 16, the Committee reported as follows:

A guiding principle for the interpretation of Article 16 was approved by the Assembly at its first meeting, in accordance with the proposals of the Committee set up last year. This principle is as follows:

It is the duty of each of the Members of the League to ascertain and to decide whether a breach of the Covenant within the meaning of Article 16 has been committed.

The principle is in agreement with the spirit of the Covenant, and with the fact that Article 16 does not recognize that any organization of the League of Nations has the power to decide, in such a way as to bind all the other Members, that a given Member is a treaty-breaking state. Such a power would not be consistent with the sovereign rights of the various states.

On the other hand, this principle certainly does not mean that the Members of the League may of their own free will withdraw from the obligations incurred in virtue of the Covenant. When cases provided for by Article 16 arise, and as soon as a Member of the League is convinced that a breach of the Covenant has occurred within the meaning of Article 16, it is bound to cooperate in the application of the sanctions provided for in this Article. This obligation is explicitly imposed by the Covenant, and must be observed by the Member of the League in accordance with the respect due to Treaties.

Nevertheless, the difficulties involved in the application of the fundamental principle which we have just stated cannot be ignored.

Differences of opinion may exist in the various countries as to the facts which would constitute a breach of the Covenant within the meaning of Article 16. As the International Blockade Committee points out, grave doubts may arise as to which country had committed the first acts of war, or whether the state which has been attacked has carried out a unanimous recommendation of the Council. Moreover, isolated attempts, aiming at the immediate application of the economic sanction, might involve the states actually making these attempts in very unfortunate consequences, without affecting the Covenant-breaking state to any appreciable degree. They may, moreover, give rise to disagreements between the states applying the economic weapon and such Members of the League as may delay in doing so.

It is therefore a question of reconciling the liberty and independence of the states in the determination of a breach of the Covenant, on the one side, with the obvious necessity, on the other, of arriving at an agreement between Members of the League as to the existence of a substantive breach of the Covenant within the meaning of Article 16, and of coordinating their action on the basis of a joint plan.

. . . It is the great moral authority of the Council, strengthened by the presence of the states concerned, which must confer upon its opinion that convincing force which is essential for bringing the Members of the League into agreement, and for inducing them to take joint action. Faced with the Council's opinion, deeming a state to have broken the Covenant, it will be very difficult for the Members of the League to evade the fulfillment of their engagements.[29]

The report of the Sixth Committee of the First Assembly had recommended, it will be recalled, that the International Blockade Commission consider what measures might be taken to give effect to the proposals submitted by the Scandinavian states at the First Assembly respecting the partial exemption of states in carrying out the obligations of Article 16.[30] The prin-

[29] *Minutes, Third Committee*, Second Assembly, pp. 384-385.
[30] See above, p. 134.

ciple laid down in Amendment 4 above was the final outcome of the deliberations on this subject. The Third Committee of the Second Assembly submitted the text which was adopted. Its Report reviewed the recommendations of the Blockade Commission on the matter and analyzed the significance of the solution which the Committee itself proposed. It is important to note that, in the view of the Third Committee, the principle expressed in Amendment 4 admits no real exemptions of Member States from the obligations under Article 16; it merely vests the Council with authority to absolve Members from the duty *immediately to carry out these obligations*. The Third Committee reported on this question in the following terms:

... The International Blockade Committee was of opinion that in the case of certain states complete and immediate participation in an economic blockade might, owing to the inadequate natural resources and the geographical position of these states, involve them in serious dangers, particularly if the blockaded state were economically very strong and one with which the states in question ordinarily maintain close commercial relations. The amendments to the Covenant submitted by the Scandinavian States refer to this case. ...

On this point there was a long discussion in your Committee. From this discussion it was ascertained that the majority of the Committee felt that it could not support the amendment proposed by the International Blockade Committee, for the reason that it did not think that it could, in principle, allow any real exception to the obligations laid down in Article 16 to be granted. ... [31]

[31] The International Blockade Committee had proposed the following amendment:

But the majority of your Committee considered that account must to a certain extent be taken of the particular conditions and requirements of certain countries, and that situations might arise in which it would be recognized as expedient to postpone, in the case of certain states, either wholly or in part, and for fixed periods, the effective application of the economic sanctions laid down in Article 16. . . .

It will be admitted that under given circumstances the application of the economic measures may be carried out with a certain gradation, not in any particular interest, but in the general interest of the success of the economic pressure on the defaulting state. It might happen, for instance, that in view of the particular situation of a state, if this state were to break off all

---

"The Council may, however, at the request of a Member which can show that the facilities demanded are essential for its economic or political security, grant such exemptions as, in its opinion, will not conflict with the aims of Article 16 of the Covenant."

Commenting on this proposal, M. Schanzer, Rapporteur of the Third Committee, spoke before the Assembly as follows:

"This amendment contemplates the possibility of a derogation in certain definite cases. Your Committee was of opinion that it was not possible for any state to withdraw from the engagements laid down in Article 16, and that a derogation even in special cases was inadmissable. . . . We adopted an amendment which does not absolutely allow of exemptions from the obligations of the Covenant, but which lays down that, under certain circumstances, the Council may, in the case of particular Members, decide upon the postponement of any of these measures for a specified period where it is satisfied that such postponement will facilitate the attainment of the desired object, or that it is necessary in order to minimize the loss and inconvenience which will be caused to such Members. But we have not admitted that a state can withdraw from its obligations under Article 16, or that any exemptions from them can be contemplated." *Plenary Meetings*, Second Assembly, pp. 406-407.

relations with a defaulting state, the latter would be induced to commit acts endangering the success of the common action of the League—for example, to take possession of certain strategic points of the first state. . . .

The view was expressed in the Committee that this solution was contrary to the principle laid down in the first paragraph of Article 16; that is to say, that the Members of the League undertake *immediately* to break off all relations with the defaulting state. But, as has already been stated in the preceding chapter in connection with the moment at which the economic pressure is to be applied, the expression "immediately" used in Article 16 must, in the opinion of the majority of your Committee, be interpreted as meaning that the act constituting a breach of the Covenant entails an *immediate obligation* for all Members of the League to break off their relations with the defaulting state. This, however, does not mean that, as far as time is concerned, certain states may not, by common agreement and in the general interest, be absolved from the immediate *carrying out of this obligation*.[32]

On the same date upon which the Second Assembly adopted the proposed amendments to Article 16, it voted the following interpretative resolutions concerning the Economic Weapon of the League:

1. The resolutions and the proposals for amendments to Article 16 which have been adopted by the Assembly, shall, so long as the amendments have not been put in force in the form required by the Covenant, constitute rules for guidance which the Assembly recommends, as a provisional measure, to the Council and to the Members of the League in connection with the application of Article 16.

2. Subject to the special provisions of Article 17, the economic measures referred to in Article 16 shall be

[32] *Minutes, Third Committee,* Second Assembly, pp. 387-388.

applicable only in the specific case referred to in this Article.

3. The unilateral action of the defaulting State cannot create a state of war: it merely entitles the other Members of the League to resort to acts of war or to declare themselves in a state of war with the Covenant-breaking State; but it is in accordance with the spirit of the Covenant that the League of Nations should attempt, at least at the outset, to avoid war, and to restore peace by economic pressure.

4. It is the duty of each Member of the League to decide for itself whether a breach of the Covenant has been committed. The fulfilment of their duties under Article 16 is required from Members of the League by the express terms of the Covenant, and they cannot neglect them without breach of their Treaty obligations.

5. All cases of breach of Covenant under Article 16 shall be referred to the Council as a matter of urgency at the request of any Member of the League. Further, if a breach of Covenant be committed, or if there arise a danger of such breach being committed, the Secretary-General shall at once give notice thereof to all the Members of the Council. Upon receipt of such a request by a Member of the League, or of such a notice by the Secretary-General, the Council will meet as soon as possible. The Council shall summon representatives of the parties to the conflict and of all States which are neighbours of the defaulting State, or which normally maintain close economic relations with it, or whose co-operation would be especially valuable for the application of Article 16.

6. If the Council is of opinion that a State has been guilty of a breach of Covenant, the Minutes of the meeting at which that opinion is arrived at shall be immediately sent to all Members of the League, accompanied by a statement of reasons and by an invitation to take action accordingly. The fullest publicity shall be given to this decision.

7. For the purpose of assisting it to enforce Article 16, the Council may, if it thinks fit, be assisted by a *technical* Committee. This Committee, which will remain in permanent session as soon as the action decided on is taken, may include, if desirable, representatives of the States specially affected.

8. The Council shall recommend the date on which the enforcement of economic pressure, under Article 16, is to be begun, and shall give notice of that date to all the Members of the League.

9. All States must be treated alike as regards the application of the measures of economic pressure, with the following reservations:

(a) It may be necessary to recommend the execution of special measures by certain States;

(b) If it is thought desirable to postpone, wholly or partially, in the case of certain States, the effective application of the economic sanctions laid down in Article 16, such postponement shall not be permitted except in so far as it is desirable for the success of the common plan of action, or reduces to a minimum the losses and embarrassments which may be entailed in the case of certain Members of the League by the application of the sanctions.

10. It is not possible to decide beforehand, and in detail, the various measures of an economic, commercial and financial nature to be taken in each case where economic pressure is to be applied.

When the case arises, the Council shall recommend to the Members of the League a plan for joint action.

11. The interruption of diplomatic relations may, in the first place, be limited to the withdrawal of the heads of Missions.

12. Consular relations may possibly be maintained.

13. For the purposes of the severance of relations between persons belonging to the Covenant-breaking State and persons belonging to other States Members of the League, the test shall be residence and not nationality.

14. In cases of prolonged application of economic pressure, measures of increasing stringency may be taken. The cutting off of the food supplies of the civil population of the defaulting state shall be regarded as an extremely drastic measure which shall only be applied if the other measures available are clearly inadequate.

15. Correspondence and all other methods of communication shall be subjected to special regulations.

16. Humanitarian relations shall be continued.

17. Efforts should be made to arrive at arrangements which would ensure the cooperation of States non-Members of the League in the measures to be taken.

18. In special circumstances and in support of economic measures to be taken, it may become advisable: (a) to establish an effective blockade of the seaboard of the Covenant-breaking State; (b) to entrust to some Members of the League the execution of the blockade operations.

19. The Council shall urge upon all the States Members of the League that their Governments should take the necessary preparatory measures, above all of a legislative character, to enable them to enforce at short notice the necessary measures of economic pressure.

CHAPTER V

ATTEMPTS TO EXTEND CERTAIN PRINCIPLES OF THE COVENANT

1. THE DRAFT TREATY OF MUTUAL ASSISTANCE

I

The proposed amendments of Article 16 were approved by the Second Assembly (1921); the interpretative resolutions on Article 10 were voted upon, with the results already noted, two years later by the Fourth Assembly. The effect of the discussions within the League on these Articles, and the position assumed by certain states toward the nature and scope of the obligations contained therein was not such as to reassure the Members of the League primarily concerned with the problem of security. In fact, the outcome of the whole proceedings had emphasized the indefinite character of the guarantees provided in the Covenant and had revealed the difficulties of organizing through the existing machinery of the League a definite scheme of mutual assistance for a state which was the victim of sudden aggression. It was still recognized that the Covenant had set up a body of general guarantees well in advance of those provided by the general principles of international law. Under Article 10, as M. Rolin had pointed out, "the Members of the League had the right to expect that they had all agreed to assure the political independence and territorial integrity of each state."[1] Moreover, the Assembly had declared that if a state went to war before the safeguards for peace provided in the Covenant had been observed, the Members of the League were required to fulfil their duties under Article 16 and could not neglect them "without a breach of their treaty obligations." In the case of Article 10, however, the question of who was to decide when a *casus fœderis* had arisen had been left unsettled, but, from the decision of the Assembly upon a similar question under Article 16, it might logically be held that this decision should rest with the individual Members upon whom the obligations of that Article lay. And, furthermore, under Article 10 there was still no specified definition of the "means" through which assistance would be rendered. The Council might "recommend" various measures, but it was manifestly within the competence of each state to decide for itself the form and degree of assistance which it would contribute.

In the case of Article 16, the proposed new draft stated that the Council should give an opinion "whether or not a breach of the Covenant had taken place," but for the guidance of the Members of the League, the Assembly had likewise resolved that "it was the duty of each Member of the League to decide for itself whether a breach of the Covenant had been committed."[2] Little progress had been made toward work-

[1] See above, p. 100.
[2] See above, p. 148.

ing out a concerted plan of action to apply the coercive measures provided for in this Article. The Council was to recommend a date for the enforcement of economic pressure, but apart from this, there was no prearranged plan to give precision and effectiveness to the measures to be applied against a state which resorted to war in violation of the Covenant. The activity of various states during this period in seeking security through special alliances outside the League was sufficient evidence that the provisions of the Covenant were considered inadequate as security measures and that specific guarantees and determinate forms of assistance were still the considerations uppermost in many quarters.[3]

II

In the meanwhile the problem of state security had come before the League in connection with another issue, namely, that of disarmament. It had come to the foreground through the efforts of the League to apply the provisions of Article 8 of the Covenant. This Article, itself, recognizes the relation between "national safety" and the reduction of armaments. It provides, in part, as follows:

The Members of the League recognize that the maintenance of peace requires the reduction of arma-

[3] The Franco-Polish and the Polish-Rumanian treaties were negotiated in 1921. For the construction of the *Little Entente*, (1920-1921) see A. J. Toynbee, *Survey of International Affairs, 1920-1923*, pp. 287-303.

ments to the lowest point consistent with national safety and the enforcement by common action of international obligations.

The Council, taking account of the geographical situation and circumstances of each state, shall formulate plans for such reduction for the consideration and action of the several Governments.

At a meeting of the Temporary Mixed Commission[4] of the League in July, 1922, Lord Robert Cecil had brought forward his notable resolutions which emphasized this interdependence of security and disarmament. These proposals as adopted by the Temporary Mixed Commission at this time were as follows:

1. No scheme for the reduction of armaments can ever be really successful unless it is general.

[4] The Temporary Mixed Commission was instituted by the Council in February, 1921, upon the recommendation of the First Assembly that a Temporary Commission be instructed "to prepare for submission to the Council in the near future reports and proposals for the reduction of armaments as provided for by Article 8 of the Covenant." The Commission thus created by the Council consisted of six persons of recognized ability in political, economic and social matters; six members of the Permanent Advisory Commission for naval, military and air questions; four members of the League Provisional Economic and Financial Committee; and six members of the Governing Body of the International Labor Office—three employer representatives and three workmen representatives.

The Permanent Advisory Commission was established in May, 1920, in accordance with Article 9 of the Covenant, and was vested with the function of advising the Council on military, naval, and air questions. It is essentially a technical Commission, consisting of delegations composed of military, naval, and air representatives from each of the states represented on the Council.

2. In the present state of the world, the majority of Governments would be unable to accept the responsibility for a serious reduction of armaments unless they received in exchange a satisfactory guarantee of the safety of their countries.

3. Such a guarantee can be found in a general defensive agreement between all the countries concerned, binding them to provide immediate and effective assistance in accordance with a pre-arranged plan in the event of one of them being attacked, provided that the obligation to render assistance to a country attacked shall be limited in principle to those countries situated in the same part of the globe. In cases, however, where, for historical, geographical, or other reasons, a country is in special danger of attack, detailed arrangements shall be made for its defence in accordance with the above-mentioned plan.

4. It is understood that the whole of the above resolutions are conditional on a reduction of armaments being carried out on lines laid down beforehand, and on the provision of effective machinery to insure the realization and the maintenance of such a reduction.[5]

With the submission of these proposals, the work of the League, as it related to the problems of disarmament and security, entered upon a phase which, culminating in the Geneva Protocol, has appropriately been designated as an "effort to close the fissures of the Covenant." It was not proposed, however, that the program of extending certain principles of the Covenant should necessarily apply to all the Members of the League on a common basis. The restive attitude of certain states under the obligations of Articles 10 and 16 appeared to have induced the conclusion that,

[5] *Minutes, Third Committee,* Third Assembly, p. 69.

rather than insist upon a rigid interpretation of these provisions, it would be more expedient to develop supplementary agreements to meet the requirements of states especially exposed and to limit the obligations contained therein to an area which was manifestly one of common interest.

The Cecil Resolutions proposed to achieve this result by a general defensive agreement between all countries immediately concerned which would provide immediate assistance in accordance with a pre-arranged plan, and to limit the application of this agreement to countries situated in the same part of the globe. But the Resolutions indicated, as well, that even this general defensive agreement might have to be supplemented by precise and detailed arrangements for the defence of states which for various reasons were in special danger of attack. In the subsequent development of this system, it was contended that these "detailed arrangements" must take the form of special military conventions, supplementary to the general defensive agreement, which the Members specially threatened might conclude between themselves with a view to arranging in advance the mutual assistance to be rendered in the event of aggression.

The report of the Temporary Mixed Commission on the proposals of Lord Robert Cecil were referred by the Third Assembly (1922) to its Third Committee—the Committee on Armaments. The debates which developed in this Committee revealed the sharp difference of opinion existing between the various representatives at Geneva respecting measures which their respective Governments were prepared to support in the interest of mutual security. Here, in fact, was renewed the old controversy which had been waged at Paris during the framing of the Covenant between the advocates of material guarantees and those who distrusted precise commitments for fulfillment in future and ill-defined contingencies.[6]

The Resolutions under consideration proposed a general defensive agreement, but stated that the obligation to render assistance thereunder should be limited in principle to countries situated in the same part of the globe. Such an exemption would have little reality for the British Empire. Mr. Fisher (British Empire) drew attention to its peculiar situation:

The third resolution presented certain difficulties: Great Britain was one member of the commonwealth of free peoples known as the British Empire. When the British Empire was at war, Canada or New Zealand was at war. When the British Empire was at

[6] See above Chap. IV, for the conflict between the French on the one hand and the British and Americans on the other respecting proposals for the enforcement of the provisions of the Covenant. It is interesting to note, however, in this connection, Sir Edward Grey's defence of the conversations which went forward prior to 1914 between the French and British military and naval staffs: "But modern war may be an affair of days. If there were no military plans made beforehand we should be unable to come to the assistance of France in time, however strongly public opinion in Britain might desire it. We should in effect not have preserved our freedom to help France, but have cut ourselves off from the possibility of doing so, unless we had allowed the British and French staffs to concert plans for common action." *Twenty-Five Years*, I, p. 73.

peace, all its members were at peace. Regional agreements, however, such as seemed to be contemplated by Resolution 3 in favor of a Treaty of Mutual Guarantee, might prove quite unacceptable to the British Empire since the mere fact that one member of the British Empire was a party to a regional arrangement would automatically involve the Empire as a whole.

This resolution implied that the guarantee insisted upon might possibly entail a military convention. He was not there to accept a commitment for the whole British Empire to detailed military conventions of the kind which might be prescribed in virtue of the third resolution.[7]

Canada, which at that moment was concerned with the possible military obligation implied in Article 10, was likewise disturbed at the trend of this fresh proposal:

Mr. Fielding (Canada), while heartily sympathizing with the general purpose and spirit of the resolution, was somewhat alarmed at the phrase "binding them to provide immediate and effective assistance" contained in Resolution 3. He would ask Lord Robert Cecil whether he contemplated that the parties concerned should fulfill that obligation without consulting their Parliaments. Any country in the British Dominions was bound to admit the right of Parliament to determine whether a war should be entered into.[8]

The preceding Assembly (1921), it will be recalled, had approved modifications of Article 16 along the lines advocated by the Scandinavian Delegations when that Article was under discussion at Paris. Here was a new program which proposed obligations even more

[7] *Minutes, Third Committee*, Third Assembly, p. 35.
[8] *Ibid.*, p. 17.

rigid than those which had been embodied in the Covenant. It was a system which these states could scarcely be expected to endorse. M. Lange (Norway) was explicit with reference to the attitude of his own country:

> The geographical situation of Norway was such that all guarantees of a military nature as regards other countries would have to be excluded. Norway, in fact, which demanded no guarantees for herself, should not be forced to guarantee the security of any other country.[9]

M. Oldenberg (Denmark) admitted that the proposals of Lord Robert Cecil were in conformity with Article 8 of the Covenant:

> But at the same time he must point out that it was difficult for Denmark to undertake obligations other than those contained in Article 16 of the Covenant. In his opinion, the danger of war might be averted by other means in which small states could collaborate, such as the laying down of the principle that no acquisition of territory should be allowed as a result of war and that any indemnity to be paid by the vanquished to the victor should be fixed by the Council of the League, which would, if necessary, refer the matter to the Permanent Court of International Justice.[10]

M. Unden (Sweden) pointed out that a general reduction of armaments itself constituted an important guarantee for the security of states:

> He was further of opinion that this proposal should take into account the other side of the problem put forward by M. Lange, *i. e.*, that, if the majority of states were not disposed to reduce their armaments without receiving guarantees, others would find them-

[9] *Ibid.*, p. 13.
[10] *Ibid.*, p. 15.

selves heavily handicapped by the obligations created by a Treaty of Guarantee. He did not think that Sweden would favorably regard any engagement which would prevent the eventual reduction of her military budgets.[11]

Was it expedient for the League of Nations to adopt the thesis that disarmament must necessarily proceed on a general basis? Very substantial progress had already been made for reduction merely through regional agreements. The point was raised by M. Rivas-Vicuna (Chile):

As a member of the Temporary Mixed Commission, he had accepted the proposals put forward by Lord Robert Cecil as being in the general interest of humanity. At the same time he felt that the value of regional agreements should not be disregarded. The League of Nations desired universal peace and general disarmament; until such an ideal could be reached, its Members must guarantee the peace of each region of the world and encourage the efforts of those who were anxious to conclude partial agreements. It might be that, in order to maintain the equilibrium of Europe, a general agreement between all the nations would be necessary, but the same did not apply in other parts of the world, as was illustrated by the happy results attending the agreement between Great Britain and the United States in regard to armed forces on the Canadian lakes, or the Treaty of 1902 between Chile and the Argentine Republic. . . . The South American Republics, though strangers to the political conflicts of other continents, nevertheless felt themselves to be bound up in their destinies and were willing to collaborate with them in bringing about that universal peace which they all desired.[12]

[11] *Ibid.*, p. 16.
[12] *Ibid.*, p. 15.

The Draft Treaty of Mutual Assistance 161

A prolonged debate took place in the Committee between the delegate of France, M. de Jouvenel, and Lord Robert Cecil. The latter contended that *effective* reduction should take place at the time of the acceptance of the *principle* of guarantee; M. de Jouvenel asked that the principle of reduction should be accepted at the same time as the principle of guarantee, but that *effective* reduction should correspond to *effective* guarantees. He proposed a new reading of Paragraph 4 to embody this idea:

The reduction of national armaments should be proportionate to the guarantees afforded by the treaty.[13]

The paragraph was re-drafted in a compromise form between these respective contentions. Reduction of armament was to proceed on a two-fold basis; in the one case from a General Treaty, and in the other from the partial treaties; in the former case the Treaty was to carry a general reduction of armaments; in the latter the reduction was to be proportionate to the guarantees afforded by the treaties.

The Resolutions were further amended to specify that any regional treaties of guarantee which were to be concluded should be open to all states, in order to avoid, if possible, the development of alliances directed against one or more countries. But even with these changes the whole scheme carried, it was asserted, weaknesses and dangers which were contrary to the purpose of the League. A statement by M. Lange (Norway) at the conclusion of the discussions expressed this viewpoint with considerable vehemence:

[13] *Ibid.*, (Annex 6).

The whole system outlined in the report of the Temporary Mixed Commission was still really founded on the old Roman adage "Si vis pacem, para bellum"; the danger of this had been demonstrated by the late war, but this military principle had fortunately not yet been imported from national into international spheres. It was necessary to guard against this danger. He therefore asked the T. M. C. to insert, in the preamble of its scheme, a text which would make it possible for states to adhere to the Treaty of Mutual Guarantee and thus to obtain the advantages of a reduction of armaments and of the guarantee.[14]

M. Lange rejected also the idea put forward by the Temporary Mixed Commission that the test for aggression might be found in the deliberate violation of the territory of another state:

Could they rely on purely military criteria? There was such a thing as pacific action—as was the case with France in 1914—when a state, at a time when a conflict was threatening, withdrew its troops 10 kilometers from the frontiers; from this action alone it became clear who was the aggressor. But it seemed impossible to insert such a provision in a treaty, more especially as the violation of the frontier by patrols, for instance, did not in itself constitute an act of premeditated aggression.

There would be no time to appeal to the Council of the League of Nations to institute an enquiry. The test would have to be sought in another direction.

This test was found by the clear and synthetic minds of two Frenchmen, M. Gaston Moch, pacifist and officer, and Jean Jaurès, the first victim of the war, who laid down in his book "The New Army," a test similar to that which was later to be sanctified by the Covenant; the aggressor state is the one which refuses

[14] *Ibid.*, p. 38.

THE DRAFT TREATY OF MUTUAL ASSISTANCE 163

to submit the dispute to juridical procedure. That was a juridical test, clear and easily determined. He asked that the two points that he had just raised should be submitted to the Temporary Mixed Commission by the Committee.[14]

The Resolutions as finally adopted after the debates in the Third Committee and those in the Plenary Sessions of the Assembly were as follows:

The Assembly, having considered the report of the Temporary Mixed Commission on the question of a General Treaty of Mutual Guarantee, being of opinion that this report can in no way affect the complete validity of all the Treaties of Peace or other agreements which are known to exist between states; and considering that this report contains valuable suggestions as to the methods by which a Treaty of Mutual Guarantee could be made effective, is of the opinion that:

1. No scheme for the reduction of armaments, within the meaning of Article 8 of the Covenant, can be fully successful unless it be general.

2. In the present state of the world, many Governments would be unable to accept the responsibility for a serious reduction of armaments unless they received in exchange a satisfactory guarantee of the safety of their country.

3. Such a guarantee can be found in a defensive agreement which should be open to all countries, binding them to provide immediate and effective assistance in accordance with a pre-arranged plan in the event of one of them being attacked, provided that the obligation to render assistance to a country attacked shall be limited in principle to those countries situated in the same part of the globe. In cases, however, where, for historical, geographical, or other reasons, a country is

[14] *Ibid.*, p. 38.

in special danger of attack, detailed arrangements should be made for its defence in accordance with the above-mentioned plan.

4. As a general reduction of armaments is the object of the three preceding statements, and the Treaty of Mutual Guarantee the means of achieving that object, previous consent to this reduction is therefore the first condition of the Treaty.

This reduction could be carried out either by means of a general Treaty, which is the most desirable plan, or by means of partial treaties, designed to be extended and open to all countries. In the former case the Treaty will carry with it a general reduction of armaments. In the latter case, the reduction will be proportionate to the guarantees afforded by the Treaty.

The Council of the League, after having taken the advice of the Temporary Mixed Commission, which will examine how each of these two systems could be carried out, should further formulate and submit to the Governments for their consideration and sovereign decision, the plan of the machinery, both political and military, necessary to bring them clearly into effect.

The Assembly requests the Council to submit to the various Governments the above proposals for their observations, and requests the Temporary Mixed Commission to continue its investigations and, in order to give precision to the above statements, to prepare a Draft Treaty embodying the principles contained herein.[15]

[15] This text is taken from the *Minutes, Third Committee, Fourth Assembly,* p. 125.

"This resolution, as its involved wording alone would indicate, was a compromise reached between the conflicting tendencies of two clearly defined groups of States. The one, represented notably by the British Empire, striving toward disarmament as an end, considered a general treaty of mutual guarantee as the normal means to that end, and reluctantly accepted the special treaties as an unfortunately necessary concession. The other

III

During the next year the Temporary Mixed Commission proceeded with the task of drawing a Draft Treaty to embody the principles contained in the foregoing Resolutions. A certain number of Governments replied promptly to the request of the Council for opinions on the system proposed. The nature of the arguments in support of the new program and the objections which it encountered may be had by citing extracts from a few representative replies from the Governments consulted.

Mutual assistance, the French Government stated, "involves the preparation explicitly indicated in Paragraph 3 of the Resolution," and "reduction of armament must always take place as a sequel to the measures adopted for mutual assistance and can in no case precede these measures." But the protection afforded by the proposed General Treaty was regarded as being little in advance of that already provided by the Covenant:

> As regards the method known as the General Treaty, the Government of the Republic considers that such a Treaty would exercise a favorable influence on the maintenance of peace, but would, of itself, only furnish

---

group, headed by the France of Poincaré, looked upon security as the one important end, relied on the special treaties as the safest means of attaining it, were content to agree to a general treaty as offering a subsidiary guarantee, and as for disarmament, relegated it into a happily hazy future."

W. E. Rappard, *International Relations as Viewed from Geneva*, p. 154.

security of a doubtful and indeterminate character and would thus be unlikely to lead to a more rapid or more complete reduction of armaments than has already been carried by the majority of Governments during the last four years.

The chief prospects of success lay in the Partial Treaties:

A consideration of the second method, known as that of partial treaties, has persuaded the Government of the Republic that military assistance, pre-arranged by means of definite conventions between the states which are exposed to one or more common dangers, might justify a reduction of their armaments in time of peace.[16]

The same thesis was developed by the Belgian Government:

It is open to question whether the conditions essential to render a treaty of mutual guarantee effective can be combined in a general treaty. In the opinion of experts, such a treaty would have to be one which could be executed immediately; it would have to provide complete assistance, both military, economic and financial; would have to include a "pre-arranged plan" incorporated in the treaty itself, and would have to be periodically supervised and revised.

The Belgian Government recognizes that, in order to be fully effective, any plan for the reduction of armaments must be general; it believes, however, that this result can only be attained step by step, by means of partial defensive treaties, concluded between states which are exposed to common dangers. . . .

Partial treaties and regional agreements, however, do not by any means present to the same degree the difficulties inherent in a general treaty. The possibili-

[16] See Annex IV.

ties of conflicts are less numerous, the preparation of schemes of defence is easier, the actual assistance can be furnished much more rapidly, the value of such assistance can readily be determined, and consequently the extent to which armaments can be reduced can be fixed in proportion to the securities afforded by the treaties.[17]

The most decisive opposition to the system projected by Resolution XIV was set forth in carefully reasoned replies submitted by Holland and the Scandinavian states. The system of partial alliances, for example, so vigorously supported by the French and Belgian Governments, was interpreted by these northern European states as a return to the old system of competitive alliances which it was the purpose of the League to displace. Thus, on this aspect of the proposal, the Government of The Netherlands observed:

As regards the partial Treaties of Guarantee indicated in the Resolution, the Royal Government is of opinion that, by adopting this system, the League of Nations would sanction a return to the system of military alliances which, so far from insuring peace, have in the past been a contributory cause in inducing states to increase their armaments. It would be a retrograde step, contrary to the ideal of the League of Nations, and disastrous to future international organization.[18]

The same line of criticism was put forward in the reply of the Danish Government:

Might not a system of groups of defensive military alliances within the League also contain the germ of

[17] Annex IV.
[18] Annex IV.

fresh conflicts of interest and fresh controversy? Even if all the Members of the League were to enter into these alliances, the results would be at least to weaken that community of interest which it was desired to establish between all Members of the League. But we have also to reckon with the very strong possibility that certain Members of the League would prefer to keep to the present provisions of the Covenant. The result might be to produce a serious split, by ranging Members of the League which belonged to defensive alliances against other Members which did not belong to these alliances, and the situation would cause the whole framework of the League of Nations to collapse. We should thereby bring about the continuance of military alliances and strengthen the position of those very coalitions which it was one of the principal aims of the League of Nations to abolish.[19]

The Resolutions proposed a general defensive agreement, binding states to provide immediate and effective assistance to a member thereof which was the victim of aggression. But what assurance, the Netherlands Government inquired, did the system provide that this assistance would be given only to those states which were in a position rightfully to claim it. In short, what was to be the test of aggression?

The Royal Government desires at this early stage to point out that it would feel great hesitation in joining in a system of military cooperation which did not provide the necessary legal guarantees that the assistance to be given shall only be granted to states in a position to claim it rightfully. According to the system established by the Covenant, it is the violation of the Covenant which sets the machinery for penalties in motion. What guarantees are there in the system recommended

[19] Annex IV.

in the Resolution to ensure that collective action will not serve other ends than those of right and justice? The Royal Government fears that the legal guarantees, which are already too vaguely set forth in the Covenant—a fact which has hitherto prevented the organization of collective action to resist aggression—are lacking, or are present in a less effective form, in the system recommended in the Assembly's resolution.[20]

The Norwegian Government likewise expressed this demand for strengthening the juridical aspects of the Covenant. And, furthermore, this Government declared, "in order to enable a state to benefit by a guarantee, there should be the preliminary assurance that that state, in the conduct of its foreign policy, will be guided by the principles upon which the Covenant of the League of Nations is based."[21]

The Danish Government took occasion to question the fundamental assumptions of the Cecil proposals, namely, that additional guarantees were essential to a program for the reduction of armaments. Had not the Covenant already established a body of guarantees and imposed obligations on all the Members of the League?

If we adopted the principles embodied in Lord Robert Cecil's new proposals, that any reduction of armament necessarily presupposes a guarantee of another kind, not only shall we *ipso facto* recognize the principle that present-day armaments are justified so long as no guarantee of another kind exists—a point of view which the Danish Delegation considers dangerous and contrary to the meaning of Article 8 of the

[20] Annex IV.
[21] Annex IV.

Covenant—but we shall also be greatly underestimating the importance, and, consequently, diminish the value of the provisions of guarantee in the Covenant, which its authors considered adequate to permit of an effective reduction of armaments.[22]

At a meeting of the Temporary Mixed Commission at Geneva in February, 1923, Lord Robert Cecil presented a draft treaty to carry forward the principles of Resolution XIV. The Temporary Commission referred this draft to the Permanent Advisory Commission, which examined the proposal and decided that it did not present a satisfactory basis for disarmament. During the succeedings months, the draft prepared by Lord Robert Cecil was the subject of further study and amendment by a Sub-Committee of the Temporary Mixed Commission, meeting in London, which endeavored to overcome the objections raised by the Permanent Advisory Commission.

In the meanwhile, the Temporary Mixed Commission was forwarded a draft proposal by one of its own members—Colonel Réquin, of the French Delegation—which endeavored to give effect to the requirement of the army and naval experts of the Permanent Advisory Commission. The essential element in Colonel Réquin's plan was an elaboration of the scheme for special treaties of mutual defense through which assistance could be provided in accordance with a pre-arranged plan.[23] A single draft, combining the Cecil and the

[22] Annex IV.

[23] The Réquin plan is explained and acutely criticized by Professor Shotwell in *"A Practical Plan for Disarmament,"* International Conciliation Pamphlet, No. 201.

Réquin plan was drawn up by the Temporary Mixed Commission in August, 1923, and submitted by it to the Fourth Assembly at the September meeting.

The draft thus prepared was referred to the Third Committee of the Assembly. M. Lebrun (France), Chairman of the Temporary Mixed Commission, made a statement before the Third Committee of the principles which had guided the Temporary Mixed Commission in preparing the draft treaty. With respect to the attitude of the Permanent Advisory Commission on the principles expressed in Resolution XIV, he said:

From the technical point of view, the members of the Permanent Advisory Commission, although in agreement on a number of general considerations, were divided in their conclusions. The majority recognized that a general treaty offered certain advantages to countries which were attacked, but drew attention to certain difficulties, notably, the impossibility of setting in motion immediate assistance in accordance with a pre-arranged plan. Consequently, the immediate assistance suggested in Resolution XIV would not be given, and it would therefore be impossible to prevent invasion in certain countries.

The majority of the Commission thought that the easiest and most definite solution of these different problems was to be found in partial agreements. The minority held that the general Treaty of Mutual Assistance alone would possess the necessary moral value for insuring the reduction of armaments. . . .

What was the chief difficulty with which the Commission had had to contend? It had been summarized in the declaration made by the Italian Delegation, which feared that these partial conventions would assume the form of pre-war treaties of alliance, and would therefore be more calculated to stimulate than to restrain the race of armaments. The Delegation had greater faith in the general treaty, which seemed in this respect to be the best, if not the only method.

M. Lebrun continued with a summary of the results obtained from consulting the various Governments on Resolution XIV:

From the political point of view, no decisive result had been achieved by consulting the various Governments. Out of the fifty-two states members of the League, twenty-six only expressed their opinion: Of these, some accepted the general principle without discussing the essential question at issue. Amongst those who did go to the root of the matter, the majority inclined toward the general treaty with partial agreements in addition. The minority rejected partial agreements on the grounds that they resembled pre-war alliances. It would seem, on the whole, that Governments inclined to one side or to the other, according to the risks which they personally incurred.

He called atttention to two interesting tendencies. Certain Governments said that, although it was natural that countries whose political situation was delicate should find advantage in concluding conjointly a Treaty of Mutual Assistance, it was no less natural that other countries more favored in this respect should hesitate to do so.

Other Governments wondered whether it was not somewhat Utopian to seek outside the Covenant for a means of attaining a reduction of armaments. If, they said, this result had not so far been attained, it was due to the fact that a certain number of great nations were not as yet Members of the League of Nations, that we were too near the last war, and, finally, that the League of Nations had not been long enough in existence to enable it to ensure the security of those placed under its protection.[24]

[24] *Minutes, Third Committee*, Fourth Assembly, p. 12.

Despite these manifestly conflicting viewpoints, the Third Committee proceeded with the examination of the draft submitted by the Temporary Mixed Commission. A month of difficult negotiations followed, but eventually the Committee presented to the Assembly a proposal entitled the "Draft Treaty of Mutual Assistance," with the recommendation that it be submitted to the Members of the League for their observations and replies.

The Report submitted by the Third Committee in connection with the Draft began with a rehearsal of the efforts of the League to proceed with plans for a reduction of armaments as provided in Article 8 of the Covenant. The Temporary Mixed Commission had been instituted for the purpose of formulating such proposals, but had found itself at once confronted with the problem of national security:

Faced by the necessity for preparing the way for the reduction of armaments, the Commission began by realizing that a certain number of states are not in a position to contemplate a reduction of their armaments without receiving in exchange a guarantee of their security. The necessity, therefore, arises of strengthening the sentiment of international confidence by defining more clearly everything in the Covenant which may be regarded as an endeavour to obtain a mutual guarantee of security. A certain connection thus becomes apparent between the work of disarmament and certain Articles of the Covenant, such as Articles 10 and 16.[25]

Resolution XIV of the Third Assembly had recog-

[25] *Report of the Third Committee*, Fourth Assembly.

nized the principle that disarmament and guarantee were interdependent; this was likewise the foundation of the rule upon which the Draft Treaty was based. The Report proceeded to contrast the purpose of the Draft Treaty with that of the Covenant:

> The purpose of the Draft is obviously narrower than that of the Covenant. The Covenant is directed toward the pure ideal of world peace and justice; the draft merely aims at the reduction of armaments. . . . The obligations and the corresponding rights embodied in the draft are narrower, and at the same time more definite, than those contained in the Covenant. In the draft the right to the guarantee in case of aggression is absolute, subject to reciprocity (Article 17). . . . In this respect the draft, though narrower and more definite, may be regarded—as one of the most diligent of its authors, Senator Lebrun, has so happily phrased it—as a prolongation of the Covenant.

But the authors of the Draft pointed out that this particular form of prolongation did not receive the endorsement of the representatives of certain states which were contending for an extension of the Covenant along other lines. The Report continued:

> Mention should be here made of the attitude adopted by certain members of the Committee who consider that the draft, which was solely directed toward the extension of the Covenant by material guarantees, would represent a one-sided development of the League. In the view of these delegations, the legal and moral aspects of the Covenant should be developed side by side with this development of material guarantees. They particularly emphasize the importance of asking those countries which would, under the present scheme, have the advantage of the guarantee offered

by the Draft Treaty for guarantees of a "reasonable" policy (that is to say, they should observe the obligations contained in the Covenant regarding the registration and publication of international treaties and regarding adhesion to the optional clause of the Statute of the Court of International Justice).

Attention should be directed here to certain outstanding provisions of the Treaty which illustrate the nature of the proposed development. Article I of the Treaty declared aggressive war an "international crime," and the High Contracting Parties severally undertook that no one of them would be guilty of its commission. No definition of "aggressive war" was provided in the Treaty, but, under Article IV, the Council of the League was given authority to decide within four days after the opening of hostilities which of the High Contracting Parties were the objects of aggression and whether they were entitled to claim the mutual assistance provided in the Treaty. The High Contracting Parties undertoook to accept this decision of the Council (Article IV).

In the event of any one of the High Contracting Parties becoming the object of a war of aggression, the other High Contracting Parties jointly and severally undertook to furnish mutual assistance in the form determined by the Council as the most effective, and to take all appropriate measures without delay in the order of urgency demanded by the circumstances. (Articles II and V.)

In particular, the Council might (Article V):

(a) decide to apply immediately to the aggressor State the economic sanctions contemplated by Article 16 of the Covenant, the Members of the League not signatory to the present Treaty not being, however, bound by this decision, except in the case where the State attacked is entitled to avail itself of the Article of the Covenant;

(b) invoke by name the High Contracting Parties whose assistance it requires. No High Contracting Party situated in a continent other than that in which operations will take place shall, in principle, be required to co-operate in military, naval, or air operations;

(c) determine the forces which each State furnishing assistance shall place at its disposal;

(d) prescribe all necessary measures for securing priority for the communications and transport connected with the operations;

(e) prepare a plan for financial co-operation among the High Contracting Parties with a view to providing for the State attacked and for the States furnishing assistance the funds which they require for the operation;

(f) appoint the Higher Command and establish the object and the nature of his duty.

For the purpose of rendering mutual assistance immediately effective, the High Contracting Parties were permitted to conclude "either as between two of them or as between a larger number, agreements complementary to the present Treaty exclusively for the purpose of their mutual defence and intended solely to facilitate the carrying out of the measures prescribed in this Treaty, determining in advance the assistance which they would give to each other in the event of any act of aggression." (Article VI.) These complementary agreements were, before registration, to be examined by the Council[26] with a view to deciding whether or not they were in accordance with the principles of the Treaty and of the Covenant. When recognized, the agreements were to be registered at the League; they were to be regarded as complementary to the General Treaty and in no way to limit "the general obligations of the High Contracting Parties nor the sanctions contemplated against the aggressor state under the terms of this Treaty." (Article VII.)

The Parties to these complementary agreements might undertake to put into immediate execution, in the cases of aggression contemplated in them, the plan of mutual assistance agreed upon. The Council of the League was to be immediately informed concerning the measures which had been undertaken in execution of the complementary agreements. The Council was thereupon to discharge its function under Article IV of determining the aggressor state, and, if the parties to the complementary agreements were, themselves, found to be the aggressors, they were liable to the sanctions set forth in the General Treaty. (Article VIII.)

The most noteworthy advance marked by the Draft Treaty by way of extending the principles embodied in Articles 10 and 16 of the Covenant was in connec-

---

[26] "Partial treaties cannot benefit by the general guarantee, until the Council has recognized that they are not contrary to the spirit of the Covenant and that they are in harmony with the General Treaty of Mutual Assistance." *Report of the Third Committee*, Fourth Assembly.

tion with the increased authority of the Council. Explicit provision was made for the Council to render a decision as to whether or not the crime of "aggressive war" had been committed. This decision was to be binding on the signatory power. A reading of the authority vested in the Council with respect to the use of sanctions shows the substantial increase in the Council's powers as compared with those which it possesses in a similar connection under Articles 10 and 16 of the Covenant.[27] The Treaty represented, in fact, the furthest advance of the efforts of the League toward constructing a system of state security based primarily upon material guarantees. The security which Lord Robert Cecil's proposals had stated as the essential prerequisite to disarmament was interpreted by certain Members of the League to mean security derived primarily from definitely organized force which could be immediately and effectively applied against a state which was guilty of aggressive warfare.[28] In deference to these demands, the system projected by the Draft Treaty permitted the conclusion of partial treaties which might become operative upon the initiative of parties thereto. Under this arrangement it

[27] Cf. Article V of the Treaty.

[28] "Certain states, which, for various reasons, regarded themselves as being especially threatened, whilst not denying the great moral and political value of the general guarantee, insisted on the impossibility of risking a reduction of their armaments in exchange for a general guarantee of assistance, the technical preparation, speed and effectiveness of which would be problematical." *Report of the Third Committee*, Fourth Assembly.

would be possible for the individual states to declare that an act of aggression had been committed, and to institute measures of mutual assistance, in advance of decision by the Council on the issue. There was thus the possibility of disagreement between the Council and the states parties to a special treaty over the fact of the existence of aggression, and this possible conflict was subsequently criticized by a number of Governments as one of the fundamental defects of the system.

But if the purpose before the League was really to extend the principles of the Covenant, should not the development proceed along lines more in keeping with the spirit of the Covenant? Throughout the debates in the Third Committee when the Draft Treaty was in process of elaboration, this viewpoint was urged, especially by the representatives of the Scandinavian states. Thus M. Lange (Norway) declared:

> The Covenant did not merely require the abolition of material force. It set up a legal system of arbitration and conciliation. . . . Ought they to add to this noble edifice a new building which would be out of keeping with the original architecture? They should add moral and legal guarantees to material guarantees and should require states to respect the idea of law.[29]

He continued by enumerating the direction which a further elaboration of the Covenant should take:

> It would be premature to attempt to establish a complete and definite supervision of the international policy of states, but might they not lay down certain definite criteria for the political guidance of states?

Only one condition was laid down for the guarantee

[29] *Minutes, Third Committee*, Fourth Assembly, p. 16.

in Article 2, *i. e.*, that the state attacked should have reduced its armaments in conformity with the Treaty. Would it not be possible to add other conditions, for instance, that this state should have sent to the Secretariat of the League for registration and publication all its international engagements as required by the Covenant; that it should have adhered to the provision inserted in Article 36 of the Statute of the Court of International Justice concerning compulsory arbitration, and, finally—for states which were Members of the League—that they should have adhered to one of the procedures referred to in Article 15?[29]

M. Lange was supported in these arguments by M. Branting (Sweden):

The Draft Treaty exceeded the scope of the Covenant as far as military assistance was concerned. Further, it was not in accordance with the system of conciliation and arbitration provided for by the Covenant. It prohibited wars of aggression, but provided no means for settling disputes when the Covenant's conciliation procedure failed.

The speaker recalled that certain Governments, including that of Sweden, had pointed out how difficult it would be for them to enter into undertakings of a military character while the present political situation lasted. The reply they had received was that the Treaty would create a sense of security and also that a Treaty of Mutual Guarantee presupposed more friendly international relations. Those were two ideas which formed a vicious circle.[30]

Criticisms of this order which the Treaty met both in the Third Committee and in debates of the Plenary Session of the Assembly did not augur well for its subsequent acceptance by the Members of the League.

[29] *Minutes, Third Committee*, Fourth Assembly, p. 16.
[30] *Ibid.*, p. 20.

The Assembly voted, however, to submit the Draft to the various Governments for observations and replies and the ensuing months revealed an opposition to the scheme which was decisive.

The Draft was rejected by the Scandinavian states and by Holland in a group of replies which reiterated the objections previously offered to Resolution XIV. France and Belgium endorsed the scheme; it was rejected, however, by certain of the exposed states of Central Europe on the ground that the guarantees provided—and especially the procedure for setting them in motion—were insufficient to justify a reduction of armaments.[31] The criticisms of the British Government were chiefly directed against the inadequacies of the guarantees, the system of partial treaties, and the unsatisfactory means devised for determining the aggressor state. But perhaps the most fundamental reason for the rejection of the Draft was the unwillingness of the United Kingdom and of the Dominions to assume the additional international obligations contained therein.

This element in the situation has been stated by Mr. Toynbee in the following terms:

From the French point of view, the draft supplied the three great omissions in the British version of an Anglo-French Pact: it embraced Eastern as well as Western Europe in its purview; it sanctioned (under certain conditions of review and control by the League) the free formation of special groups of alliances to supplement the general agreement; and it permitted

[31] Cf. The reply of the Government of Jugo-Slavia, Annex VI.

the parties to these special alliances to concert military plans in advance. From the British point of view, again, the draft offered undoubted advantages over the project of a bilateral Pact as French statesmen had conceived it ... but it broke down over the same crux as the project for an Anglo-French Pact, namely, the fact that the area within which it was to take effect was not commensurate with Europe. Given the insularity of the British outlook, a system of security based on a bilateral Pact between Great Britain and France could cover only a fraction of Europe. On the other hand, owing to the universality of the League of Nations, which possessed Members in every region of the world, a scheme based on the League organization was bound to embrace not only Europe but the Middle East, Africa, the Far East and Pacific, and the American Continent, and this meant that the overseas members of the British Commonwealth, as well as the United Kingdom, would necessarily be involved.[32]

II. Protocol for the Pacific Settlement of International Disputes

I

The decisive rejection of the Draft Treaty of Mutual Assistance left unfulfilled one of the major objects which the League of Nations had set out to accomplish. The Draft Treaty, it will be recalled, was the product of activity on the part of the League which had started with reduction of armaments as the end in view. The emphasis on security had come forward with the promulgation of the thesis that reduction of armaments could not proceed without adequate guar-

[32] *Survey of International Affairs, 1924*, pp. 28-29.

THE GENEVA PROTOCOL 183

antees of national safety. This was the implication of the Covenant, it was pointed out; the Covenant enjoined a reduction of armament "to the lowest point consistent with national safety and the enforcement by common action of international obligations." For two years the question of disarmament and security had been uppermost in the deliberations of the League and from these a definite principle had evolved. The progress was summarized by M. Benes when in September, 1924, the Fifth Assembly once more approached the arduous problem:

After prolonged, detailed and, sometimes, heated discussion, we succeeded in establishing one definite principle which has since played an important part in the policy of the League and, indeed, in European policy. This principle is that the reduction of armaments should go hand in hand with the establishment of some system providing security for countries which have hitherto been obliged to protect their national indepedence and liberty by means of armaments.[33]

What principles, however, should serve as the basis of this system of security which it was deemed essential to devise? Should there be a continued reliance primarily on force or could other methods be devised more in harmony with the pacific ideals of the League of Nations? In a notable address which opened the debates of the Fifth Assembly, the British Prime Minister, Mr. Ramsay MacDonald, sounded a note of warning on the emphasis which lately had been placed on force as a means of establishing state security:

[33] *Plenary Meetings*, Fifth Assembly, p. 61.

The danger of supreme importance which is facing us now is that national security should be regarded merely as a military problem and based solely on the predominance of force. For a moment this may serve. For a moment it may lull to sleep. For a moment it may enable large nations and small to believe that their existence will no longer be challenged. But, my friends, there is an evolution in every plan and a consequence of every idea, and if, after all the appalling evidence in history that military force cannot give security, we today go back and repeat the follies of our ancestors, then the security we give for the day is only a betrayal of the nation that we lull to sleep under it.

But even more significant was Mr. MacDonald's advocacy on this occasion of the development of the juridical aspects of the Covenant along the lines supported by the ex-neutral states of northern Europe since the time of the drafting of the Covenant. As the spokesman of the British Delegation, he declared:

I am in favor of arbitration. I see nothing else for the world. If we cannot devise a proper system of arbitration, then do not let us fool ourselves that we are going to have peace. Let us go back to the past! Let us go back to competitive armaments! Let us go back to that false, whited sepulchre of security through military pacts—there is nothing else for us—and let us prepare for the next war, because that is inevitable.

On the difficult question of providing an effective test to designate the aggressor state, he proposed that the League accept the juridical test which, it will be recalled, had been urged in 1922 by M. Lange before the Third Committee in the discussion of the Cecil Resolutions:

The one method by which we can secure, the one method by which we can approximate to an accurate attribution of responsibility for aggression is arbitration, the setting up of a court, or, rather, courts—because one court will not suffice for the purpose. . . . The test is: Are you willing to arbitrate? The test is: Are you willing to explain? The test is: Will you come before us and tell us what you propose to do? The test is: Will you expose your commitments? Are you afraid of the world? Are you afraid of daylight, a lover of darkness and timorous lest the world should know what is in your mind? Such is the test, the only test.[34]

The French Delegation at Geneva in 1924 readily accepted these proposals for a more comprehensive system of arbitration, and was disposed, as well, to modify the requirements for precise military guarantees which up to this time had been such a conspicuous element in all French programs for security.[35] And yet, in the opening debates of the Assembly, M. Herriot took occasion to point out that security implied something more than the covenant of states to arbitrate all disputes:

Arbitration is essential [he said] but it is not suffi-

[34] *Plenary Meetings*, Fifth Assembly, pp. 41-45.

[35] As a result of the General Election of May, 1924, in France, the Poincaré Ministry had been succeeded by the Radical-Socialist Government of M. Herriot. This change of Ministry was symptomatic of what Mr. Toynbee terms a "psychological transformation" in France which, he says, "was so important in itself that it doubtless accounted, more than any other single factor, for the great step forward which the Fifth Assembly actually found itself able to take as the result of a month's deliberation." *Survey of International Affairs, 1924*, pp. 37-38.

cient. . . . It does not entirely fulfill the intentions of Article 8 of the Covenant, which, if I may again remind you, are security and disarmament.

We in France regard these three terms—arbitration, security, and disarmament—as inseparable. . . . Arbitration must not be made a snare for trustful nations. We Frenchmen believe—and in speaking thus I am expressing a moral rather than a political idea—we Frenchmen believe that a nation which accepts arbitration, which, notwithstanding the uncertainties and risks that still exist in the world, sets this example of willingness to accept the dictates of justice; we Frenchmen believe that such a nation, be it great or small, has a right to security.[36]

At the conclusion of the preliminary debates on the problem, the French and British Delegations offered jointly the following resolution which was adopted by the Assembly:

The Assembly, noting the declarations of the Governments represented, observes with satisfaction that they contain the basis of an understanding tending to establish a secure peace, decides as follows:

With a view to reconciling in the new proposals the divergencies between certain points of view which have been expressed and, when agreement has been reached, to enable an international conference upon armaments to be summoned by the League of Nations at the earliest possible moment:

1. The Third Committee is requested to consider the material dealing with security and the reduction of armaments, particularly the observations of the Governments on the Draft Treaty of Mutual Assistance, prepared in pursuance of Resolution XIV of the Third Assembly and other plans prepared and presented to the Secretary-General since the publication of the

[36] *Plenary Meetings*, Fifth Assembly, pp. 52-53.

Draft Treaty, and to examine the obligations contained in the Covenant of the League in relation to the guarantees of security which a resort to arbitration and a reduction of armaments may require:

2. The First Committee is requested:
   (a) To consider, in view of possible amendments, the articles in the Covenant relating to the settlement of disputes;
   (b) To examine within what limits the terms of Article 36, paragraph 2, of the Statute establishing the Permanent Court of International Justice might be rendered more precise and thereby facilitate the more general acceptance of the clause;

and thus strengthen the solidarity and the security of the nations of the world by settling by pacific means all disputes which may arise between states.

II

The product of the joint efforts of the First and Third Committees was the Protocol for the Pacific Settlement of International Disputes, unanimously approved by the Fifth Assembly on October 2, 1924.[37]

[37] In the preparation of the Protocol, the First and Third Committees of the Assembly had before them a Draft Treaty of Mutual Assistance prepared by an American group which the Council of the League had submitted as an official document to the Fifth Assembly. The American Draft was characterized by the emphasis placed upon the juridical test to designate the aggressor state and by the principle of optional or voluntary sanctions. A distinguished group of Americans, including Professor James T. Shotwell, General Tasker H. Bliss, and Mr. David Hunter Miller collaborated in the preparation of the Draft. The text is given in the *Minutes of the Third Committee*, Fifth Assembly, Annex 4.

From the standpoint of this study, only three general features of the Protocol need be examined: First, the restraint it proposed to introduce upon the resort to war by the signatories thereto; secondly, the methods it provided for the pacific settlement of international disputes; and, thirdly, its application of the principle of sanctions.

With regard to the first of these principles, it may be said that the general object of the Protocol was the complete abolition of aggressive war. The tests employed by the Protocol for the identification of aggressive war will be noted later. But it was the prohibition of aggressive war only that the Protocol sought to establish. It was recognized that the state still retained the right of legitimate self-defence. "The state attacked retains complete liberty to resist by all means in its power any act of aggression of which it may be a victim." Furthermore, under the Protocol there might be the authorization of war in two additional cases. A state might employ force under the provisions of the Covenant and those of the Protocol in aid of a Member state which was the victim of aggression; "or a state may employ force with the authorization of the Council or the Assembly in order to enforce a decision given in its favor." But in all of these cases the state resorting to war would be regarded as acting not on its private initiative, "but in a sense as the agent and organ of the community."[38]

[38] General Report on the Protocol by M. Politis and M. Benes.

THE GENEVA PROTOCOL

The system set up by the Protocol for the pacific settlement of international disputes was designed to provide means for the adjustment by one means or another of all international disputes between the signatories thereto.[39] To accomplish this result, two main lines of development were followed: the first was the provision in the Protocol for a more general acceptance by the signatory states of the compulsory jurisdiction of the International Court of Justice; and the second was the extension of the principles laid down in Article 15 of the Covenant in order to provide settlement, either by the Council or by compulsory arbitration, for all disputes which did not fall within the jurisdiction of the Court.

Under Article 3 of the Protocol, the signatory states agreed to accept as compulsory, ipso facto, and without special agreement, the jurisdiction of the Court in the cases covered by paragraph 2 of Article 36 of the Court Statute. This acceptance of the jurisdiction of the Court was subject, however, to two general limi-

[39] "While the Draft Treaty concentrated attention and effort upon the second phase in an international dispute, the Protocol transferred the emphasis to the first phase. The Draft Treaty was primarily concerned to secure, to a state which had reduced its armament, the certainty of receiving precise, immediate, and effective military assistance in the event of it being attacked by another party. The Protocol was primarily concerned to provide exhaustively for the compulsory settlement of all international disputes, so that no loophole should be left for the waging of a 'private' war between states which would not be stigmatized and penalized as an act of aggression." A. J. Toynbee, *Survey of International Affairs, 1924*, p. 49.

tations which were set forth in the Protocol.[40] The first was the competence of the signatory states to conclude special arbitration agreements for the adjustment of a particular dispute—or for all disputes—and these agreements might take precedence, as a mode of settlement, over the jurisdiction of the Court. This limitation resulted from Article 21 of the Covenant which provided that nothing in the Covenant should "affect the validity of international engagements such as treaties of arbitration"—a principle which was reaffirmed in Article 19 of the Protocol.

The second limitation on the jurisdiction of the Court was the provision in Article 3 of the Protocol that, in acceding to the compulsory jurisdictional clause of the Court Statute, the signatories to the Protocol should retain the right without prejudice "to make reservations compatible with the said clause."[41] In theory, this latter proviso might have operated to nullify practically the whole scope of the compulsory jurisdiction of the Court. The second paragraph of

[40] In summarizing these provisions, the author has been guided largely by the authoritative analysis of the Protocol by Professor P. J. Noel Baker in his work on *The Geneva Protocol for the Pacific Settlement of International Disputes*, London, 1925.

[41] The reservation was inserted at the insistence of the British Delegation in order to safeguard the "liberty of the British fleet," *i. e.* to prevent an enemy state—presumably one which had violated the provisions of the Covenant or the Protocol—from referring to the Court a dispute arising out of naval operations. Under paragraph 7, Article 4, of the Protocol, disputes of this nature were likewise exempted from the other processes of compulsory settlement instituted by the Protocol.

Article 36 of the Court Statute enumerates the classes of legal disputes comprised by the compulsory jurisdiction of the Court, and provides, moreover, that in adhering to this provision, states may accept compulsory jurisdiction in respect of all or any of these classes of disputes. A reservation, therefore, compatible with the compulsory jurisdictional clause of the Statute might exempt, as Professor Baker points out,[42] any (though not all) of these four classes. But in practice it is improbable that reservations of this nature would have been made since under the Protocol all disputes which did not go before the Court must eventually come before the Council, and could then, at the request of any party, be submitted to arbitration. The Committee of Arbitrators could then, at the request of any party, obtain an advisory opinion from the Court upon any points of law in dispute. (Article 4, parag. 2 (c), of the Protocol.) It is reasonable to assume that the arbitrators would be guided by the Court's opinion, and the results in such instances would be the settlement of justiciable disputes on purely legal grounds. A state, therefore, which sought to limit the jurisdiction of the Court under the above power of reservations would have to reckon with the supplementary provisions of the Protocol, which at some stage or other utilized juridical procedure. In substance, it may be said that, whatever might have been the practical effects of these possible limitations on the compulsory jurisdiction of the Court, they were not

[42] *The Geneva Protocol*, p. 66.

deemed to modify the comprehensiveness of the system set up by the Protocol for the ultimate pacific settlement of all disputes of an international character.

III

For the settlement of disputes which did not fall within the jurisdiction of the Court, and which were not amicably adjusted by the parties themselves, the Protocol proposed (Article 4) four modes of settlement which may be regarded as going forward in successive stages until some one of the methods resulted in a settlement: First, mediation by the Council as provided in paragraph 3, Article 15, of the Covenant; second, compulsory arbitration at the request of one of the parties to the controversy; third, unanimous decision by the Council if neither party requested arbitration; and, fourth, final compulsory arbitration enjoined by the Council if the dispute had not been settled by some one of the preceding methods.[43]

The Protocol accepted the principle expressed in paragraph 8, Article 15, of the Covenant, which exempted disputes of a domestic nature from settlement by the Council. It also applied this principle to the processes of compulsory arbitration provided for in

[43] "If the Council's efforts at conciliation fail in the first instance, it can go further and exercise its authority, first, by recommending arbitration, and secondly, if the parties refuse to accept it, by imposing on them its own decision, provided that decision is unanimous, or, if it is not unanimous, by making the parties once more submit to arbitration." M. Loudon (Netherlands) *Plenary Meetings*, Fifth Assembly, p. 200.

the Protocol. If, during the course of an arbitration, one of the parties to the dispute claimed that the dispute, or a portion thereof, was a matter solely within the domestic jurisdiction of a state, the arbitrators were to ask on this point the advice of the Permanent Court of International Justice. The opinion of the Court was to be binding on the arbitrators, and, if the opinion were affirmative, the arbitrators were to confine themselves to so declaring in their award. In the proceedings of the Council, under the Protocol, the provisions of paragraph 8, Article 15, of the Covenant, relating to domestic questions were to continue to apply (Article 5).

Article 5 of the Protocol carried, however, the following further proviso:

If the question is held by the Court or by the Council, to be a mattter solely within the domestic jurisdiction of the state, this decision shall not prevent consideration of the situation by the Council or by the Assembly under Article 11 of the Covenant.

The foregoing provision was an amendment to the original draft of this Article, and its final adoption marked the adjustment of a crisis which for a time jeopardized the whole constructive program of the Fifth Assembly. The original draft of Article 5, as it was reported by a Sub-Committee of the First Committee, followed the principle of paragraph 8, Article 15, of the Covenant, and exempted from settlement by the pacific procedure of the Protocol those questions which, in the manner prescribed by the Protocol, had been declared to be within the domestic jurisdiction of states. But at this stage of the proceedings the Japanese Delegation offered, as an amendment to Article 5, the following proviso:

> The above provisions leave unaffected the Council's duty of endeavouring to conciliate the parties so as to assure the maintenance of peace and of a good understanding between nations.[44]

The purpose of this amendment, M. Adatci (Japan) explained to the Committee, "was to fix and define the duty of the Council in a question regarded as forming a part of the jurisdiction of states." But the general purpose of the Japanese Delegation at the Fifth Assembly was, in fact, to achieve an expansion of the peaceful procedure of the Covenant and of the Protocol to apply to all classes of disputes, including domestic questions, which might arise between the signatories thereto. This purpose was clearly set forth in a statement of M. Adatci before the First Committee, when prospects of a compromise on the issue which had thus been raised were none too favorable:

> It is the profound conviction of the Japanese Delegation that the League should, in fulfillment of its moral and political duties, allow the application of the procedure laid down in Articles 12, 13, and 15 of the Covenant in the case of all disputes which may arise between Members of the League. In paragraph 8 of Article 15 alone is it provided that such procedure shall not apply to a certain class of questions which may arise between the various states. The League of Nations should fulfill its regular duty by making all

[44] *Minutes, First Committee*, Fifth Assembly, p. 105.

such questions subject to the procedure laid down in the Covenant, whenever the peace of the world is seriously endangered, in order to facilitate a pacific settlement and a just and equitable solution of the dispute. There would be otherwise this absurd consequence, that the League of Nations will remain quite indifferent to the fact that the most flagrant acts of injustice are being committed under the purely technical and juridical cover of the alleged domestic jurisdiction of a state which is a Member of the League.

And, yet, the Committee has desired to maintain a disconcerting and absolute inactivity on the part of the League in disputes which may arise between the Members in connection with any of the problems which are vaguely covered by paragraph 8 of this Article.

Very regretfully we yield to your wishes, for the time has perhaps not yet come to insist upon this provision.[45]

The First Committee had also before it at this time a draft Article (Article 6, which became Article 10 in the final text) which set up the presumption of aggression against a state which engaging in hostilities had disregarded a unanimous report of the Council, a judicial sentence, or an arbitral award recognizing that the dispute between it and the other belligerent state arose out of a matter which by international law was solely within the domestic jurisdiction of the latter state. The Japanese Delegation had made partial concessions in their program, but they were not prepared to accept this presumptive conviction of a state which might resort to war over an issue for which no relief could be found through the peaceful procedure of the Covenant. The statement of M. Adatci continued:

[45] *Ibid.*, pp. 80-81.

But what is so illogical and unjust is that any party should incur the risk of being declared the aggressor because it takes action when flagrant injustice has given rise to disputes between the Members of the League and the latter has categorically refused, in virtue of purely technical and juridical considerations, to deal with the matter. The most elementary logic and equity should preclude such a method of procedure, for the League should not threaten to declare guilty any party which takes action, precisely when the League offers no solution, when a dispute has arisen between that party and another state which threatens to disturb international peace or the good understandings between nations.

It is in order to do away with this anomaly that the Japanese Delegation formally proposes the deletion, in number I of Article 6 of the Protocol, of the words: ". . . or has disregarded a unanimous report of the Council, a judicial sentence or an arbitral award recognizing that the dispute between it and the other belligerent state arises out of a matter which, by international law, is solely within the domestic jurisdiction of the latter state."

The adjustment reached on methods of designating the aggressor state will be noted below,[46] but it is appropriate at this point to say a word respecting the implication of this final paragraph of Article 5. It did, indeed, as M. Adatci desired, "fix and define" the duty of the Council on domestic questions, and despite the subsequent rejection of the Protocol, the discussions on the matter were an important contribution to the evolution of Article 11 of the Covenant. The amendment was a formal recognition of the right and duty

[46] See below, p. 200.

of the Council, under Article 11 of the Covenant, to exercise its conciliatory functions, though not its power of recommending solutions, on all questions threatening international peace and good understanding between nations, even though the question at issue had been the subject of a substantive verdict declaring it to lie within the exclusive jurisdiction of states. But that the amendment added nothing to the authority which the Council already possessed under the Covenant was the subject of an explicit declaration to the First Committee by the representative of Great Britain:

It is the understanding of the British Delegation, in accepting this amendment, that the text now adopted, which it is proposed to add to Article 5, safeguards the right of the Council to take such action as it may deem wise and effectual to safeguard the peace of nations in accordance with the existing provisions of Article 11 of the Covenant. We accept it because we believe that it does not confer new powers or functions on either the Council or the Assembly. Those powers are already defined in the Covenant as it exists today, and we do not add to them by this text.[47]

IV

The signatory states undertook to carry out in full good faith any judicial sentence or arbitral award which might be rendered and to comply with the solutions recommended by a unanimous decision of the Council. In the event of a state failing to comply with

[47] Statement by Sir Cecil Hurst, *Minutes, First Committee*, p. 87.

a settlement rendered through some one of the pacific methods, the Council was first to exert all its influence to secure compliance therewith, and failing therein, it was to propose what steps should be taken to give effect to the settlement in accordance with the provision contained at the end of Article 13 of the Covenant. No provision is made under this Article respecting the nature of the steps which the Council shall propose to secure compliance with an award, nor did the Protocol propose specific measures. The Report on the Protocol notes, however, that "the party in favor of which the decision has been given, might, however, employ force against the recalcitrant party if authorized to do so by the Council." But in the event of a state resisting an award by a resort to war, the Protocol specifically provided that "the sanctions provided for by Article 16 of the Covenant, interpreted in the manner indicated in the present Protocol, shall immediately become applicable to it." (Article 4.)

The Protocol provided that the Council should call upon the signatory states to apply forthwith against an aggressor state the sanctions which were provided by that instrument. (Article 10.) Before inquiring into the nature and scope of these sanctions it will be well to note the definition of the "aggressor state" embodied in the Protocol, and the means provided for determining the existence of aggression. The aggressor state is one "which resorts to war in violation of the undertakings contained in the Covenant or in the present Protocol." (Article 10.) Violation of the

The Geneva Protocol

rules laid down in the Protocol for demilitarized zones were to be held as equivalent to a resort to war. It may be observed, therefore, that in the actual definition of aggression, the Protocol made no advance over the Covenant or the Draft Treaty of Mutual Assistance. In each of these systems it is the resort to war which constitutes aggression. It was, however, a relatively easy matter, as the authors of the Protocol pointed out, to define aggression; a more complex problem was that of ascertaining the *existence* of aggression and of designating with certainty the state which was *first actually guilty of a resort to war*. The Covenant does not adequately provide for the determination of these questions, and, under Article 16, it is left to the individual Members to decide whether the Covenant has been violated and whether they shall render assistance to the state which claims to be attacked. Under the Draft Treaty of Mutual Assistance, the Council of the League was given authority to designate the aggressor state and the signatory states were to be bound by its decision. This verdict was to be rendered within four days after the opening of hostilities and could be given only by a unanimous vote of the Council. We have noted above the criticism which this arrangement evoked from the opponents of the Treaty.

But on this problem of identifying the aggressor state, the framers of the Protocol set up a system of automatic procedure which it was believed would go far toward eliminating the necessity of decision on the question by the Council. To this end they adopted a set of "presumptive tests" which were designed to identify automatically the aggressor state to the satisfaction of the Council and the signatories to the Protocol. Thus at the outbreak of hostilities, a state would be presumed to be an aggressor, unless the Council unanimously decided otherwise, if it:

1. Refused to submit the dispute to the procedure of pacific settlement provided by Articles 13 and 15 of the Covenant as amplified by the present Protocol, or to comply with a judicial sentence or arbitral award or with a unanimous recommendation of the Council, or has disregarded a unanimous report of the Council, a judicial sentence or an arbitral award recognizing that the dispute between it and the other belligerent state arises out of a matter which by international law is solely within the domestic jurisdiction of the latter state; nevertheless, in the last case the state shall only be presumed to be an aggressor if it has not previously submitted the question to the Council or the Assembly, in accordance with Article 11 of the Covenant.

2. If it has violated provisional measures enjoined by the Council for the period while the proceedings are in progress as contemplated by Article 7 of the present Protocol. (Article 10.)

The authors of the Protocol proceeded on the assumption that in view of the above provisions the facts themselves would generally establish the state guilty of aggression and that a decision by the Council on the problem would not be required; unless, indeed, by unanimous decision, the Council decided that the presumed aggressor was in reality innocent. But upon the possibility that this automatic procedure did not, to the satisfaction of the Council, identify the aggressor, the Protocol further provided that "if the Council does not at once succeed in determining the aggressor, it shall be bound to enjoin upon the belligerents an armistice, and shall fix the terms, acting, if need be, by a two-thirds majority and shall supervise its execution." (Article 10.) Any belligerent which refused to accept the armistice or violated its terms would be deemed to be the aggressor, and the Council was to call upon the signatory states to apply forthwith against such a state the sanctions provided by the Protocol. In reporting the work of the First Committee, M. Politis outlined the manner in which these various provisions were presumed to operate:

Where a presumption has arisen and is not rejected by a unanimous decision of the Council, the facts themselves decide who is an aggressor; no further decision by the Council is needed and the question of unanimity or majority does not present itself; the facts once established, the Council is bound to act accordingly.

Where there is no presumption, the Council has to declare the fact of aggression; a decision is necessary and must be taken unanimously. If unanimity is not obtained, the Council is bound to enjoin an armistice, and for this purpose no decision, properly speaking, has to be taken; there exists an obligation which the Council must fulfill; it is only the fixing of the terms of the armistice which necessitates a decision, and for this purpose a two-thirds majority suffices.

The final clause of paragraph 1, above,[48] represents the compromise effected on the second of the amendments offered by the Japanese Delegation when Arti-

[48] See above, p. 200.

cles 5 and 10 were under consideration by the First Committee. The Japanese objected to the original proposal of the Committee that the presumption of aggression should rest against a state which went to war with another over an issue which had been declared to be within the reserved domain of the latter state. These objections were met by this reference in Article 10 of the Protocol to Article 11 of the Covenant. Under this clause a state which resorted to war against another state over a question which had been declared to be within the domestic jurisdiction of the latter state was not to suffer the "presumption of aggression" if previously it had submitted the questions to the Council or to the Assembly in accordance with Article 11 of the Covenant. But a subsequent resort to war over the issue was not legitimized. It was merely the presumptive tests of aggression which fell to the ground. In the event of hostilities, it remained for the Council to determine the aggressor state, rendering, under these circumstances, its opinion by a unanimous vote. If unanimity was not obtained, the Council was then bound to enjoin an armistice, and the party rejecting or violating the terms of the armistice was to be deemed the aggressor state. The Report of M. Politis analyzes the significance of this provision in the following words:

After very careful consideration it appeared that it would be unreasonable and unjust to regard as *ipso facto* an aggressor a state which, being prevented through the operation of paragraph 8 of Article 15 from urging its claims by pacific methods and being thus left to its own resources, is in despair driven to war.

It was considered to be more in harmony with the requirements of justice and peace to give such a state which has been non-suited on the preliminary question of the domestic jurisdiction of its adversary, a last chance of arriving at an amicable agreement by offering it the final method of conciliation prescribed in Article 11 of the Covenant. It is only if, after rejecting this method, it has recourse to war that it will be presumed to be an aggressor.

This attenuation of the rigid character of paragraph 8 of Article 15 has been accepted, not only because it is just, but also because it opens no breach in the barrier set up by the Protocol against aggressive war; it in no way infringes the principle—which remains unshaken—that a war undertaken against a state whose exclusive jurisdiction has been formally recognized is an international crime to be avenged collectively by the signatories of the Protocol.

V

It has often been said of the Protocol that it made no provision for sanctions beyond those laid down in the Covenant. In principle this is true with the reservation in mind that since all classes of disputes were to be settled under the Protocol, there might have arisen new occasion for the employment of sanctions. And yet the Protocol sought to supply certain fundamental omissions which have appeared in the system of penalties set up by the Covenant and to avoid certain obvious contingencies under which the whole machinery of organized and collective punishment under the League system may fail to function. Consider, for instance, the possibilities in this connection which exist today. In the event of the outbreak of war, the Council of the League may fail to reach unanimous agreement respecting the aggressor state, or, reaching unanimity on this point, it may fail to arrive at unanimous agreement concerning a recommendation to Member states as to the material forces which should be contributed to protect the covenants of the League. But conceding that the Council functions smoothly in these circumstances, the Member states, themselves, are still competent to decide whether a breach of the Covenant has been committed; whether the opinion of the Council is justified, and whether their obligations under Article 16 of the Covenant shall become operative.

Under the Protocol the effort was made to identify automatically the party guilty of aggression either by the arbitration tests discussed above, or by the failure of a state to observe the terms of an armistice which the Council had enjoined. A state which engaged in hostilities without observing the arbitral procedure of the Protocol was presumed to be an aggressor unless by unanimous decision these presumptions were rejected by the Council. In the absence of these presumptions, or, if they were rejected by the Council, that body was then to designate the state guilty of aggression. If unable to do so by unanimous decision, the Council was required under the terms of the Protocol to declare an armistice; this was an imperative duty which the Council must fulfill, and the state which failed to obey the terms thereof was to be regarded as an aggressor state. Thus it was sought to make good the omissions of the Covenant and to eliminate the possibility of non-cooperation on the part of Member states on the plea that an act of aggression had not occurred.

Given the existence of aggression, the signatories of the Protocol agreed to cooperate *loyally and effectively* in the application of the sanctions of all kinds mentioned in paragraphs 1 and 2 of Article 16 of the Covenant. This criterion, it may be said, was merely an attempt to give precision to the nature and extent of the obligations which exist already under the Covenant. But the Protocol introduced a formula which was to provide a "certain elasticity" in carrying out the obligations to apply sanctions. A Member was to render aid "in the degree which its geographical position and its particular situation as regards armaments allows." (Article 11.) Obligated by the standards of loyal and effective cooperation, each Member remained, nevertheless, the judge of the manner and degree to which it would participate in the application of sanctions. The gist of Article 11, paragraphs 1 and 2, said the authors of the Protocol, might be expressed as follows:

> Each state is the judge of the manner in which it shall carry out its obligations but not of the existence of those obligations—that is to say, each state remains the judge of what it will do, but no longer remains the judge of what it should do.

CHAPTER VI

THE LOCARNO AGREEMENTS

I

By the end of December, 1924, seventeen states had followed the recommendation of the Fifth Assembly and signed the Protocol for the Pacific Settlement of International Disputes. Among these were France, Belgium, Czechoslovakia, Jugoslavia, and Poland. Two of the Baltic Republics, namely, Latvia and Esthonia, had signed; Finland and Spain presented their signatures in December; the Latin American Republics were represented by the adhesion of Brazil, Chile, Paraguay, and Uruguay.[1] By a number of states of continental Europe, whose prime concern since the close of the World War had been the problem of national security, the Protocol was apparently regarded as a substantial guarantee of protection and peace. The question was now one of going forward with the third element in that formula—arbitration, security, and disarmament—which of late had been so frequently voiced at Geneva.

In the meanwhile there had been a change of Government in England. The November elections had returned an impressive Conservative majority to the House of Commons, and the Second Ministry of Mr. Baldwin was now subjecting to a searching examina-

[1] *Monthly Summary of the League of Nations*, December, 1924.

tion the work which Mr. MacDonald and his colleagues had done so much to inspire at the Fifth Assembly. At the December meeting of the Council of the League in Rome, the representative of the British Government requested a postponement of discussions relating to the work which the Council was presumed to take in furtherance of the scheme set up by the Protocol. The Conservative Ministry, it was explained, had been so recently returned to power that additional time was necessary before a policy could be announced concerning that intricate and important document. When the Council convened at Geneva in March, 1925, the British Government presented its views on the question. His Majesty's present advisers, the Rt. Hon. Austen Chamberlain reported, after discussing the subject with the self-governing Dominions and India, saw insuperable obstacles to signing and ratifying the Protocol in its present shape. They were in sympathy with the purpose which the Protocol was intended to serve; they were not opposed in principle to schemes "for clarifying the meaning of the Covenant or strengthening its provisions." But the Protocol as it stood was not the most suitable means of achieving that end.

A brief reference[2] has been made already to the considerations set forth by the British Government in rejecting the momentous labors of the Fifth Assembly. A further recapitulation here of these objections will contribute to an understanding of the British point of view. The chief points raised by Mr. Chamberlain may be summarized as follows:

[2] See above, p. 38.

1. The framers of the Covenant, in elaborating their peace-preserving machinery, had rejected the simple idea of compulsory arbitration of all international difference, "presumably because they felt, as so many states Members of the League have felt since, that the objections to universal and compulsory arbitration might easily outweigh its theoretical advantages." The objections of His Majesty's Government to compulsory arbitration were increased rather than diminished, "owing to the weakening of those reservations in clause 15 of the Covenant, which were designed to prevent any interference by the League in matters of domestic jurisdiction."

2. Under the Protocol, "fresh classes of disputes are to be decided by the League; fresh possibilities of defying its provisions are thereby created; fresh occasions for the application of coercive measures follow as a matter of course." Was it not unwise to add to the liabilities already incurred under the Covenant for the application of sanctions, "without taking stock of the degree to which the machinery of the Covenant has been already weakened by the non-membership of certain great states. There were powerful economic communities, notably the United States, outside the limits of the League. The economic weapon, therefore, "might force trade into unaccustomed channels, but it could hardly stop it; and, though the offending state would no doubt suffer, there is no presumption that it would be crushed or even that it would suffer most."

3. Articles 7 and 8 of the Protocol prohibited the parties to a dispute from making any warlike preparations between the moment when the dispute arises and the moment when proceedings for a pacific settlement have been concluded. However laudable the intentions of these provisions may have been, "they may embarrass the victim of aggression even more than the aggressor." The provisions were particularly objectionable when applied to the case of forces at sea. "The whole value of a fleet depends upon its mobility. . . .

To suggest that, directly a dispute arises which in any way concerns a maritime power, its ships are to remain immovably fixed on the stations where the chance conveniences of peace may happen to have placed them, is asking the threatened state to make a surrender of its inalienable right of self-defence, to which it is never likely to submit."

4. Article 15 of the Protocol contains two provisions. By the first, the aggressor state is required to pay all the costs of the war for which it is responsible, and full reparation for all damages, public or private, which the war has caused. By the second, it is protected from any alteration of its frontiers, and all interference with its internal affairs. His Majesty's Government was in general sympathy with these two provisions, but "they cannot think it wise to embody these generalities in dogmas of inflexible rigidity, designed to control the action of the League in all circumstances and for all time. In the sternest codes of law, mitigating circumstances are allowed to modify the judgments of the courts; and His Majesty's Government fail to see why the League of Nations should deliberately deprive itself of a discretion which all other tribunals are free to exercise."

5. The Protocol purports to be little more than a completion of the work begun but not perfected by the authors of the Covenant. But surely this is a very inadequate description of its effects. The additions which it makes to the original document do something quite different from merely clarifying obscurities and filling in omissions. They destroy its balance and alter its spirit. The fresh emphasis laid upon sanctions, the new occasions discovered for their employment, the elaboration of military procedure, insensibly suggest the idea that the vital business of the League is not so much to promote friendly cooperation and reasoned harmony in the management of international affairs as to preserve peace by organizing war, and (it may be) war on the largest scale.

What expedient remains? the British memorandum queried after having amassed this formidable array of criticisms. Could not the feeling of security be attained through some alternative more desirable and effective than the Protocol? "The brooding fears that keep huge armaments in being," said Mr. Chamberlain, "have little relation to the ordinary misunderstandings inseparable from international (as from social) life." They were the product of exceptional fear and distrust on the part of certain nations—"they spring from deep-lying causes of hostility which, for historic or other reasons, divide great and powerful states." Would it not be wiser to deal with these extreme cases as entities in themselves and through a series of special remedies seek to accommodate special needs? He concluded his statement with the following constructive proposal:

Since the general provisions of the Covenant cannot be stiffened with advantage, and since the "extreme cases" with which the League may have to deal will probably affect certain nations or groups of nations more nearly than others, His Majesty's Government concludes that the best way of dealing with the situation is, with the cooperation of the League, to supplement the Covenant by making special arrangements in order to meet special needs. That these arrangements should be purely defensive in character, that they should be framed in the spirit of the Covenant, working in close harmony with the League and under its guidance, is manifest. And, in the opinion of His Majesty's Government, these objects can best be attained by knitting together the nations most immediately concerned, and whose differences might lead to a renewal of strife, by means of treaties framed with the sole object of maintaining, as between themselves, an unbroken peace. Within its limits no quicker remedy for our present ills can easily be found or any surer safeguard against future calamities.[3]

At the conclusion of Mr. Chamberlain's statement, the French representative on the Council, M. Briand, told the Council that his Government remained definitely attached to the Protocol, but that it would not refuse "to enter into any discussions for improving it."[4] But the discussions in which the French Government soon found itself engaged were destined to conclude not in a revision of the Protocol, but in the series of agreements initialed at Locarno on October 16, 1925.

II

As a matter of fact, the British advocacy of the principle of regional pacts of security had, in the meanwhile, been expressed in another quarter. On February 9, 1925, the German Ambassador at Paris communicated to M. Herriot, President of the French Council and Minister for Foreign Affairs, a memorandum from which the following extract is taken:

In considering the various forms which a pact of security might at present take, one could proceed with an idea cognate to that from which the proposal made in December, 1922, by Dr. Cuno sprang. Germany could, for example, declare her acceptance of a pact by virtue of which the Powers interested in the Rhine,

[3] *Official Journal*, April, 1925, pp. 446-450.
[4] *Ibid.*, p. 453.

above all, England, France, Italy, and Germany, entered into a solemn obligation for a lengthy period (to be eventually defined more specifically) *vis-a-vis* the Government of the United States of America as trustee not to wage war against a contracting state. A comprehensive arbitration treaty, such as has been concluded in recent years between different European countries, could be amalgamated with such a pact. Germany is also prepared to conclude analogous arbitration treaties providing for the peaceful settlement of juridical and political conflicts between all other states as well.

The memorandum went on to propose a series of additional agreements which might contribute to a system of security for the region under review. A pact expressly guaranteeing the present territorial status of the Rhineland would be acceptable to Germany. The interested states might bind themselves reciprocally to observe the inviolability of the existing territorial status on the Rhine and jointly and individually guarantee the observance of this obligation. In the same sense, the signatory powers could guarantee in this pact the fulfillment of the obligation to demilitarize the Rhineland which Germany had undertaken in Articles 42 and 43 of the Treaty of Versailles. Into the system there might also be interwoven the comprehensive arbitration treaties which Germany was ready to conclude with other states similarly disposed. Perhaps the ideas underlying this proposal might have application in other regions. The possible evolution of the scheme was suggested in the following terms:

It would be well worth considering whether it would not be advisable to so draft the security pact that it would prepare the way for a world convention to include all states along the lines of the "Protocole pour le Règlement pacifique de Différends internationaux" drawn up by the League of Nations, and that, in case such a world convention was achieved, it could be absorbed by it or worked into it.[5]

The above memorandum was acknowledged by M. Herriot on February 20, with the assurance that it would be carefully examined, but that a detailed reply must be deferred until France had consulted with her Allies respecting the establishment of a system of security within the framework of the Treaty of Versailles. The negotiations which then followed between France and her Western Allies reached a final and satisfactory phase in the early summer of 1925. On May 28, the British Government returned to Paris a final revision of a French text of a reply to Germany with the statement that the text thus submitted was believed to be the expression of a policy common to both countries.

The degree of British participation in the projected system was the subject of explicit elucidation in this note of May 28th to the French Government. With reference, for example, to the proposed system of arbitration treaties, the British note observed:

They [the British Government] therefore welcome any treaties of arbitration or conciliation which the continental powers concerned may be prepared to enter into, provided only that such treaties do not affect the

[5] "Papers respecting the Proposals for a Pact of Security made by the German Government on February 9, 1925." *Great Britain Parl. Papers*, Miss. No. 7 (1925) Cmd. 2435, p. 4.

rights and obligations attaching to membership of the League of Nations under the Covenant. But the position of His Majesty's Government is somewhat different from that of those powers. In view of the position of the British Empire, with its world-wide responsibilities, His Majesty's Government are bound to regard the question of participation in treaties of this description from a different point of view to that of powers whose interests lie mainly or exclusively in Europe. And as regards the proposals for the maintenance of peace which are now under discussion, His Majesty's Government feels that, while for the continental powers concerned the conclusion of the suggested arbitration treaties forms, as is stated in the French draft reply, the natural complement of a Rhineland pact, that is not equally the case with Great Britain.[6]

And the suggestion of a British guarantee of the entire system of arbitration conventions elicited the following statement:

"Though His Majesty's Government are not prepared to go so far as the French Government suggest, yet they are prepared in principle (and, of course, subject to a careful examination of the actual terms ultimately proposed) to give a guaranty, flowing logically from the territorial guarantee of the Rhineland, of arbitration treaties which may be concluded between Germany and her Western neighbors, signatories of the pact. The type of guarantee which they have in mind would operate in the event of a failure on the part of one of the parties to refer a dispute to arbitration (using the term in its widest sense to cover both judicial awards and conciliation tribunals) or to carry out an award, if such failure were coupled with a resort to hostilities. The guaranty would be, so to speak, defensive; it would not entail upon His

[6] *Ibid.*, p. 20.

Majesty's Government—as they conceive it—any obligation to resort to force elsewhere than in the areas covered by the proposed Rhineland pact; and would not operate in any event in favor of the party which had refused arbitration or had refused to give effect to an arbitral award.[7]

With certain minor changes, the British version of the proposed reply was accepted by the French, and on June 16 was forwarded to Berlin.

The chief elements of expansion of the original German proposal upon which the French insisted in this note of June 16 were five in number: (1) No agreement could be achieved unless Germany on her side assumes the obligations and enjoys the rights laid down in the Covenant of the League of Nations; (2) Belgium should be included as a state directly interested in the proposed Rhineland pact; (3) the search for guarantees could not involve any modifications of the existing treaties of peace, and the Allies could not surrender the right to oppose any failure to observe the stipulations of these treaties, even if the stipulations in question do not directly concern them; (4) Germany should conclude, as had been suggested, comprehensive arbitration pacts with her neighbors who, without being parties to the suggested Rhineland pact, were signatories to the Treaty of Versailles; and (5) the proposed arbitration pacts between Germany and Belgium and Germany and France, guaranteeing a peaceful settlement of juridical and political conflicts, should have the joint and several guarantee of the powers

[7] *Ibid.*, p. 20.

participating in the Rhineland pact, "so as to bring this guarantee into immediate operation, if one of the parties, refusing to submit a dispute to arbitration or to carry out an arbitral award, resorts to hostile measures. Where one of the contracting parties, without resorting to hostile measures, fails to observe its undertakings, the Council of the League of Nations shall propose what steps should be taken to give effect to the treaty."[8]

The German reply of July 20 agreed in principle to certain of these proposals, but in respect to others it requested further elucidation. The German Government was especially concerned with the French reservations respecting the enforcement of the provisions of the Treaty of Versailles and with the circumstances under which the guarantee of the proposed arbitration treaties would become operative:

What chiefly attracts attention are the cases of exception provided for by the Allied Governments in which coercive action by one state against another state is to be permitted. In this respect, the German Government, judging by the terms of the note of the 16th of June and the correspondence published between the French and His Britannic Majesty's Government, cannot but assume that in those cases, in the opinion of the Allied Governments, coercive action can take place without any regular procedure laid down in advance, either by arbitral or some other international procedure.

Under this arrangement, the German memorandum proceeded to point out, the question of admissibility

[8] *Ibid.*, p. 50.

or inadmissibility of reprisals on reparation accounts would be left to the unilateral decisions of the Allied Governments. Similarly, the Allied Governments would be free to take military measures against Germany whenever in their sole judgments Germany had infringed the provisions regarding the demilitarization of the Rhineland. And equally serious would be the consequences flowing from the form of guarantee of the arbitration treaties which the French proposed:

Although the intervention of the guarantor would be dependent upon definite conditions, he would nevertheless be entitled to decide on his own free judgment whether, in the case under consideration, these conditions, in fact, exist. This would mean that should a conflict arise, it would be for the guarantor to decide which of the two contracting parties to the treaty of arbitration is to be considered the aggressor, and he would have the right to decide, even if he was bound to one of the contracting parties by a special alliance.

It is quite clear that the system of guarantees would, by such constructions, be invalidated to the sole detriment of Germany. . . . According to the Covenant, the question whether a disturbance of peace exists has to be decided by a carefully regulated procedure, and the application of coercive measures is subject to conditions which have to be conclusively established, all these decisions, according to the system outlined in the French note, would be put into the hands of one of the contracting parties. Such a system would not maintain peace and might even give rise to the danger of serious complications.[9]

The French rejoinder to this communication was

[9] *Great Britain Parl. Papers*, Miss. No. 7 (1925) Cmd. 2468, pp. 7-8.

made on August 24th. It reiterated the principle that the Treaty of Versailles and the rights acquired by the Allied Governments thereunder must not be impaired; "nor can the guarantee of its execution and the provisions which govern the application of these guarantees (and in certain cases contemplate their alleviation) be modified by proposed agreements any more than the treaty itself can be modified." But an effort was made to relieve the apprehensions of the German Government on the subject of the operations of the guarantee of the proposed arbitration agreements:

"It would not seem impossible to establish provisions adapting the operation of the guarantee (whoever be the guarantor and whether the guaranty applies to frontiers or to arbitration) to the nature of the violation and to the circumstances and degree of urgency which might necessitate the immediate execution of this guaranty. In this connection an examination might be made whether some means could be found of safeguarding the impartiality of the decisions come to, without diminishing the immediate and efficacious operation of the guarantee itself."

At the conclusion of this dispatch, the French Government observed that further progress on essentially delicate questions could scarcely be made by a further interchange of notes and invited the German Government to enter into more definite negotiations which might result in the conclusion of a definite treaty. The prompt acceptance of this proposal by Germany led to a conference of legal experts of Germany, France, Belgium, and Great Britain in London from September 1 to 4, and agreement on tentative drafts prepared on this occasion resulted in the final conference at Locarno.

III

What are the essential elements in this regional system of national security inaugurated by the Locarno treaties? In the Rhineland region two basic principles have been applied—a guarantee of territorial integrity and a guaranteed process of arbitration—the same two methods through which the framers of the Covenant six years previously approached the problem of state security. The Treaty of Mutual Guarantee between Germany, Belgium, France, Great Britain, and Italy represents a "stiffening" of these original principles of the Covenant to meet the requirements of a certain region. The principle of territorial guarantee is embodied in Article 1 of that Treaty, in which the High Contracting Parties collectively and severally guarantee the maintenance of the territorial status quo resulting from the frontiers between Germany and Belgium and Germany and France, and the inviolability of the said frontiers as fixed by or in pursuance of the Treaty of Versailles.[10] This affirmative guarantee is supplemented by a self-denying covenant on the part of Germany and Belgium and Germany and France, expressed in Article 2, through which these powers

[10] This Article also provides a joint and several guarantee of the observance of the stipulations of Arts. 42 and 43 of the treaty of Versailles concerning the demilitarized zone.

mutually undertake that they will in no case attack or invade each other or resort to war against each other.[11]

The means of fulfillment of the guarantee of territorial integrity noted above is outlined in Article 4 of the Guaranty Treaty. This Article endeavors to meet two requirements, relating to the use of material sanctions, which have been repeatedly advanced in League discussions on the problem of security. The one is that mutual assistance in order to be effective must be immediately available; and the other is that coercive action by one state against another should be controlled through some sort of international procedure. Under Article 4, the state which alleges that a violation of territorial integrity has been committed, *i. e.*, a violation of Article 2, shall at once bring the question before the Council of the League of Nations. The international procedure, therefore, is instituted in the first

---

[11] This stipulation does not, however, apply in the following cases:

1. The exercise of the right of legitimate defense, that is to say, resistance to the violation of the undertaking contained in the previous paragraph or to a flagrant breach of Arts. 42 or 43 of the said treaty of Versailles, if such breach constitutes an unprovoked act of aggression and by reason of armed forces in the demilitarized zone immediate action is necessary.

2. Action in pursuance of Art. 15 of the Covenant of the League.

3. Action as a result of a decision taken by the Assembly or by the Council of the League of Nations or in pursuance of Art. 15, parg. 7, of the Covenant of the League of Nations, provided that in this last event the action is directed against a state which was the first to attack.

stage of the dispute. The Council proceeds with its inquiry, and when satisfied that a violation or breach has been committed, it will notify its findings without delay to the signatories of the Treaty, who have agreed that in such case they will each come immediately to the assistance of the power against whom the violation has been committed. But mutual assistance may have been already set in motion. In the case of a *flagrant violation* of the provisions of Article 2, each of the Contracting Parties have agreed to come immediately to the assistance of the party which has been attacked as soon as it is able to satisfy itself that the violation in question constitutes an unprovoked act of aggression. Evidences of such aggression are the crossing of the frontier; the outbreak of hostilities; or the assembly of armed forces in the demilitarized zone. This unilateral application of sanctions is, however, subject to revision and control through the procedure of the League Council. As soon as the Council has issued its findings, the Contracting Parties undertake to act in accordance with the recommendations of the Council, provided that they are concurred in by all the members other than the representatives of the parties engaged in hostilities.

As the natural complement to this Rhineland pact, the Treaty of Mutual Guarantee outlines the general stipulations for a guaranteed process of arbitration. Germany and Belgium and Germany and France agree to settle by peaceful means all questions of every kind which may arise between them which it may not be possible to settle by the normal methods of diplomacy (Article 3). This agreement is guaranteed by the Contracting Parties in the following manner: If one of the parties refuses to submit a dispute to peaceful settlement or to comply with an arbitral award or a judicial decision, and resorts to war, *i. e.*, violates the provisions of Article 2, the sanctions provided in Article 4 become effective, subject to the procedure laid down in that Article. Where without committing a breach of Article 2 of the Treaty, one party refuses to utilize the accepted measures for pacific settlement, the other party to the dispute shall refer the question to the Council of the League, and the Council shall propose what steps shall be taken; the Contracting Parties agreeing to comply with these proposals. (Article 5.)

IV

The Guaranty Treaty expresses only in general terms the agreement between Germany on the one hand and Belgium and France on the other for the peaceful settlement of all disputes. Detailed arrangements for effecting these peaceful settlements are contained in the special arbitration conventions concluded between these respective Powers. The peace-preserving machinery set up in these two conventions need be only briefly alluded to. The two conventions are identical in form and establish procedure for the settlement of both justiciable and non-justiciable questions. Justiciable disputes are referred to as disputes between the parties "as to their respective rights," including, in particular, those mentioned in Article 13 of the Covenant of the League of Nations.[12] These are to be submitted for decision either to an arbitral tribunal or to the Permanent Court of International Justice. (Article 1.) But before a resort is made either to the arbitral tribunal or to the Court, the dispute may, by agreement between the parties, be referred to a Permanent Conciliation Commission. The organization, procedure, and function of this Commission is the subject of detailed arrangements in the conventions. The primary tasks of the Commission are to elucidate the question in dispute; to endeavor to bring the parties to an agreement; and it may inform the parties of the terms of a settlement which it deems suitable. (Article 8.) If the Conciliation Commission is unable to propose a settlement acceptable to the parties, the dispute shall then be submitted, by special agreement between the parties, either to the Permanent Court or to an arbitral tribunal under the conditions and procedure laid down by the Hague Convention of October 18, 1907. (Article 16.) If the parties are unable to agree upon the terms of this special agreement, one or the other may bring the dispute before the Permanent Court by means of an application. (Article 16.)

[12] The second paragraph of Article 13 reads as follows:

"Disputes as to the interpretation of a treaty, as to any question of international law, as to the existence of any fact which, if established, would constitute a breach of any international obligation, or as to the extent and nature of the reparation to be made for any such breach, are declared to be among those which are generally suitable for submission to arbitration or judicial settlement."

All questions between the parties to these conventions, for which settlement cannot be attained by the foregoing procedure, or through other conventions in force between them, are to be submitted to the Permanent Conciliation Commission. In the case of these non-justiciable questions, it is the duty of the Commission to propose an acceptable solution and in any case to present a report. (Article 17.) If the parties do not accept this proposed solution within a month after the termination of the labors of the Commission, the question shall, at the request of either party, be brought before the Council of the League of Nations, which shall deal with it in accordance with Article 15 of the Covenant of the League. (Article 18.)

V

It was the purpose of the Locarno agreements not only to establish a system of national security in Western Europe, but to promote this feeling between Germany and her Eastern neighbors as well. But the methods applied in this latter area are less comprehensive in scope than are those employed in the Rhineland region. The element of an affirmative guarantee of the existing territorial status quo is lacking, and the principle of guaranteed arbitration is less adequately developed. Germany and Poland and Germany and Czechoslovakia are parties to arbitration conventions identical with the Rhineland arbitration pacts, and containing, in addition, the following proviso:

The present treaty, which is in conformity with the Covenant of the League of Nations, shall not in any way affect the rights and obligations of the High Contracting Parties as Members of the League of Nations and shall not be interpreted as restricting the duty of the League to take whatever action may be deemed wise and effectual to safeguard the peace of the world.

In one sense, the above provision may be regarded as affirming the principle that the arbitral conventions introduce no restriction on the parties thereto to take coercive action against one another in fulfillment of the obligations contained in Articles 10 and 16 of the Covenant. In fact, such coercive action on the part of Poland and of Czechoslovakia against Germany, on behalf of France, is the subject of specific arrangement through the special alliances which these respective Powers concluded at Locarno with France. Furthermore, it appears that under this provision the arbitration conventions do not limit the right of Germany as a Member of the League of Nations to raise under Articles 11 and 18 of the Covenant the question of a revision of her Eastern frontiers.

The element of guarantee which Poland and Czechoslovakia acquire for their arbitration agreements with Germany is likewise derived from these special alliances which they have contracted with France. Each of these alliances carries, as Article 1, a provision for reciprocal mutual assistance in the event that the non-observance of the arbitration pacts is accompanied by an unprovoked recourse to arms. The Article in question, from the Franco-Polish alliance, is quoted below:

In the event of Poland or France suffering from a failure to observe the undertakings arrived at this day between them and Germany with a view to the maintenance of the general peace, France and reciprocally Poland, acting in application of Article 16 of the Covenant of the League of Nations, undertake to lend each other immediately aid and assistance, if such a failure is accompanied by an unprovoked recourse to arms.

In the event of the Council of the League of Nations, when dealing with a question brought before it in accordance with the said undertakings, being unable to succeed in making its report accepted by all its members other than the representatives of the parties to the dispute, and in the event of Poland or France being attacked without provocation, France or reciprocally Poland, acting in application of Article 15, paragraph 7, of the Covenant of the League of Nations, will immediately lend aid and assistance.

Such are the main principles of the Locarno system which represents the final product of a prolonged and assiduous effort to create within the framework of the Covenant a system of supplementary guarantees of national safety. The real antecedents of these treaties lie in the Covenant, the Draft Treaty of Mutual Assistance, and the Geneva Protocol. In the area over which they operate these agreements combine the various elements which at one time or another had been advocated at Geneva as fundamental to an adequate program of security. Territorial guarantee, demilitarized zones, provisions for mutual assistance, immediately available, and guaranteed processes of arbitration—all of these devices have evolved from security proposals which have been put forward during the past six years, and all are utilized in the Locarno system.

CHAPTER VII

Conclusion

I

It seems appropriate to offer some general comments as a conclusion to this study. It was stated at the outset that an effort would be made to review certain aspects of the movement within recent years for a more effective juridical order in the society of states and to indicate the attitude of the members of this society toward some of the new legal relations established by the Covenant of the League of Nations.

The framers of the Covenant, in response to widespread demands and aspirations, sought to strengthen the international legal order by embodying in the Covenant certain definite juridical principles. Among these principles was the declaration of Article 10: the members of the League undertook to respect and preserve as against external aggression the territorial integrity and political independence of one another. They accepted, furthermore, restraints on a traditionally asserted right to wage war at their own discretion, and they agreed to observe certain processes for the peaceful settlement of their disputes before an eventual resort to war. They assumed obligations to apply conjointly measures of redress to a state which went to war in violation of the provisions of the Covenant.

To what extent are these foregoing principles supported by opinion in the society of nations and what is the probability of their acceptance as the actual rules of conduct of the Governments concerned?

It would be premature to offer definite conclusions along these various lines. Students of the law of nations find it no easy task to specify rules upon which there is definite and universal assent; even more difficult is it to say that along certain lines there exists a profound and unmistakable international opinion. Likewise with respect to the principles incorporated in the Covenant of the League, it is difficult to appraise their actual strength in the international community today and to say in what measure they have been accepted by those who direct and condition the international policies of states. In the preceding pages extensive use has been made of the declarations of Governments and of their representatives on the issue raised at Geneva, but it can hardly be assumed that the viewpoints expressed have unerringly interpreted the sentiment of the various nations. Account must assuredly be taken of the fact that from time to time Governments of diverse political objectives and beliefs bespeak the policy of a given nation in world affairs. Moreover, the League of Nations is still young and the understanding and acceptance of its institutions will be no easy nor rapid process.

And yet in these first few years of the existence of the League certain important developments have come about. In many instances fairly well-defined positions

CONCLUSION

have been taken by states or groups of states on the principle of collective guarantees of territorial integrity and political independence; on schemes for the organization and application of sanctions; on proposals for expanding the peace-preserving machinery of the Covenant. The more adequately the positions of states on these questions are revealed the more trustworthy will be our appraisal of opinion in the community of nations and the more clearly will the existing problems of international organization be set forth.

The events at Geneva which we have undertaken here to survey fall logically into two main categories. The first are those which centered around Articles 10 and 16 of the Covenant, effecting an elucidation of the meaning of these provisions and attempting a prolongation of the principles which they express. The second comprise the efforts made to expand those features of the Covenant which relate to the peaceful settlement of international disputes. In the one case, chief emphasis was placed on the concept of mutual assistance between states, implying the use of material sanctions to guarantee the observance of international agreements; in the other, effort was concentrated on the development of peaceful procedure and on advancing the reign of law in the community of nations. From all of this endeavor certain results have issued; they help to clarify the present status of international organization; they point to difficulties encountered, and they are provocative of thought as to the proper lines of future advance.

II

Let us turn first to this idea of mutual assistance and the use of penalties which it implies. What of its progress, and what are the existing limitations to its furtherance? It has doubtless already become apparent that in the construction of the obligations under Articles 10 and 16 there was a significant assertion of the autonomy and independence of the Members of the League. It is true that it was argued on behalf of certain states that the Council of the League possessed the juridical authority to determine when the obligations under these Articles should become operative and that the recommendations of the Council for their fulfillment should possess of their own account a legal quality. But the prevailing and dominant sentiment was otherwise; it was emphasized that the Covenant had not set up a super-state nor had it created an organ with the legal competence to determine the scope of the obligations of the Members for enforcing the provisions of the Covenant. Each state was to remain the judge of the circumstances calling for its action and of the degree to which it would employ its material resources in the fulfillment of its obligations.

The whole proceedings at Geneva on Articles 10 and 16, and the efforts to expand the principles of these provisions in the Draft Treaty of Mutual Assistance, give rise to considerable reflection on this matter of material guarantees to assure the observance of international agreements. One or two general observations on the subject may possibly be in point. Through the

Conclusion

Covenant of the League there was transferred from the national to the international sphere the concept of penalties for the violation of accepted legal rules, but in the nature of the case it was merely a principle that was carried over—not its detailed application. The efforts of the League of Nations, however, to formulate a plan for the use of its coercive weapon have demonstrated that in the present stage of international organization the proposed use of penalties raises problems of extreme complexity. It is apparent, of course, that the application of sanctions in the international sphere involves their usage in a field in many respects dissimilar from the one in which they have evolved. For example, in the municipal sphere penalties deal directly with the individual, but in the international sphere they are applicable to states and to states moreover which may be capable of offering very effective resistance. Within the state sanctions of law are administered through especially constituted agents of the community, and ordinarily only these are involved, while in the society of nations the application of sanctions, at least as postulated in the Covenant, would presumably involve the entire body of states. It need hardly be pointed out that coercive action by one state against another presents a wholly different problem from that of the exercise of public authority over the individual; it represents, indeed, the clash of highly organized and powerful forces with consequences which are far-reaching and unpredictable. Such factors as these may mean that while the principle of sanctions for international agreements may be regarded as desirable or essential even, there may be inherent limitations to their effective exercise in a society composed of states, and their development may have to proceed along lines other than those at present contemplated.

It is worth while to recall at this point the formula for mutual assistance which has been put forward by those states which by reason of their exposed positions have most energetically supported the principle of mutual guarantees. Mutual assistance, it has constantly been affirmed, must be the subject of definite and explicit understanding; arrangements for its application must be worked out in accordance with a prearranged plan; it must become immediately and automatically operative. The logic of these requirements of the state which sees in material force the only dependable safeguard of its security is incontestable. On the other hand, given the existing limits to the feeling of solidarity among nations, the present application of a formula of this precision over an extensive area appears unlikely. The closest approximation to it has been made through the Locarno treaties, and it is noteworthy that these agreements are confined to a region of the manifestly common interest of the states concerned and that they carry the principle of universal compulsory arbitration. The relation between this latter principle—compulsory pacific settlement—and the development of adequate guarantees is believed to be a vital one to which some further reference will be made.

In the meanwhile it will be well to have before us a recapitulation of some of the more outstanding difficulties encountered by the League in its exploration of this matter of material guarantees. In the first place, there was a manifest unwillingness on the part of many Members of the League to assume, for the use of sanctions, obligations in addition to those already embodied in the Covenant. Indeed, in the light of national viewpoints expressed at Geneva, it may be concluded that states are generally unwilling to give explicit promises for mutual assistance in regions where their own apparent interests are not involved.

The question, moreover, of the proper occasion for the exercise of guarantees raised difficult problems. There was positive opposition in certain quarters to entrusting the decision on this question to an organ of the League; hence the elaborate provisions in the Protocol for an automatic test to identify the aggressor state. But if League Members were unwilling to accept the verdict of the Council on the question of aggression, they were equally reluctant to see developed under the auspices of the League schemes of coercion which could become operative upon the unilateral decision of a given state. Objection to this possibility was forcefully advanced when the system of partial treaties associated with the Draft Treaty and with the Protocol were under discussion. It should not be overlooked, however, that on both of these problems, *i. e.*, the test for aggression and League supervision of partial treaties, substantial advance was made in the Protocol, which progress was later utilized in the Locarno agreements, and the problem of ascertaining the state guilty of violating its engagements does not appear to be one of insurmountable difficulty.

Two other important limitations were encountered by the League in this examination of the principle of mutual guarantee. It became apparent that states of secondary rank from the standpoint of material power were unwilling to expose themselves to the danger of coercive action against a powerful neighboring state. Their case was ably stated by the Scandinavian delegations, with the result that their obligations under Article 16 may be in effect suspended by the Council. And, finally, a factor of far-reaching consequence was the non-membership in the League of certain powerful nations whose absence meant, not only the loss of their positive cooperation with the League, but also a possible assertion of their interests in such fashion as would frustrate an effective application of the League's program of coercive measures.

III

Such in broad outline are some of the problems which have evolved in this brief experience of the League with the principle of mutual assistance and material guarantees. The concrete political objective of the League's endeavors was disarmament, but it was said that disarmament could not proceed without adequate guarantees of national safety, and one avenue toward security which the Covenant had outlined was this principle of collective guarantees. Its obvious limitations, however, in the present stage of international feeling, turned attention to other features of the Covenant, and arbitration as an essential element in a security program came to the fore. As a matter of fact, throughout all this effort at Geneva to elaborate plans for mutual assistance, the representatives of certain states protested against what was termed "a one-sided development of the Covenant." If states were to receive the benefits of guarantees, they should give in return, it was asserted, the assurance of a "reasonable international policy." As M. Lange said on one occasion, "states should be required to respect the idea of law," and he advocated as a price of the guarantee provided in the Draft Treaty of Mutual Assistance that the beneficiaries should have accepted the compulsory jurisdiction of the Permanent Court of International Justice.

The implications of such demands as these are far-reaching. They suggest that the growth of the principle of mutual protection among a given group of states is closely related to the development of a corresponding collective supervision of their external relations. What, it may be asked, are to be the minimum requirements of this supervision? Possibly the first primary requisite will be that states shall renounce the right to administer force on their sole initiative except for the purposes of self-defence, and that they shall unreservedly accept pacific procedure for the adjustment of their conflicting rights and interests. A reference is here in point to the principle advanced through Article 10. It has been said that President Wilson drew his inspiration for this Article "straight from the fundamental American documents,"[1] notably the provision in the Constitution of the United States that "the United States shall guarantee to every state in this Union a republican form of government and shall protect each of them against invasion." But in its new context, *i. e.*, the Covenant of the League, this principle of guaranty lacks the association of other principles which are possibly the natural and necessary complements to it. Of particular significance in this regard is the provision that controversies between the States of the American Union shall be subject to the jurisdiction of the United States Supreme Court. Here is obligatory peaceful settlement without those distinctions as to classes of cases, or reservations as to subject matter, which have thus far proved to be the limiting factors in the development of pacific procedure in international relations. And the American Constitution, it may be noted, sets up the following further supervision of the external policies of the Member States. "No state shall, without the consent of Congress . . . keep troops or ships of war in time of peace, enter into any agreement or compact with another state or with a foreign power, or engage in war, unless actually invaded or in such imminent danger as will not admit of delay."[2]

[1] R. S. Baker, *Woodrow Wilson and World Settlement*, I, p. 221.
[2] Article I, Section 10.

It does not follow that all of the above standards of supervision of the external relations of states are essential or that they are applicable in a present-day scheme of international organization. But if analogies are to be drawn at all from the American constitutional system, they would support the contention that between the principle of guarantee of the security of states and a substantial legal control of their international policies there is a close and inevitable connection.

In effect this was the thesis which eventually evolved at Geneva. There could be no disarmament without security, no security without guarantees, no willing guarantees without a respect for the idea of law. "The support demanded from different states by other states less favorably situated had placed the former under the obligations of asking for a sort of moral and legal guarantee that the states which have to be supported would act in perfect good faith and would always endeavor to settle their disputes by pacific means."[3]

It is submitted that the underlying principle of the Geneva Protocol—the universal acceptance of pacific methods for the settlement of all disputes which may arise between states—is the condition *sine qua non* for a genuine society of nations. The Protocol was doubtless defective in some of its provisions; that it went well in advance of the present state of international opinion cannot be denied; but it gave concrete expression to an ideal, and the translation of this ideal into

[3] *General Report on the Protocol*, First and Third Committees, Fifth Assembly.

reality is the chief task of the new era which the League of Nations is presumed to have ushered in. It is well to emphasize this point, to understand its implications and to see clearly the alternative to its non-realization. It may be admitted that the principle of universal and compulsory arbitration must at the present time be the subject of compromise and halfway measures; it may, indeed, be beyond the capacity of nations to achieve, but if we aspire to a society of nations solidly grounded on legal and moral rules, this is the necessary goal, and without achieving it we must be prepared to live under a régime of competing and opposing forces, exercised without the authoritative sanction of law and predestined to ultimate conflict.

IV

It is in this relation that the Protocol rendered a further service, affording as it did some test of the existing sentiment of states toward comprehensive pacific settlement and bringing into prominence obstacles which lay in the way of its realization. The Memorandum of the British Government on the Protocol is an instructive document in this respect. It subjects the Protocol to various criticisms, all of which merit consideration, but certain of the issues raised have a special bearing on the prospective development of international pacific methods. In the first place, the British Government took occasion to reject once more the principle of universal compulsory settlement of all international controversies. The objection to it, it was said, "might easily outweigh its theoretical advantages," and care was taken to point out that from time to time the British Government had entered reservations to the compulsory jurisdiction of the Permanent Court of International Justice. These observations in themselves may be regarded as objections in principle to the Protocol, apart from its detailed provisions, and a definitive declaration of policy by a great and influential Power. They cannot, however, be fairly or adequately examined apart from the context of the Memorandum. His Majesty's Government was "more immediately concerned to enquire how far the change in the Covenant effected by the Protocol is likely to increase the responsibilities already undertaken by the States Members of the League." And here follows an analysis of the present status of the League: reference to the weakening of its machinery as a result of the non-membership of certain states; the possible dislike of these states of compulsory arbitration; their distrust of League methods; and the consequent dangers to League Members in assuming additional responsibilities for enforcing the provisions of the Covenant and the Protocol. One other element in the British reply requires citation in this connection. The objections of His Majesty's Government, it was observed, to compulsory arbitration, so far from being diminished by the provisions of the Protocol, had rather been increased, "owing to the weakening of those reservations in clause 15 of the Covenant, which were designed to prevent any interference by the League in matters of domestic jurisdiction."

The foregoing points in the British Memorandum bring out certain realities of the present international situation of which it is important to take account. Among these is the fact that the British Commonwealth of Nations and, in an even more pronounced degree, the United States of America are at present unwilling to accept in any comprehensive manner the authority of an international jurisdiction. In this respect their attitude is in striking contrast with that of less powerful nations, and we are impressed once more with the traditional relationship between the possession of power by a state and its reluctance to accept the processes of arbitral justice. It is equally manifest, moreover, as the British reply rightly points out, that the failure of certain states to accept the processes and obligations of the Covenant has fundamentally altered the legal order which it was the purpose of the League to set up. In discussing the evolution of the principle of sanctions in the Covenant we have said that there has been little evidence of a willingness on the part of Member states to commit themselves to a program of coercive action solely in the interest of what may be termed League principles and beyond the radius of their national interests. Granted that with an all-inclusive League this condition would have been intrinsically the same, the obvious fact remains that any proposal of the League for coercive measures against an aggressor nation cannot remain indifferent to the presence of neutral and possibly unsympathetic states. The national interests of League Members involved in relations with such states may well be such that these interests will control the policies of League Members and reduce to a secondary position the common interest which otherwise might be supported.

But the new order envisaged through the League is even more fundamentally affected by the abstention of these non-Member states from the legal system of arbitration and conciliation established through the Covenant. There can be no real progress in the law of nations, no genuine change in those relations of states which often with warrant are designated as atomistic, anarchic, and uncivic, without a common acceptance of the arbitral principles of the Covenant. Juridical restraints on the freedom of states to resort to war; the obligatory use of processes of justice which define the causes for which force may justifiably be used, these are essential requisites of any genuinely effective legal order in the society of nations. There is no escape from these primary principles if we seek in truth to initiate a reconstruction and development of the law of nations. States which fail to accept these principles in common with other states are, in substance, rejecting the idea of a reign of law in the relasionship of states; they may seek thereby to safeguard some apparent national interest, but they are prolonging as well the precarious and unstable régime of force under which the rights and interests of nations have neither security nor permanence.

The reference in the British Memorandum to the possible encroachment through the Protocol of an international jurisdiction upon the domestic domain of states raises an issue which must necessarily be considered in all proposals for advancing international pacific settlement. In an extremely illuminating discussion of this question, Professor Brierly has recently observed that "Article 15 of the Covenant of the League of Nations has introduced into the terminology of international law a phrase which already shows signs of becoming a new catchword, and which is capable of proving as great a hindrance to the orderly development of the subject as the somewhat battered idols of sovereignty, state equality, and the like have been in the past."[4] In his examination of the meaning of the term, "matters which by international law are solely within the domestic jurisdiction of states," Professor Brierly concludes that there are in reality only two "domains," and that a matter is either (a) regulated by international law, or (b) a matter of domestic jurisdiction. And while far from advocating any radical diminution of the reserved domain of states, Professor Brierly rightly says that "the great majority of really dangerous international disputes arise out of matters which indisputably fall within the category of domestic jurisdiction, and the problem of how to deal with them is the most crucial, and unfortunately also the most intractable, of all international questions. Continuing, he states that "an essential condition of any progress is a more general

[4] "Matters of Domestic Jurisdiction," *British Year Book of International Law, 1925*, pp. 8-19.

recognition that under the phrase of 'domestic jurisdiction' are comprised a multitude of matters differing widely from one another, and that it is unreasonable to expect that disputes arising from all of them can be settled in the same way."

The adjustment of this problem of the category of interests which should be left to the reserved domain of states and those which are the proper subjects of international control presents the real test of the capacity of nations to effect a peaceful ordering of their relationships. Here there must be at once stability and processes of change; a common respect of national interests and institutions; a common willingness to recognize that for the equitable adjustment of certain matters a joint control is necessarily required. We encounter here a problem, different in content, it is true, but in principle the same as that which always recurs wherever there are associations of men or groups of men—what are the proper limits of collective authority and control; what is the sphere of individual autonomy which should be reserved to the members which compose the society? If we concede that the most menacing international disputes arise from matters now left to the exclusive determination of states, it is essential to the advance of pacific procedure that these matters be brought under an international jurisdiction competent to provide a definitive settlement of the questions at issue. The creation of this jurisdiction and the proper determination of its content presents a task with which the future international organization must necessarily deal.

ANNEX I

SELECTED ARTICLES FROM THE COVENANT OF THE LEAGUE OF NATIONS

Article 8

The Members of the League recognize that the maintenance of peace requires the reduction of national armaments to the lowest point consistent with national safety and the enforcement by common action of international obligations.

The Council, taking account of the geographical situation and circumstances of each State, shall formulate plans for such reduction for the consideration and action of the several Governments.

Such plans shall be subject to reconsideration and revision at least every 10 years.

After these plans shall have been adopted by the several Governments, the limits of armaments therein fixed shall not be exceeded without the concurrence of the Council.

The Members of the League agree that the manufacture by private enterprise of munitions and implements of war is open to grave objections. The Council shall advise how the evil effects attendant upon such manufacture can be prevented, due regard being had to the necessities of those Members of the League which are not able to manufacture the munitions and implements of war necessary for their safety.

The Members of the League undertake to interchange full and frank information as to the scale of their armaments, their military, naval and air programs, and the condition of such of their industries as are adaptable to warlike purposes.

Article 10

The Members of the League undertake to respect and preserve as against external aggression the territorial integrity and existing political independence of all Members of the League. In case of any such aggression or in case of any threat or danger of such aggression, the Council shall advise upon the means by which this obligation shall be fulfilled.

Article 11

1. Any war or threat of war, whether immediately affecting any of the Members of the League or not, is hereby declared a matter of concern to the whole League, and the League shall take any action that may be deemed wise and effectual to safeguard the peace of nations. In case any such emergency should arise, the Secretary-General shall, on the request of any Member of the League, forthwith summon a meeting of the Council.

2. It is also declared to be the friendly right of each Member of the League to bring to the attention of the Assembly or of the Council any circumstances whatever affecting international relations which threatens to disturb international peace or the good understanding between nations upon which peace depends.

Article 12

1. The Members of the League agree that, if there should arise between them any dispute likely to lead to a rupture they will submit the matter either to arbitration or judicial settlement or to enquiry by the Council and they agree in no case to resort to war until three months after the award by the arbitrators or the judicial decision, or the report by the Council.

2. In any case under this Article, the award of the arbitrators or the judicial decision shall be made within a reasonable time, and the report of the Council shall be made within six months after the submission of the dispute.

Article 13

1. The Members of the League agree that, whenever any dispute shall arise between them which they recognize to be suitable for submission to arbitration or judicial settlement, and which cannot be satisfactorily settled by diplomacy, they will submit the whole subject-matter to arbitration or judicial settlement.

2. Disputes as to the interpretation of a treaty, as to any question of international law, as to the existence of any fact which, if established, would constitute a breach of any international obligation, or as to the extent and nature of the reparation to be made for any such breach, are declared to be among those which are generally suitable for submission to arbitration or judicial settlement.

3. For the consideration of any such dispute, the court to which the case is referred shall be the Permanent Court of International Justice, established in accordance with Article 14, or any tribunal agreed on by the parties to the dispute or stipulated in any convention existing between them.

4. The Members of the League agree that they will carry out in full good faith any award or decision that may be rendered, and that they will not resort to war against a Member of the League which complies therewith. In the event of any failure to carry out such an award or decision, the Council shall propose what steps should be taken to give effect thereto.

Article 15

1. If there should arise between Members of the League any dispute likely to lead to a rupture, which is not submitted to arbitration or judicial settlement in accordance with Article 13, the Members of the League agree that they will submit the matter to the Council. Any party to the dispute may effect such submission by giving notice of the existence of the dispute to the Secretary-General, who will make all necessary arrangements for a full investigation and consideration thereof.

2. For this purpose the parties to the dispute will communicate to the Secretary-General, as promptly as possible, statements of their case, with all the relevant facts and papers, and the Council may forthwith direct the publication thereof.

3. The Council shall endeavor to effect a settlement of the dispute and, if such efforts are successful, a settlement shall be made public giving such facts and explanations regarding the dispute and the terms of settlement thereof as the Council may deem appropriate.

4. If the dispute is not thus settled, the Council, either unanimously or by a majority vote, shall make and publish a report containing a statement of the facts of the dispute and the recommendations which are deemed just and proper in regard thereto.

5. Any Member of the League represented on the Council may make public a statement of the facts of the dispute and of its conclusions regarding the same.

6. If a report by the Council is unanimously agreed to by the Members thereof other than the Representatives of one or more of the parties to the dispute, the Members of the League agree that they will not go to war with any party to the dispute which complies with the recommendations of the report.

7. If the Council fails to reach a report which is unanimously agreed to by the Members thereof, other than the Representatives of one or more of the parties to the dispute, the Members of the League reserve to themselves the right to take such action as they shall consider necessary for the maintenance of right and justice.

8. If the dispute between the parties is claimed by one of them, and is found by the Council, to arise out of a matter which by international law is solely within the domestic jurisdiction of that party, the Council shall so report, and shall make no recommendation as to its settlement.

9. The Council may in any case under this Article refer the dispute to the Assembly. The dispute shall be so referred at the request of either party to the dispute, provided that such request be made within fourteen days after the submission of the dispute to the Council.

10. In any case referred to the Assembly, all the provisions of this Article and of Article 12 relating to the action and powers of the Council shall apply to the action and powers of the Assembly, provided that a report made by the Assembly, if concurred in by the Representatives of those Members of the League represented on the Council and of a majority of the other Members of the League, exclusive in each case of the Representatives of the parties to the dispute, shall have the same force as a report by the Council concurred in by all the Members thereof other than the Representatives of one or more of the parties to the dispute.

ARTICLE 16

1. Should any Member of the League resort to war in disregard of its covenants under Articles 12, 13, or 15, it shall ipso facto be deemed to have committed an act of war against all other Members of the League, which hereby undertake immediately to subject it to the severance of all trade or financial relations, the prohibition of all intercourse between their nationals

and the nationals of the covenant-breaking State, and the prevention of all financial, commercial or personal intercourse between the nationals of the covenant-breaking State and the nationals of any other State, whether a Member of the League or not.

2. It shall be the duty of the Council in such case to recommend to the several Governments concerned what effective military, naval or air force the Members of the League shall severally contribute to the armed forces to be used to protect the covenants of the League.

3. The Members of the League agree, further, that they will mutually support one another in the financial and economic measures which are taken under this Article, in order to minimise the loss and inconvenience resulting from the above measures, and that they will mutually support one another in resisting any special measures aimed at one of their number by the covenant-breaking State, and that they will take the necessary steps to afford passage through their territory to the forces of any of the Members of the League which are co-operating to protect the covenants of the League.

4. Any Member of the League which has violated any covenant of the League may be declared to be no longer a Member of the League by a vote of the Council concurred in by the Representatives of all the other Members of the League represented thereon.

Article 19

The Assembly may from time to time advise the reconsideration by Members of the League of treaties which have become inapplicable, and the consideration of international conditions whose continuance might endanger the peace of the world.

ANNEX II

LETTER OF PRESIDENT WILSON TO SENATOR GILBERT M. HITCHCOCK, WITH REFERENCE TO ARTICLE 10[1]

THE WHITE HOUSE,
Washington, 8 March, 1920.

MY DEAR SENATOR HITCHCOCK: I understand that one or two of your colleagues do me the honor of desiring to know what my views are with reference to Article X of the League of Nations and the effect upon the League of the adoption of certain proposed reservations to that Article. I welcome the opportunity to throw any light I can upon a subject which has become so singularly beclouded by misapprehensions and misinterpretations of every kind.

There is no escaping the moral obligations which are expressed in positive terms in this Article of the Covenant. We won a moral victory over Germany far greater even than the military victory won on the field of battle, because the opinion of the whole world swung to our support and the support of the nations associated with us in the great struggle. It did so because of our common profession and promise that we meant to establish "an organization of peace which should make it certain that the combined power of free nations would check every invasion of right and serve to make peace and justice the more secure by affording a definite tribunal of opinion to which all must submit and by which every international readjustment that cannot be amicably agreed upon by the peoples directly concerned shall be sanctioned." This promise and assurance were written into the preliminaries of the Armistice and into the preliminaries of the peace itself and constitute one of the most sacred obligations ever assumed by any nation or body of nations. It is unthinkable that America should set the example of ignoring such a solemn moral engagement.

For myself, I feel that I could not look the soldiers of our gallant armies in the face again if I did not do everything in my

[1] Reprinted from *Congressional Record*, 66th Congress, Second Session, pp. 4354-4355.

power to remove every obstacle that lies in the way of the adoption of this particular Article of the Covenant, because we made these pledges to them as well as to the rest of the world and it was to this cause they deemed themselves devoted in a spirit of crusaders. I should be forever unfaithful to them if I did not do my utmost to fulfill the high purpose for which they fought.

I think, my dear Senator, we can dismiss from our minds the idea that it is necessary to stipulate in connection with Article X the constitutional methods we should use in fulfilling our obligations under it. We gain nothing by such stipulations and secure nothing which is not already secured. It was understood as a matter of course at the conference in Paris that whatever obligations any government assumed or whatever duties it undertook under the treaty would of course have to be fulfilled by its usual and established constitutional methods of action. Once or twice in meetings of the conference, when the treaty was under consideration, "reservations" were made to that effect by the representatives of individual powers, and those "reservations" were invariably received in the way in which men who have met for business and not for talk always receive acts of scrupulous supererogation,—listening to with indifferent silence, as such men listen to what is a matter of course and was not necessary to say.

There can be no objection to explaining again what our constitutional method is and that our Congress alone can declare war to determine the cause or occasions for war, and that it alone can authorize the use of the armed forces of the United States on land or on the sea. But to make such a declaration would certainly be a work of supererogation.

I am sorry to say that the reservations that have come under my notice are almost without exception, not interpretations of the Articles to which it is proposed to attach them but in effect virtual nullifications of those Articles.

Any reservation which seeks to deprive the League of Nations of the force of Article X cuts at the very heart and life of the Covenant itself. Any League of Nations which does not guarantee as a matter of incontestable right the political independence and integrity of each of its members might be hardly more than a futile scrap of paper, as ineffective in operation as the agreement between Belgium and Germany which the Germans violated in 1914. Article X as written into the Treaty of Versailles represents the renunciation by Great Britain and Japan, which before the war had begun to find so many interests in common in the Pacific; by France; by Italy—by all the great fighting powers of the world of the old pretensions of political conquest and territorial aggrandizement. It is a new doctrine in the world's affairs and must be recognized or there is no secure basis for the peace which the whole world so longingly desires and so desperately needs. If Article X is not adopted and acted upon, the governments which reject it will, I think, be guilty of bad faith to their people whom they induced to make the infinite sacrifices of the war by the pledge that they would be fighting to redeem the world from the old order of force and aggression. They will be acting also in bad faith to the opinion of the world at large to which they appealed for support in a concerted stand against the aggressions and pretensions of Germany. If we were to reject Article X or so to weaken it as to take its full force out of it, it would mark us as desiring to return to the old world of jealous rivalry and misunderstandings from which our gallant soldiers have rescued us, and would leave us without any vision or new conception of justice and peace. We would have no lesson from the war but gained only the regret that it had involved us in its maelstrom of suffering. If America has awakened, as the rest of the world has, to the vision of a new day in which the mistakes of the past are to be corrected, it will welcome the opportunity to share the responsibilities of Article X.

It must not be forgotten, Senator, that this Article constitutes a renunciation of wrong ambition on the part of powerful nations with whom we were associated in the war. It is by no means certain that without this Article any such renunciation will take place. Militaristic ambitions and imperialistic policies are by no means dead even in the counsels of the nations whom we most **trust and with whom we most desire to be associated in the tasks** of peace. Throughout the sessions of the conference in Paris it was evident that a militaristic party, under the most influential leadership, was seeking to gain ascendency in the counsels of France. They were defeated then, but are in control now. The chief arguments advanced in Paris in support of the Italian claims on the Adriatic were strategic arguments, that is to say, military arguments, which had at their back the thought of naval supremacy in that sea. For my own part, I am as intolerant of imperialistic designs on the part of other nations as I was of such designs on the part of Germany.

The choice is between two ideals: on the one hand, the ideal of democracy, which represents the rights of free peoples everywhere to govern themselves, and on the other hand, the ideal of imperialism which seeks to dominate by force and unjust power, an ideal which is by no means dead and which is earnestly held in many quarters still. Every imperialistic influence in Europe was hostile to the embodiment of Article X in the Covenant of the League of Nations, and its defeat now would mark the complete consummation of their efforts to nullify the treaty. I hold the doctrine of Article X to be the essence of Americanism. We cannot repudiate it or weaken it without at the same time repudiating our own principles.

The imperialist wants no League of Nations, but if, in response to the universal cry of the masses everywhere, there is to be one, he is interested to secure one suited to his own purposes, one that will permit him to continue the historic game of pawns and peoples,—the juggling of provinces, the old balances of power, and the inevitable wars attendant upon these things. The reservation proposed would perpetuate the old order. Does anyone really want to see the old game played again? Can anyone really venture to take part in reviving the old order? The enemies of a league of nations have by every instinct centered their efforts against Article X, for it is undoubtedly the foundation of the whole structure. It is the bulwark, and the only bulwark, of the rising democracy of the world against the forces of imperialism and reaction.

Either we should enter the League fearlessly, accepting the responsibility and not fearing the role of leadership which we now enjoy, contributing our efforts towards establishing a just and permanent peace, or we should retire as gracefully as possible from the great concert of powers by which the world was saved. For my own part, I am not willing to trust to the counsel of diplomats the working out of any salvation of the world from the things which it has suffered.

I believe that when the full significance of this great question has been generally apprehended, obstacles will seem insignificant before the opportunity, a great and glorious opportunity, to contribute our overwhelming moral and material force to the establishment of an international régime in which our own ideals of justice and right may be made to prevail and the nations of the world be allowed a peaceful development under conditions of order and hitherto impossible.

I need not say, Senator, that I have given a great deal of thought to the whole matter of reservations proposed in connection with the ratification of the treaty, and particularly that portion of the treaty which contains the Covenant of the League of Nations, and I have been struck by the fact that practically every so-called reservation was in effect a rather sweeping nullification of the terms of the treaty itself. I hear of reservationists and mild reservationists, but I cannot understand the difference between a nullifier and a mild nullifier. Our responsibility as a nation in this turning point of history is an overwhelming one, and if I had the opportunity I would beg everyone concerned to consider the matter in the light of what it is possible to accomplish for humanity rather than in the light of special national interests.

If I have been truly informed concerning the desire of some of your colleagues to know my views in this matter, I would be very glad if you should show this letter to them.

Cordially and sincerely yours,

WOODROW WILSON.

Hon. GILBERT M. HITCHCOCK,
United States Senate.

ANNEX III

EXTRACTS FROM THE REPLIES OF CERTAIN GOVERNMENTS ON THE AMENDMENT TO ARTICLE 10 OF THE COVENANT

PROPOSED BY
THE CANADIAN DELEGATION TO THE THIRD ASSEMBLY[1]

REPLY FROM ALBANIA

According to general opinion, Article 10 constitutes the corner-stone of the Covenant and the very foundation of the League.

[1] Reprinted from *Minutes, First Committee,* Fourth Assembly.

Therefore, any modification in the direction indicated by the Canadian proposal would be regarded as weakening the guarantee of peace provided by the Covenant. This applies in particular to the second paragraph, which it is desired to add to Article 10. In these circumstances, to make compliance with the advice of the Council dependent upon the wish which Members might have to entertain it and upon their desire to conform to it would be to render such advice too ineffective.

The Albanian Government, however, considers that the disadvantages found to exist in the proposed amendment would be greatly mitigated if the proposed Treaty of Mutual Guarantee, which is at present being examined by the competent organisations of the League, were to become a reality.

For that reason, the Albanian Government considers that it would be desirable to postpone, for the moment, the consideration of the Canadian proposal.

Reply from Belgium

The Belgian Government notes with keen satisfaction that the Canadian Delegation to the Third Assembly has not only withdrawn its demand that Article 10 should be omitted from the Covenant, but has formally recognised the value of the arguments brought forward in favour of its retention. The Delegation now merely asks that this provision, the meaning of which appears to have been rendered obscure through various, and often contradictory, interpretations of the text, shall be modified by an amendment in which it shall be laid down that the "advice" to be given by the Council in the eventuality provided for by Article 10 cannot oblige a Member of the League of Nations "to engage in any act of war without the consent of its Parliament, Legislature or other representative body."

The discussions which took place in the Committees and Commissions during the Session of the Assembly and at other times have clearly shown that the Canadian Government's main objection to Article 10, which led it to ask that this Article should be omitted, was not justified as regards the interpretation given to this provision by the Members of the League of Nations.

The object of the collective guarantee contained in this Article is not to perpetuate the political or territorial status quo; its aim is simply to ensure that States which are victims of external aggression shall obtain the assistance of the other Members of the League in order to maintain or restore the state of affairs threatened or subverted by armed force, without in any way prejudicing the fundamental legality of territorial claims, and leaving every avenue open for resort to such pacific procedure as may lead to a solution.

The new Canadian proposals still show a tendency to exaggerate the scope of the obligations arising out of Article 10. In pointing out to the Council that it should take the political and geographical circumstances of each State into special account, and in emphasising the fact that the advice it might give concerning the method of giving effect to the collective guarantee should not have the force of an obligation for the various States, the Canadian amendment merely brings out certain aspects of the present text which all the delegates were unanimous in recognising.

It may therefore be asked whether such considerations can appropriately be cast in the form of an amendment. Such a form presents the considerable drawback of leading people to suppose that the meaning of the Article has been modified. Public opinion throughout the world would consider—though wrongly, no doubt—that such an amendment constituted a weakening of Article 10, which is generally regarded as the keystone of the Covenant. The proposed amendment would, moreover, be subjected to all the uncertainties and delays inherent in the procedure of ratification provided for in the Covenant, and would leave the present text unaltered for a period which might be considerable. It would consequently become far more difficult in the meantime to interpret it in the sense which the Canadian Delegation desires. It would therefore appear to be more desirable, and more in conformity with the Canadian Government's object, to dispel any apprehension it may still feel concerning the present text of Article 10 by the adoption of an interpretative resolution.

* * * * *

The Belgian Government noted with considerable apprehension that, during the discussions raised by the Canadians proposals, certain delegates to the Assembly or Members of

Committees defended interpretations of Article 10 which would have the effect of reducing the force of this Article to a far greater extent than is demanded by the Canadian Government to-day.

According to their point of view, the *external aggression* which would bring into play the guarantee of independence and integrity to be afforded to all the Members could be nothing but the unlawful resort to war for which provisions is made in Article 16. The effect of this would be to reduce Article 10 to a mere vague statement of the principle which is developed in Articles 15, 16 and 17, regulating the way in which the League shall intervene in the case of unlawful wars.

There is no doubt that the scope of Article 10 is far wider than this. Any act of war on the part of a foreign State constitutes external aggression, excepting such acts as may be in execution of a judgment pronounced by the Permanent Court of International Justice or are the result of an unanimous recommendation of the Council. The aim in view is to render it impossible for the States to increase their territory by acts of *violence*, and to remove all incentives to do so. They must not be authorised to commit such acts, merely because they have resorted to mediation by the Council in connection with some dispute, and have then made this a pretext for war, when efforts at mediation have failed.

The Belgian Government is strengthened in its opinion that such is the real object of this provision in the Covenant by the fact that, when the matter was being discussed in the League of Nations Committee at the Peace Conference, M. Hymans, the Belgian delegate, formally proposed that the guarantee given under Article 10 should be extended to include the *invioliability* of States. This proposal was not adopted. The explanations submitted on this occasion showed that it was intended to guarantee the inviolability of States Members only in the case of unlawful aggression, as provided for in Article 15 *et seq*; their integrity, on the other hand, was to be protected in all cases of external aggression.

The Belgian Government is glad to note that the Canadian delegates have never at the Sessions of the Assembly departed from such an interpretation, which has also received the very authoritative approval of Professor Struycken.

Reply from Bulgaria

If the high ideals of the League of Nations are to be attained, there must be an article of guarantee, and consequently the omission of Article 10 would weaken the very foundations of the League of Nations.

The idea has therefore arisen of submitting certain amendments, to define more clearly the obligations assumed by the different States, and to limit the risks by fixing the exact meaning of certain points. Amendments having this object in view cannot be otherwise than welcome if the obligation provided for in Article 10 is preserved.

The opinion of the Bulgarian Government concerning the amendments which have been submitted by the Canadian Delegation is as follows:

The first amendment is intrinsically right. The question is one of finding the best formula, but we think that all States should not be placed on the same footing, and that circumstances should be taken into account.

The second amendment entirely respects the sovereignty of the different nations so long as no true international sovereignty and force exist, and various constitutions, such as that of the French Republic, lay down that war cannot be declared without the approval of the representative body. "An act of war" is so important a matter and may have such terrible consequences that we consider very legitimate the desire to preserve for each nation the right only to engage in war of its own free will and after consideration of the circumstances. This is a principle which the new democratic Bulgaria also admits.

Reply from China

The Chinese Government is in favour of maintaining this Article exactly as it stands. It does not think it will be desirable to modify it in any way unless, in the supreme interests of the League, such modifications may be rendered necessary in the future by the urgency of events.

Reply from France

According to the present wording of Article 10, the Council has to "advise upon the means by which this obligation shall be fulfilled"—the obligation being the one referred to in the first sentence. The Council is perfectly free to prescribe the means which it thinks best adapted to attain the required object; it will doubtless take account, in particular, of the geographical and political circumstances of each State. The recommendations which it makes will be the more readily accepted in proportion as they are framed with regard to the national circumstances of the several States. But it is desirable that the powers assigned to the Council should not be restricted by the insertion of any formula in Article 10. The Council must be free to take account of all the special circumstances of any State, not only of its political and geographical circumstances, but also of its economic or other circumstances. The Council must even be able, in certain cases, to look beyond the considerations which are peculiar to certain States and to be guided solely by the higher considerations of the interest of the world's peace in the recommendations which it makes with a view to securing respect for, and preservation of, territorial integrity and political independence of the States Members of the League as against any aggression—and also as against the threat or danger of such aggression.

The paragraph which it is proposed to add gives rise to the following observations:

(a) The word "opinion" given in the text does not correctly interpret the nature of the decision which has to be taken by the Council in accordance with the second sentence of Article 10. The words "the Council shall advise upon the means . . ." mean that "the Council takes all necessary steps. . ." Moreover, its decision will ordinarily take the form of a recommendation ad-addressed to the different States. Therefore, there is no question of an "opinion" but of "recommendations" or of "measures advocated."

(b) It cannot be doubted that the States Members will give most serious consideration to these recommendations and will "use their utmost endeavours to conform" to them. Such an attitude would be in conformity with the spirit of Article 10, the first sentence of which lays a certain obligation upon the States while the second sentence merely instructs the Council to advise upon the means by which this obligation shall be fulfilled. Thus, the first portion of the paragraph proposed by the Canadian Government merely expresses in a new form the general intention of this article.

(c) In the second portion of the additional paragraph, we read: "no Member shall be under the obligation to engage in any act of war without the consent of its Parliament, legislature or other representative body." Although Article 10 of the Covenant imposes an obligation on the States Members to respect and preserve as against external aggression the territorial integrity and political independence of other Members, it is obvious that effect can only be given to this obligation in conformity with the constitutional rules of the respective States. The approval given to the Covenant, and consequently to Article 10 at the time of its ratification by a Parliament, legislature or other representative body could not, it appears, be considered as implying a permanent mandate to the Government—in case of aggression, or threat or danger of aggression, against a State Member to take measures which would ordinarily require the authorisation of the said Parliament, legislature or other representative body. It may, however, be pointed out that, if the machinery for affording mutual aid in certain hypothetical cases of aggression were specially instituted by partial agreements between certain States, these partial agreements would become operative within the general limits of Article 10.

(d) In conclusion, the French Government is of opinion that the procedure for amendments, being protracted and complicated, should only be resorted to for the purpose of making substantial alterations in the Covenant; and it therefore considers that the Canadian proposals contained in the additional paragraph, which gives special expression to general principles, are not sufficient grounds for setting in motion the machinery for amendments.

REPLY FROM GREECE

The Greek Government considers that Article 10 of the Covenant is one of the foundations of the League of Nations and constitutes one of the most essential guarantees for world peace; it therefore considers that this Article is of the highest importance and that any proposal tending to abolish this guarantee would be a heavy blow to the prestige of the League of Nations, would deprive it of an essential source of strength and would subsequently render it practically, if not absolutely, impotent. The principle laid down in Article 10, of providing a guarantee for the States Members "to preserve their territorial integrity or political independence as against all external aggression," could not, in the opinion of the Greek Government, be weakened without very seriously affecting the whole fabric of the League of Nations.

It is true that the interpretation of Article 10, particularly in its relations with Article 12 *et seq.* of the Covenant, presents serious difficulties, which it would doubtless be desirable to overcome by rendering the text of the Article clearer or by an authoritative interpretation, but it is equally evident that the object of Article 10 is to prevent territorial changes as a result of war. According to Article 10, the territorial *status quo* should only be altered by peaceful methods. It seems that only by rendering the application of Article 10 effective can wars of aggression for the purpose of bringing about territorial aggrandisement be avoided in the future.

Reply from Hungary

In the view of the Royal Hungarian Government, the Canadian proposal contains a valuable idea, which it appreciates all the more because Article 10, in the form proposed, would be in closer conformity with the Hungarian Constitution, which lays down that the assent of Parliament is required before the Hungarian army may be employed outside the frontiers of the State. . . .

* * * * *

In the view of the Royal Hungarian Government, the obligation to employ the armed forces of the nation outside the country, without having obtained previous authorization from Parliament, lays so grave a responsibility on the respective Governments, and particularly on those of the Powers not represented on the Council, that the Government of a constitutional country could not assume it without the greatest difficulty.

Reply from Italy

After examining the draft, the Royal Government is of opinion that no discussion of the Canadian proposal could lead to practical and tangible results until the negotiations have been concluded which are now in progress with regard to the questions of the Treaty of Mutual Guarantee and the reduction of armaments, with which such a proposal is intimately connected.

The Royal Government therefore considers that the amendment to Article 10 of the Covenant proposed by Canada could only be examined, if at all, when decisions have been taken respecting the two afore-mentioned problems.

REPLY FROM THE NETHERLANDS

As it is understood, and is a matter of course, that the Council of the League of Nations will have to take into consideration, the political and geographical circumstances of every State when giving its advice, as laid down in Article 10, the Royal Government considers that it is unnecessary to insert in the Covenant an explicit mention of this obligation. Moreover, as such a mention might give rise to the impression that the Council would not need to take count of other circumstances—e. g., economic circumstances—the desirability of the amendment appears open to question.

The paragraph which it is proposed to add to Article 10 would have the advantage of emphasising the purely advisory character of the recommendation made by the Council by virtue of this Article. However, the Government of the Netherlands doubts whether it is desirable to make distinctions, from the point of view of their importance, between the various forms of advice given by the Council. Further, Her Majesty's Government does not feel able to agree with the latter portion of the proposed paragraph. The relation between Governments and their parliaments is entirely a matter of domestic concern, and could not be regulated or settled by the Covenant. Moreover, the words employed are open to the interpretation that there are no other grounds which might justify a Government in deciding not to give effect to the advice of the Council.

In these circumstances the Royal Government does not feel able to recommend the adoption of the amendment.

REPLY FROM PERSIA

The People and Government of Persia cannot in any way agree to an *amendment* modifying the spirit of Article 10 of the Covenant, nor can they adhere to any provision which would lessen the efficacy of this Article.

Reply from Poland

The Polish Government is of opinion that, for the reasons given below, it would be advisable, under the present circumstances, to retain Article 10 as it stands.

If, as it would appear, the first proposal introduces no new factor into the provisions of Article 10, it offers no advantages. Indeed, it is difficult to see how the Council of the League of Nations could "advise upon the means" which it might consider necessary for respecting and preserving the territorial integrity and political independence of a Member of the League which was attacked, without seriously taking into account the political and geographical circumstances, both of the State attacked and of all States which would be obliged to assist it. If, however, the first Canadian proposal tended in any way to lessen the efficiency of the guarantees provided under Article 10, the Polish Government would feel all the more bound to oppose the adoption of the amendment.

The second proposal would tend to nullify the value of the guarantees laid down in Article 10, as it would make the taking of any action in support of a State attacked—and this action could only be effective if it were certain and immediate—conditional upon the approval of the representative bodies of each State Member of the League of Nations.

From the legal point of view, this proposal gives rise to very grave objections as it completely transforms Article 10. In ratifying the Covenant of the League of Nations, each Parliament, legislature or representative body explicitly gave its approval in advance to the enforcement of measures which are the logical consequence of the obligations entered into by the Members of the League of Nations. It would therefore appear obvious that acceptance of the Canadian Delegation's second amendment would be tantamount to the unconditional abolition of Article 10, as previously proposed by that Delegation. In view of these considerations, the Polish Government thinks it desirable to state its point of view with regard to the problem raised by Article 10 in its present aspect. The Polish Government considers that the terms of Article 10 constitute one of the fundamental principles of the Covenant of the League of Nations as at persent constituted, and further, that the undertaking entered into mutually by all Members of the League of Nations to respect and preserve their territorial integrity and political independence is one of the corner-stones on which the whole organisation of the League of Nations rests. Indeed, on all occasions on which the question of creating a society of States, such as the League of Nations, has been considered, the principle of the mutual and collective guarantee of territorial integrity and political independence has always been regarded either as the aim and object of such a society or as one of the essential conditions for its formation. It should also be pointed out that, whenever public opinion has had an opportunity of expressing its views in support of the idea of the League of Nations, it has always closely associated the principle of guarantees with the question of the usefulness of an international organisation of this type.

Further, it is necessary again to draw attention to a point which has repeatedly been emphasised, i. e., that Article 10 in no way excludes the possibility of territorial changes, but that its sole object is to prevent such changes being brought about by foreign aggression. Under these conditions, the mutual and collective guarantee given under the provisions of Article 10 would appear to be a logical consequence of, and essential factor in, the system upon which the League of Nations is at present organised. The effect of abolishing stipulations of this type and scope would be completely to transform the character of the League and the outcome would be the revision of the entire Covenant, seeing that its various clauses are so closely related one to another that it is impossible to modify the bearing of one without coincidently changing the bearing of another. Accordingly, if we adopted the Canadian proposals, we should be obliged to revise all the provisions in the Covenant defining the objects of the League of Nations in addition to those which refer to the rights and obligations of the States Members of the League.

It is indisputable that the Covenant of the League of Nations imposes upon its Members certain obligations which *de facto* constitute important restrictions upon the exercise of their sovereign rights. The States Members have declared their willingness to submit to the control of the League of Nations, not only in regard to their foreign relations, but also, to a certain extent, in regard to matters of a domestic nature; they have agreed to accept the interference of the League in all matters in which its intervention might be required, owing to apprehension of any danger to peace (e. g., Articles 11 and 19 of the Covenant).

The States which constitute the League of Nations would probably never have consented to all these restrictions if they had not believed that they would find a compensation and a makeweight in the mutual guarantee of their territorial integrity and political independence. In consequence, if the obligation imposed by the mutual guarantee is to be cut out from the Covenant of the League of Nations, we shall be obliged to take into account the possibility of revising all clauses in virtue of which the League of Nations has the right to intervene in the foreign relations between States Members and sometimes in their home affairs.

One of the most important duties assumed by the Members of the League of Nations is the realisation of the reduction of armaments (Article 8). The undertakings in this matter are logically bound up with the guarantees provided in Article 10, since States could not be required seriously to contemplate the question of the reduction of armaments unless they were assured of their territorial integrity and political independence. Even within the limits of Article 8 as it stands, any scheme for reduction must be compatible with the national safety of each State. Were the guarantees withdrawn, it would be necessary to leave each State free to decide what armaments were necessary to its safety, and, as the League of Nations could offer its Members no effective guarantee, it would no longer have any authority in the matter. Accordingly, the effect of cancelling Article 10 might well be the abandonment of the scheme for the reduction of armaments, the more so since it might be interpreted as proof that the territorial integrity of the Members of the League of Nations cannot or need not necessarily be preserved.

The outcome might be that international relations, which are not yet by any means peaceful and give no assurance of the safety required by all States, might be further disturbed by a lack of confidence, the effect of which would certainly not tend towards the realisation of the reduction of armaments.

Reply from Portugal

The Portuguese Government is of opinion that as Article 10 constitutes the most adequate expression of the high ideals which inspired the constitution of the League of Nations and the drawing up of the Covenant, and as it is a fundamental Article, it should be preserved in its original form. If, however, the Assembly decides that the objections raised by the Canadian Delegawere sufficiently cogent to render a modification of this Article necessary, the Portuguese Government will not raise any objection to the adoption of the two amendments proposed by the Canadian Delegation.

Reply from Roumania

We consider that Article 10 of the League of Nations constitutes the most effective guarantee against all attempts at aggression with the object of modifying the territorial position established under the Treaties of Peace. To suppress the Article would be equivalent, therefore, to depriving the Covenant of one of its main attributes; moreover, to lessen its force by means of clauses under which its application would depend on the decision of the Council called upon to examine "the political and geographical circumstances of each State," would be to weaken the scope and effect of the clause of Mutual Guarantee.

The Royal Government, however, does not raise any objection to the reservation that no Member should be obliged to engage in any act of war without the consent of its Parliament.

Reply from Spain

In accordance with my instructions, I have the honour to inform you that, as the question of the Treaty of Guarantee is now under consideration by the League of Nations, the Royal Government is of opinion that any discussion of the amendment to Article 10 of the Covenant would be premature, since this quesquestion is closely allied to that of the Treaty of Guarantee. If effect were given to the idea of the Treaty of Guarantee, this might involve certain modifications in Article 10 of the Covenant, and in that case alone would it be possible, when all the facts are known, for amendments to be proposed and adopted, with a view to bringing out more clearly the true signification of Article 10, having regard, on the one hand, to the effectiveness of the guarantee provided and, on the other hand, to the nature of the obligations imposed by the Treaty of Guarantee.

Reply from Sweden

The Sweden Government does not share the opinion as to the legal interpretation of Article 10 on which the Canadian proposal is based. In its opinion, no Member of the League of Nations is, at present, obliged to conform to a recommendation of the Council to intervene by force of arms in any conflict, independently of the question whether parliamentary authorisation for such intervention may be necessary under the constitution of the State in question. The obligation of Members of the League to take punitive steps is fully defined in Article 16 of the Covenant. If this point of view is accepted, the Canadian proposal would not constitute any fundamental modification of Article 10.

As the Draft Treaty of Mutual Guarantee is at present under consideration by the competent organs of the League of Nations, and the realisation of the idea of such a treaty may render necessary other amendments to Article 10, the Swedish Government considers that it would be preferable to defer consideration of the Canadian proposal until later.

ANNEX IV

EXTRACTS FROM THE REPLIES OF CERTAIN GOVERNMENTS REGARDING RESOLUTIONS XIV OF THE THIRD ASSEMBLY[1]

Reply from Belgium

It is open to question whether the conditions essential to render a treaty of mutual guarantee effective can be combined in a general treaty. In the opinion of experts, such a treaty would have to be one which could be executed immediately, it would have to provide complete assistance, both military, economic and financial, would have to include a pre-arranged plan, incorporated in the treaty itself, and would have to be periodically supervised and revised.

It would not appear possible in practice for a general treaty of guarantee to comply with these conditions and "to provide immediate and effective assistance in accordance with a pre-ar-

[1] Reprinted from *Minutes, Third Committee*, Fourth Assembly.

ranged plan" so as to afford really effective aid in case of attack. Moreover, the impossibility of foreseeing the nature and extent of the hostilities which may break out, and the value and nature of the assistance to be afforded in each by the guarantor States, the inevitable slowness with which the machinery of mutual assistance would be set in motion—all these factors make it impossible to estimate with any degree of accuracy the securities afforded to each individual signatory State of a general defensive treaty, or to determine the consequent extent to which armaments could be reduced.

The Belgian Government recognises that, in order to be fully effective, any plan for the reduction of armaments must be general; it believes, however, that this result can only be attained step by step, by means of partial defensive treaties concluded between States which are exposed to common danger; these treaties would be designed so as to be capable of gradual extension and and would be open to other countries without reservation as to specific conditions, and would, after conclusion, lead to a reduction of armaments by stages. Those small States which are weakest and most exposed can in this respect merely follow the example of the great Powers, which should precede them on the path of disarmament.

Partial treaties and regional agreements, however, do not by any means present to the same degree the difficulties inherent in a general treaty. The possibilities of conflicts are less numerous, the preparation of schemes of defence is easier, the actual assistance can be furnished much more rapidly, the value of such assistance can readily be determined, and, consequently, the extent to which armaments are to be reduced can be fixed in proportion to the securities afforded by the treaties, and the reduction can follow immediately upon their entry into force. Moreover, such partial treaties would not appear to be in any way incompatible with a general treaty defining and fixing the general obligations laid down in Articles 10 and 16 of the Covenant of the League of Nations.

The Belgian Government is glad to note that special measures are provided for the defence of countries which, "for historical, geographical or other reasons" are in special danger of attack.

Reply from Canada

The Canadian Government strongly favours a general policy of reduction of armaments as suggested in Resolution XIV, and is willing to consider any proposal tending to the achievement of such an aim; but with regard to the adoption of a treaty of Mutual Guarantee binding the parties to it to render assistance to a country which is attacked, the peculiar national conditions and geographical situation of the Dominion make it difficult for Canada to agree to such a Treaty without much consideration and reservation. It is intended that the obligation to render assistance shall be limited in principle to those countries situated in the same part of the globe. While Canada is situated in the North American continent, she is a nation forming part of the British Empire, and it seems difficult to devise a scheme which would give due effect to these conflicting considerations. In any case, it seems very unlikely that the Canadian people, in the present circumstances, would pe prepared to consent to any agreement binding Canada to give assistance as proposed to other nations, and the Government therefore does not see its way to a participation in the Treaty of Mutual Guarantee.

Reply from Czechoslovakia

The Government of the Czechoslovak Republic fully agrees with the principles laid down in Resolution No. XIV adopted by Third Assembly of the League of Nations.

Since, under present political conditions, the desired confidence between two States does not exist in a sufficient measure—a fact which was recognised even by the Third Committee of the 1922 Assembly—the Czechoslovak Government is of opinion that only the conclusion of a Treaty of Mutual Guarantee in the form of partial treaties designed to be extended and open to other countries could, under present circumstances, be attempted with any hope of success.

A clear definition of the term "aggression," taking into account all possible eventualities, is of the utmost importance. The criterion chosen, *i. e.*, violation of territory would appear too simple, as the experiences gained during the last war have shown.

The "political and military machinery" necessary to ensure the execution of the stipulations of a Treaty of Guarantee should be such that the measures provided for are capable of actual realisation. That would not seem to be the case, since it is provided that the Council should decide by a three-fourths majority within a period of four days from the day on which an appeal has been submitted to the League of Nations which State should be considered the aggressor.

REPLY FROM DENMARK

Points 2 and 3, which are the fundamental principles of the Draft, are based on the conception that States having reduced their armaments must be afforded a new guarantee, for which provision has not been made in the Covenant, and that this guarantee should consist of defensive alliances established between countries situated in the same part of the globe.

The members of the Danish Delegation do not in any way desire to ignore the great difficulties which various States will encounter in bringing about an effective reduction of their armaments, but they consider that these difficulties can in no sense absolve States from the clear and unconditional obligations imposed upon them by Article 8 of the Covenant, which prescribes a reduction of armaments, without affording States which have agreed to this reduction any guarantee or security apart from that already afforded by the provisions of the Covenant itself, and, in particular, by Articles 10, 11 and 16.

If we adopt the principle, embodied in Lord Robert Cecil's new proposals, that any reduction of armaments necessarily presupposes a guarantee of another kind, not only shall we *ipso facto* recognise the principle that present-day armaments are justified so long as no guarantee of another kind exists—a point of view which the Danish Delegation considers dangerous and contrary to the meaning of Article 8 of the Covenant—but we shall also be greatly under-estimating the importance, and, consequently, diminishing the value of the provisions of guarantee in the Covenant, which its authors considered adequate to permit of an effective reduction of armaments.

* * * * *

The policy which Denmark has long pursued, and which she has always held to be necessary to preserve the existence and independence of the country, has been a policy of impartial neutrality, for she sought her international guarantee rather in the development of law than in armed force.

If Denmark, when she entered the League of Nations and adhered to Articles 10, 11, 16 and 17 of the Covenant, undertook certain obligations which do not entirely accord with her conception of neutrality, in the generally accepted meaning of the word, it was because she originally supposed that the League of Nations would very shortly include all the countries of the world, or at any rate all countries of any considerable political or military importance. It is therefore evident that small States are in a very difficult position to-day when confronted with the question of defensive alliances involving far greater military commitments than those provided for in Article 16 of the Covenant. These difficulties are obviously increased by the fact that the League of Nations is still so far from being universal that great military and political States like the United States of America, Germany and Russia are not yet members.

Under these conditions it would be very dangerous for a State like Denmark, with its limited resources, to adhere to a system of military alliances which might conceivably be utilised to counterbalance the opposing policies of great Powers. It is in fact impossible at the present time to foresee what would be the consequences for Denmark of obligations of this character.

Might not a system of groups of defensive military alliances within the League also contain the germ of fresh conflicts of interest and fresh controversy? Even if all the Members of the League entered into these alliances, the result would be at least to weaken that community of interest which it was desired to establish between all Members of the League. But we have also to reckon with the very strong possibility that certain Members of the League would be willing to accept the new obligations while others would prefer to keep to the present provisions of the Covenant. The result might be to produce a serious split, by ranging Members of the League which belonged to defensive alliances against other Members which did not belong to these alliances, and the situation might cause the whole framework of the League of Nations to collapse. We should thereby bring about the continuance of military alliances and strengthen the position of those very coalitions which it was one of the principal aims of the League to abolish.

Reply from France

.... These points being clear, the general survey which the Government of the Republic has made of this question, both from a political and a technical point of view, has led it to the following conclusions:

(1) The reductions of armaments contemplated by Resolution XIV can only be accepted in exchange for external support which must be of the same effective value and available with the same rapidity. This leads to the conclusion that:

(a) Mutual assistance involves *the preparation* explicitly indicated in paragraph 3 of the Resolution.

(b) The assistance in question will nevertheless depend, even at the best, on certain factors of a partly speculative character, so that no country can consider itself relieved of the duty of being able to provide for its security, in case of necessity, by means of its own resources.

(c) Any attempt to lay down a scale of armaments *a priori* must be abandoned.

(d) Lastly, reductions of armaments must always take place as a sequel to the measures adopted for mutual assistance and can in no case precede those measures.

(2) As regards the method known as that of the general treaty, the Government of the Republic considers that such a treaty would exercise a favourable influence on the maintainance of peace but would, of itself, only furnish security of a doubtful and indeterminate character and would thus be unlikely to lead to a more rapid or more complete reduction of armaments than has already been carried out by the majority of Governments during the last four years.

(3) A consideration of the second method, known as that of partial treaties, has persuaded the Government of the Republic that military assistance, pre-arranged by means of definite conventions between the States which are exposed to one or more common dangers, might justify a reduction of their armaments in peace time.

(4) The Government of the Republic is of opinion that the object aimed at by the Assembly cannot be attained by the *exclusive* choice and application of either of these methods and that the best solution would be to combine, in a general conven-

tion, two forms of mutual assistance corresponding to the condtions of modern war and to the diversity of the problems confronting the different States. These forms of assistance would be:
(a) For those States which desire it, *immediate military* assistance, becoming operative up to a certain point automatically, to be furnished by partial conventions which would be concluded with special regard to certain specific contingencies and would thus constitute a special machinery for giving effect to the general principal laid down by the Assembly.
(b) For all States, *general, progressive*, and *conditional* assistance, embracing all forms of support (military, economic and financial) to be furnished by means of a *general treaty which would include within its framework the special conventions referred to in the last paragraph.*

REPLY FROM THE NETHERLANDS

The Netherlands Government has given to this extremely important and complex question the full measure of attention which it deserves. It has also sought the opinion of the Advisory Committee on International Law which, after subjecting the Resolution to a very careful examination, has expressed its opinion in a report dated April 4th, 1923, a French translation of which is attached to the present letter. The Committee arrived at the conclusion that the treaties of guarantee contemplated by the Resolution would not be in accordance with the principles of the Covenant and would conflict with the normal development of the League of Nations.

* * * * *

If, as regards protection which the League of Nations gives to its Members, the present situation does not fulfil the hopes which were entertained, and if States do not regard the guarantee afforded by the League as sufficiently effective to allow them to reduce their military forces, in accordance with Article 8 of the Covenant, we are driven to ask what is the reason for this state of affairs? Should the blame be attributed solely to the system established by the Covenant? Or should we not rather conclude that, so long as there are Great Powers which are not Members of the League of Nations, the reduction of armaments cannot be of that universal character which is essential for its effective realisation? The Royal Government questions whether we are justified in assuming that universality will be achieved more easily or more rapidly by means of Treaties of Guarantee than by the agency of the League of Nations. And until it has been achieved, is there any reason to conclude that a Treaty of Guarantee, such as is contemplated in the Assembly's Resolution, will lead to that reduction of armaments which the system established by the Covenant seems unable to realise? The Royal Government cannot refrain from entertaining serious doubt on this matter.

* * * * *

The Royal Government desires, however, at this early stage, to point out that it would feel great hesitation in joining in a system of military co-operation which did not provide the necessary legal guarantees that the assistance to be given shall only be granted to States in a position to claim it rightfully. According to the system established by the Covenent, it is the violation of the Covenant which sets the machinery for penalties in motion. What guarantees are there in the system recommended in the Resolution to ensure that collective action will not serve other ends than those of right and justice? The Royal Government fears that the legal guarantees, which are already too vaguely set forth in the Covenant—a fact which has hitherto prevented the organisation of collective action to resist aggression—are lacking, or are present in a less effective form, in the system recommended by the Assembly's Resolution.

* * * * *

As regards the partial Treaties of Guarantee indicated in the Resolution, the Royal Government is of opinion that, by adopting this system, the League of Nations would sanction a return to the system of military alliances which, so far from ensuring peace, have in the past been a contributary cause in inducing States to increase their armaments. It would be a retrograde step, contrary to the ideal of the League of Nations, and disastrous to future international organisation. The Royal Government could not give its support to such a scheme.

Reply of Norway

The Norwegian Government nevertheless desires to draw attention to the fact that a Treaty of Guarantee, implying an absolute obligation to afford military assistance in certain contingencies, would go further than the Covenant of the League of Nations, since, according to the latter, participation in military action is subject to the consent of each Member. When the question of the adhesion of Norway to the League of Nations was decided, great importance was attached to the fact that each Member was free to decide for itself whether it would or would not participate in military action, and a treaty, which in this respect would involve greater obligations than the Covenant, would inevitably give rise to most serious misgivings.

The Norwegian Government desires to point out that, according to Article 8 of the Covenant of the League of Nations, the Members of the League are bound to endeavour to secure a general reduction of armaments, even without any other guarantees than those laid down at the time when the League was founded. It cannot be admitted, therefore, that the reduction of armaments can be subordinated to a Treaty of Mutual Guarantee; such a treaty can only be considered as one of several means of securing a reduction of armaments. The Norwegian Government cannot, therefore, share the view, which appears to be expressed in the letter from the President of the Council of the League dated October 23rd last, that a reduction of armaments can only be obtained by means of a treaty of guarantee. The Norwegian Government holds the view that the most effective guarantee of peace would consist in the actual reduction of armaments, and in the development of the system provided for in the Covenant for the solution of international disputes, and not in international sanctions of a military character which might be attached thereto.

* * * * *

As regards the preparation of a treaty of guarantee, I should like to draw attention to the dangers which, in the Norwegian Government's view, might result from the conclusion of regional agreements, when such agreements refer not only to the regional reduction of armaments but also to a regional guarantee. My

Government is of opinion that only one treaty of guarantee should be concluded, and that all States should be free to adhere to it, whether Members of the League or not.

The Royal Government further desires to point out that the treaty should take the form of a continuation of the system laid down in the Covenant for the peaceful solution of international disputes, and not that of a treaty intended to supersede or abolish the Covenant. In order to enable a State to benefit by a guarantee, there should be a preliminary assurance that that State, in the conduct of its foreign policy, will be guided by the principles upon which the Covenant of the League of Nations is based.

Reply from Poland

Final Observations

Our examination of the problem of disarmament and guarantees leads us to formulate the following proposals for the pacification of international relations, as far as present circumstances permit.

(a) Inter-State military guarantees can be effective only within the radius of the direct common interests of individual States or groups of States. This community of interests is the foundation of all associations, and constitutes a live and genuine guarantee.

(b) As a basis for its own reductions, every State must primarily consider the reductions in the forces of enemy countries which are its immediate neighbours. It would therefore be desirable to conclude regional agreements for the reduction of armaments between neighbouring States whose relations are not friendly.

Reply from Venezuela

The Ministry is of opinion that the problem of disarmament obviously affects in a direct manner the great Powers alone. The military organisation of Venezuela, being merely a guarantee if internal security, does not constitute an international danger and is not a heavy burden on the population. The country has no navy whatever, and its artillery force is confined to that required to guarantee national security. The Republic naturally regards with pleasure the reduction of the war effectives of countries in which these are very great, as it considers this reduction to be advantageous to the peace of the world. Guided by such considerations, it adhered to the above-mentioned Convention on the Traffic in Arms and Ammunition signed at Saint-Germain-en-Laye.

* * * * *

Thus the examination of the question from the supremely important point of view of the general good, from which no civilised nation can disassociate itself, leads to the conclusion that it would be desirable and useful for every country to support in principle the adoption of the proposed Treaty of Mutual Guarantee, in view of the fact that this Treaty would protect the country even more effectively from any possible attack upon its independent national existence, and would assist it, with timely and powerful resources, in successfully repelling such an attack. This is a consideration apart from the undeniable proof of moral rectitude which adherence to such an admirable instrument would provide.

But as Venezuela is, in fact, without a large army or fleet, she would be giving an undertaking of no practical utility, since she could not, if occasion arose, fulfil the obligations imposed upon her by the Treaty.

The Government has therefore the honour to observe that it views the idea of the Treaty with the highest satisfaction, though it is obliged in due frankness to point out that, for the foregoing reasons, it would be almost impossible for the Republic to fulfil the essential clauses of the Treaty. It is therefore bound to decline what it can only regard as an honour: that of becoming a party to this Treaty and thereby contributing to the maintenance of international peace.

ANNEX V

TEXT OF THE DRAFT TREATY OF MUTUAL ASSISTANCE[1]

Preamble

The High Contracting Parties, being desirous of establishing the general lines of a scheme of mutual assistance with a view to facilitate the application of Articles 10 and 16 of the Covenant of the League of Nations, and of a reduction or limitation of national armaments in accordance with Article 8 of the Covenant "to the lowest point consistent with national safety and the enforcement by common action of international obligations," agree to the following provisions:

I. Pact of Nonaggression

Article 1

The High Contracting Parties solemnly declare that aggressive war is an international crime and severally undertake that no one of them will be guilty of its commission.

A war shall not be considered as a war of aggression if waged by a State which is party to a dispute and has accepted the unanimous recommendation of the Council, the verdict of the Permanent Court of International Justice, or an arbitral award against a High Contracting Party which has not acecpted it, provided, however, that the first State does not intend to violate the political independence or the territorial integrity of the High Contracting Party.

II. General Assistance

Article 2

The High Contracting Parties, jointly and severally, undertake to furnish assistance, in accordance with the provisions of the present Treaty, to any one of their number should the latter be the object of a war of aggression, provided that it has conformed to the provisions of the present Treaty regarding the reduction or limitation of armaments.

[1] Reprinted from World Peace Foundation Pamphlet, VII, No. 8.

Article 3

Menace of Aggression

In the event of one of the High Contracting Parties being of opinion that the armaments of any other High Contracting Party are in excess of the limits fixed for the latter High Contracting Party under the provisions of the present Treaty, or in the event of it having cause to apprehend an outbreak of hostilities, either on account of the aggressive policy or preparations of any State party or not to the present Treaty, it may inform the Secretary-General of the League of Nations that it is threatened with aggression, and the Secretary-General shall forthwith summon the Council.

The Council, if it is of opinion that there is reasonable ground for thinking that a menace of aggression has arisen, may take all necessary measures to remove such menace, and in particular, if the Council thinks right, those indicated in sub-paragraphs (*a*), (*b*), (*c*), (*d*) and (*e*) of the second paragraph of Article 5 of the present Treaty.

The High Contracting Parties which have been denounced and those which have stated themselves to be the object of a threat of aggression shall be considered as especially interested and shall therefore be invited to send representatives to the Council in conformity with Articles 4, 15 and 17 of the Covenant. The vote of their representatives shall, however, not be reckoned when calculating unanimity.

Article 4

Hostilities

In the event of one or more of the High Contracting Parties becoming engaged in hostilities, the Council of the League of Nations shall decide, within four days of notification being addressed to the Secretary-General, which of the High Contracting Parties are the objects of aggression and whether they are entitled to claim the assistance provided under the Treaty.

The High Contracting Parties undertake that they will accept such a decision by the Council of the League of Nations.

The High Contracting Parties engaged in hostilities shall be regarded as especially interested, and shall therefore be invited to send representatives to the Council (within the terms of Articles 4, 13 and 17 of the Covenant), the vote of their representative not being reckoned when calculating unanimity; the same shall apply to States signatory to any partial agreements involved on behalf of either of the two belligerents, unless the remaining Members of the Council shall decide otherwise.

ARTICLE 5

Measures of Assistance

The High Contracting Parties undertake to furnish one another mutually with assistance in the case referred to in Article 2 of the Treaty in the form determined by the Council of the League of Nations as the most effective, and to take all appropriate measures without delay in the order of urgency demanded by the circumstances.

In particular, the Council may:

(a) decide to apply immediately to the aggressor State the economic sanctions contemplated by Article 16 of the Covenant, the Members of the League not signatory to the present Treaty not being, however, bound by this decision, except in the case where the State attacked is entitled to avail itself of the Articles of the Covenant;

(b) invoke by name the High Contracting Parties whose assistance it requires. No High Contracting Party situated in a continent other than that in which operations will take place shall, in principle, be required to co-operate in military, naval or air operations;

(c) determine the forces which each State furnishing assistance shall place at its disposal;

(d) prescribe all necessary measures for securing priority for the communications and transport connected with the operations;

(e) prepare a plan for financial co-operation among the High Contracting Parties with a view to providing for the State attacked and for the States furnishing assistance the funds which they require for the operations;

(f) appoint the Higher Command and establish the object and the nature of his duty.

The representatives of States recognized as aggressors under the provisions of Article 4 of the Treaty shall not take part in the deliberations of the Council specified in this Article. The High Contracting Parties who are required by the Council to furnish assistance, in accordance with subparagraph (*b*), shall, on the other hand, be considered as especially interested, and, as such, shall be invited to send representatives, unless they are already represented, to the deliberations specified in subparagraphs (*c*), (*d*), (*e*) and (*f*).

III. COMPLEMENTARY DEFENSIVE AGREEMENTS

ARTICLE 6

For the purpose of rendering the general assistance mentioned in Articles 2, 3 and 5 immediately effective, the High Contracting Parties may conclude, either as between two of them or as between a larger number, agreements complementary to the present Treaty exclusively for the purpose of their mutual defense and intended solely to facilitate the carrying out of the measures prescribed in this Treaty, determining in advance the assistance which they would give to each other in the event of any act of aggression.

Such agreements may, if the High Contracting Parties interested so desire, be negotiated and concluded under the auspices of the League of Nations.

ARTICLE 7

Complementary agreements, as defined in Article 6, shall, before being registered, be examined by the Council with a view to deciding whether they are in accordance with the principles of the Treaty and of the Covenant.

In particular, the Council shall consider if the cases of aggression contemplated in these agreements come within the scope of Article 2 and are of a nature to give rise to an obligation to give assistance on the part of the other High Contracting Parties. The Council may, if necessary, suggest changes in the texts of agreements submitted to it.

When recognized, the agreements shall be registered in conformity with Article 18 of the Covenant. They shall be regarded as complementary to the present Treaty, and shall in no way limit the general obligations of the High Contracting Parties nor the sanctions contemplated against the aggressor State under the terms of this Treaty.

They will be open to any other High Contracting Party with the consent of the signatory States.

ARTICLE 8

The States parties to complementary agreements may undertake in any such agreements to put into immediate execution, in the cases of aggression contemplated in them, the plan of assistance agreed upon. In this case they shall inform the Council of the League of Nations, without delay, concerning the measures which they have taken to ensure the execution of such agreements.

Subject to the terms of the previous paragraph, the provisions of Articles 4 and 5 above shall also come into force both in the cases contemplated in the complementary agreements and in such other cases as are provided for in Article 2 but are not covered by the agreements.

IV. DEMILITARIZED ZONES

ARTICLE 9

In order to facilitate the application of the present Treaty, any High Contracting Party may negotiate, through the agency of the Council, with one or more neighboring countries for the establishment of demilitarized zones.

The Council, with the co-operation of the representatives of the Parties interested, acting as Members within the terms of Article 4 of the Covenant, shall previously ensure that the establishment of the demilitarized zone asked for does not call for unilateral sacrifices from the military point of view on the part of the High Contracting Parties interested.

V. COST OF INTERVENTION

ARTICLE 10

The High Contracting Parties agree that the whole cost of any military, naval or air operations which are undertaken under the terms of the present Treaty and of the supplementary partial agreements, including the reparation of all material damage caused by operations of war, shall be borne by the aggressor State up to the extreme limits of its financial capacity.

The amount payable under this article by the aggressor shall, to such an extent as may be determined by the Council of the League, be a first charge on the whole of the assets and revenues of the State. Any repayment by that State in respect of the principal money and interest of any loan, internal or external, issued by it, directly or indirectly, during the war shall be suspended until the amount due for cost and reparations is discharged in full.

VI. Disarmament
Article 11

The High Contracting Parties, in view of the security furnished them by this Treaty and the limitations to which they have consented in other international treaties, undertake to inform the Council of the League of the reduction or limitation of armaments which they consider proportionate to the security furnished by the general Treaty or by the defensive agreements complementary to the general Treaty.

The High Contracting Parties undertake to co-operate in the preparation of any general plan of reduction of armaments which the Council of the League of Nations, taking into account the information provided by the High Contracting Parties, may propose under the terms of Article 8 of the Covenant.

This plan should be submitted for consideration and approved by the Governments, and, when approved by them, will be the basis of the reduction contemplated in Article 2 of this Treaty.

The High Contracting Parties undertake to carry out this reduction within a period of two years from the date of the adoption of this plan.

The High Contracting Parties undertake, in accordance with the provisions of Article 8, paragraph 4, of the Covenant, to make no further increase in their armaments, when thus reduced, without the consent of the Council.

Article 12

The High Contracting Parties undertake to furnish to the military or other delegates of the League such information with regard to their armaments as the Council may request.

Article 13

The High Contracting Parties agree that the armaments determined for each of them, in accordance with the present Treaty, shall be subject to revision every five years, beginning from the date of the entry into force of this Treaty.

VII. Protocol

Article 14

Maintenance of Existing Treaties

Nothing in the present Treaty shall affect the rights and obligations resulting from the provisions of the Covenant of the League of Nations or of the Treaties of Peace signed in 1919 and 1920 at Versailles, Neuilly, St. Germain and Trianon, or from the provisions of treaties or agreements registered with the League of Nations and published by it at the date of the first coming into force of the present Treaty as regards the signatory or beneficiary Powers of the said treaties or agreements.

Article 15

Compulsory Jurisdiction of the Court

The High Contracting Parties recognize from to-day as *ipso facto* obligatory the jurisdiction of the Permanent Court of International Justice with regard to the interpretation of the present Treaty.

Article 16

Signature

The present Treaty shall remain open for the signature of all States Members of the League of Nations or mentioned in the Annex to the Covenant.

States not Members shall be entitled to adhere with the consent of two-thirds of the High Contracting Parties with regard to whom the Treaty has come into force.

Article 17

Partial Adhesion

Any State may, with the consent of the Council of the League, notify its conditional or partial adherence to the provisions of this Treaty, provided always that such State has reduced or is prepared to reduce its armaments in conformity with the provisions of this Treaty.

Article 18

Ratification

[The present Treaty shall be ratified and the instruments of ratification shall be deposited as soon as possible at the Secretariat of the League of Nations.

It shall come into force:

In Europe when it shall have been ratified by five States, of which three shall be permanently represented on the Council;

In Asia when it shall have been ratified by two States, one of which shall be permanently represented on the Council;

In North America when ratified by the United States of America;

In Central America and the West Indies when ratified by one State in the West Indies and two in Central America;

In South America when ratified by four States;

In Africa and Oceania when ratified by two States.

With regard to the High Contracting Parties which may subsequently ratify the Treaty, it will come into force at the date of the deposit of the instrument.

The Secretariat will immediately communicate a certified copy of the instruments of ratification received to all the signatory Powers.

It remains understood that the rights stipulated under Articles 2, 3, 5, 6 and 8 of this Treaty will not come into force for each High Contracting Party until the Council has certified that the said High Contracting Party has reduced its armaments in conformity with the present Treaty or has adopted the necessary measures to ensure the execution of this reduction, within two years of the acceptance by the said High Contracting Party of the plan of reduction or limitation of armaments.]

Article 19

Denunciation

[The present Treaty shall remain in force for a period of fifteen years from the date of its first entry into force.

After this period, it will be prolonged automatically for the States which have not denounced it.

If, however, one of the States referred to in Article 18 denounces the present Treaty, the Treaty shall cease to exist as from the date on which this denunciation takes effect.

This denunciation shall be made to the Secretariat of the League of Nations, which shall, without delay, notify all the Powers bound by the present Treaty.

The denunciation shall take effect twelve months after the date on which notification has been communicated to the Secretariat of the League of Nations.

When the period of fifteen years referred to in the first paragraph of the present Article has elapsed, or when one of the denunciations made in the conditions determined above takes place, if operations undertaken in application of Article 5 of the present Treaty are in progress, the Treaty shall remain in force until peace has been completely re-established.]

ANNEX VI

EXTRACTS FROM THE REPLIES OF CERTAIN GOVERNMENTS ON THE DRAFT TREATY OF MUTUAL ASSISTANCE SUBMITTED BY THE FOURTH ASSEMBLY[1]

REPLY FROM THE BRITISH GOVERNMENT

Out of the twenty-six nations whose replies are published with the report of the Temporary Mixed Commission, only a very small number are able to express unqualified acceptance of Resolution XIV adopted at the third session of the Assembly, which forms the basis of the reports now under consideration. The objections to the various proposals for treaties of mutual guarantee or assistance which have been considered by the League are to be found in the report of the Third Committee itself, as well as in the reports of experts and the opinions of Governments included in the documents circulated to Members of the League. From these detailed criticisms there emerge certain objections of principle which up to the present time do not appear to have been adequately met.

[1] Reprinted from *Minutes, Third Committee*, Fifth Assembly.

The main criticisms of the proposed treaty fall under two heads, which may be expressed in an interrogative form: Are the guarantees contained therein sufficient to justify a State in reducing its armaments? Are the obligations to be undertaken towards other States of such a nature that the nations of the world can conscientiously engage to carry them out?

In regard to the first group of criticisms, it is generally conceded that if a treaty of mutual assistance is to prove effective in bringing about a reduction of armaments, its stipulations must be such that the parties thereto can assume with absolute confidence not only that in the contingencies for which it provides it will be brought into operation with certainty, but also that it will effectually accomplish its purpose.

The effectiveness of the scheme will be seen to depend to a considerable extent on the ability of the Council of the League to determine, by unanimous vote of all Members not concerned in the dispute, which nation is the aggressor. This difficult question has to be settled within a period of four days from the notification of hostilities to the Secretary-General. It is unnecessary here to deal at length with the difficulties which might confront the Council in reaching agreement on such a point within the stipulated time, or the likelihood that unanimity might never be reached at all on a really controversial issue, since these considerations are fully discussed in the documents circulated to the various Governments. In this connection, the "commentary on the definition of a 'case of aggression'," drawn up by a Special Committee of the Temporary Mixed Commission, in collaboration with certain technical members of the Permanent Advisory Commission, is of great interest. The commentary does not provide a solution of the difficulty. It is stated therein more than once that no satisfactory definition of what constitutes an "act of aggression" could be drawn up. Consequently, the report does not provide that element of certainty and reliability which is essential if the League of Nations is to recommend the adoption of the treaty by its Members as a basis for reduction in armaments.

Another important objection of principle is the long delay which is liable to occur before the forces at the disposal of the League of Nations can be brought into effective operation against an aggressor State. It is not until after the determination by the

Council of the question which State is the aggressor, which is likely to occupy the whole of the four days permitted by the draft Treaty, that the Council can begin to take the necessary steps for bringing pressure, whether military or economic, to bear on the aggressor. Economic pressure is admittedly slow in operation. As regards military pressure, all the technical experts who have advised the organs of the League on the subject are agreed that no military assistance can be considered immediate and effective unless it be given in accordance with a pre-arranged plan. It is obvious, however, and was recognised by the Third Committee of the Fourth Assembly, that in the case of a general treaty of assistance plans can rarely be pre-arranged. They would therefore have to be drawn up, after the question which was the aggressor State had been determined, by the naval, military or air officers designated by the Council of the League to command the international forces. The experience of the recent world-war does not justify the assumption that where the forces of several nations are involved the immediate acceptance, much less the rapid execution, of plans of operations can with certainty be counted on. The possibility will always exist that the States most favourably situated for providing the necessary force may at a given moment not be in a position to do so, owing to commitments elsewhere, the State of public opinion, or the political condition of the country at the time. The appointment of the higher command will itself involve delay. The Council will have great difficulty in reaching a unanimous decision, for no nation places its troops under a foreign command without very careful considerations. A system which involves prolonged delays before the first step in bringing military pressure to bear on an aggressor nation can be taken does not reach that standard of effectiveness which is essential.

The necessary measures to carry the general guarantees into effect are, moreover, made dependent upon the explicit consent of each individual State which may be called upon to render assistance as a permanent or *ad hoc* Member of the Council. This consideration can but strengthen His Majesty's Government in the view that the guarantee afforded by the draft Treaty is so precarious that no responsible Government will feel justified in consenting to any material reduction of its armaments in return. If, as His Majesty's Government feel convinced, this is the case, the whole object of the Treaty is lost and its conclusion is objectless. His Majesty's Government, indeed, go further. They are persuaded, after careful examination of the draft scheme, that, if the obligations created by the Treaty be scrupulously carried out, they will involve an increase rather than a decrease in British armaments. The report of the Temporary Mixed Commission for 1922 stated that, "in the case of armed assistance, certain forces, such as aircraft and warships, are the most readily available and therefore the most likely to be asked for and to be effective in the initial stages of the war." It is the considered opinion of the British Naval Staff that a treaty such as is proposed will, if properly carried out, necessitate an increase in the British naval forces. His Majesty's Government cannot avoid the belief that the position will be the same in other countries.

It was owing to the recognition of the defects inherent in any general treaty of mutual assistance that the proposal was made to super-impose on a general treaty a system of partial treaties between groups of countries. It has been urged against such partial treaties that their conclusion by one group of States is likely to bring about the formation of competing groups, and that the result will be a reappearance of the former system of alliances and counter-alliances, which in the past has proved such a serious menace to the peace of the world. The proposal to meet this objection by bringing the partial treaties under the control of the League does not overcome the difficulty, particularly so long as important nations remain outside the League, and His Majesty's Government cannot but recognise the force of the above criticism.

A further objection to the scheme for partial treaties to be embodied in the Treaty of Mutual Assistance is the opening that would be afforded for conflict between the Council of the League and individual Governments. Under Article 4 of the draft Treaty it will be the duty of the Council to decide which of two belligerents is the aggressor. Under Article 8, States parties to a partial treaty will be at liberty to decide the point for themselves, before it is decided by the Council. The possibility of disagreement between the Council and States between which a partial treaty is operative is one which cannot be contemplated with equanamity. . . .

The draft Treaty further appears to involve an undesirable

extension of the functions of the Council of the League. Under Article 16 of the Covenant, the Council can only recommend action, while even under Article 10 it can only *advise*. By Article 5 of the draft Treaty, the Council is authorised to decide to adopt various measures. Thus the Council would become an executive body with very large powers, instead of an advisory body. In any event, the Council of the League is a most inappropriate body to be entrusted with the control of military forces in operation against any particular State or States.

* * * * *

His Majesty's Government, therefore, have come to the conclusion that the adoption of the text included in the report of the Third Committee of the Fourth Assembly cannot be recommended. They are, however, far from admitting that the careful study of these questions has been fruitless. The years of patient investigation which have been devoted to this subject by the various organs of the League are themselves a proof of the desire of nations Members of the League to find a solution to the difficult question of reduction and limitation of armaments. This sentiment finds strong expression in practically all the replies of the various nations published with the report of the Temporary Mixed Commission. If this study has not so far resulted in the submission of a draft treaty of mutual assistance in an acceptable form, the reports which have been under consideration nevertheless contain some encouraging and suggestive passages as to other lines of enquiry which might be followed with useful results.

Reply from the Canadian Government

The position of Canada in the British Empire is such that, in spite of the fact that the application of the Treaty to the continent of North America is by its terms conditioned upon its ratification by the United States of America, the question of Canada's adherence to it has a more practical aspect than it would otherwise have. Apart from indications that the Government of the United States of America was likely to find the plan acceptable in principle, Canada has already indicated disapproval of the interpretation of the terms of Article 10 of the Covenant as implying an obligation upon her to intervene actively under that article. The proposed Treaty creates an obligation wider in its extent and more precise in its implications than any which Article 10 could be interpreted as imposing, and it proposes, moreover, to transfer the right to decide upon the scope of the action Canada should take from the Canadian Parliament to the Council of the League of Nations. It is true that, for the purpose of deciding upon the assistance to be given by Canada, the Council would include a Canadian representative and that the draft limits the liability of a signatory in another continent to measures not involving naval, military or air operations. But the presence of a Canadian representative on the Council would hardly compensate for the, at least nominal, transfer of authority, and, again, Canada's position in the British Empire affects the protection afforded her by the continental limitation of which in any event the utility is uncertain since it appears doubtful if hostile action can widely or indeed safely be undertaken by any State upon the principle of limited liability.

REPLY FROM THE CZECHOSLOVAK GOVERNMENT

The Czechoslovak Government considers the idea of the Treaty of Mutual Assistance capable of achieving what the League of Nations desires to achieve. The Czechoslovak Government is not aware, at the moment, of any other means by which this object can be attained and is doubtful if, indeed, other means exist. After full consideration, therefore, it accepts the idea of the Treaty of Mutual Assistance submitted to it for consideration as a basis for further efforts to bring about general disarmament and the security of nations. It accepts it as a basis, but is at the same time prepared to abandon it directly any plan is presented that is easier of realisation, more effective in result, and less open to objections than this draft Treaty. The Czechoslovak Government itself recognises these objections.

* * * * *

There is, in the first place, in the opinion of the Czechoslovak Government, a question of principle which should be further considered: in the case of aggression, the Council of the League would have to decide by unanimous vote which party is responsible for the aggression and what measures are to be taken against such party. Without considering the principle underlying this question, including the necessity of respecting the sovereignty of

States in matters of such importance, the Czechoslovak Government is in favour, in such cases, of applying the principle of a majority vote pure and simple. It ventures, therefore, to submit reservations in regard to the article in question.

* * * * *

There are certain general observations which inevitably occur to all those who, responsible to their country and to international public opinion, do not wish to treat lightly questions of such importance and are endeavoring to approach the very heart of the proposal submitted to us. From this point of view, the Czechoslovak Government has followed with the closest attention all official and unofficial expressions of opinion in the various countries regarding the question of the Treaty of Mutual Assistance and disarmament.

There is, in the first place, one important and serious objection to the principle upon which the whole text of the Treaty is based: that is, the interdependence between security and the progressive reduction of armaments. This principle signifies, indeed, that there shall be no reduction of armaments except in proportion to the security furnished to any State attacked by the guarantee of the other States.

The following objection immediately arises: Does not the Covenant in Article 8 simply and unconditionally impose upon all the Members of the League the obligation to proceed to the reduction of armaments?

The Czechoslovak Government considers that such an interpretation of the Covenant is entirely wrong. It is of opinion that Article 8 must necessarily be supplemented by Articles 10 and 16, that one cannot be applied without the other, and that Articles 10 and 16 express simply and solely the idea of security which, in the draft Treaty in question, is still further accentuated and transferred, so to speak, from the theoretical plane of the Covenant into the practical sphere of the Treaty of Mutual Assistance.

It has been said, and rightly said, that the Treaty of Mutual Assistance is "an extension of the Covenant." I would say, further, *it is the putting into concrete, practical form of the Covenant*, and more especially of Articles 10 and 16. Finally, it appears to me that the idea of interdependence between security and the reduction of armaments is essentially inherent in the Covenant and entirely in keeping with its spirit. The Czechoslovak Government has never interpreted those articles of the Covenant in any other manner.

If, therefore, the Council of the League and the Assembly are endeavoring to put into practice the principles of the Covenant, they can only follow the method indicated by the principles expressed in the Treaty of Mutual Assistance, that is to say, they can only put into force the idea of disarmament, by developing at the same time the principles contained in Articles 10 and 16.

The Czechoslovak Government cannot conceal the fact that a certain amount of anxiety has for some time past been apparent in public opinion in its country. Public opinion in Czechoslovak has not failed to note that for the last two years repeated attempts have been made in the League of Nations to reduce the importance of Article 10, to lessen its significance to the point of rendering it ineffective in the event of any real threat of aggression against a smaller country. I rather fear that these tendencies led to more or less positive results during the Fourth Assembly.

I venture to add that such tendencies appear to me contrary to the spirit of the Covenant and, in such a case, to the Covenant itself; the League of Nations would thereby lose much of its value and its real moral importance, and the very basis of the League would be jeopardised.

The Czechoslovak Government was therefore delighted to see the opposite tendency developing, the tendency to enhance the importance of the great principle of the Covenant contained in Article 10.

REPLY FROM THE GERMAN GOVERNMENT

If we really wish to promote that realisation of disarmament, of such essential import to the League of Nations, we must not follow the lines laid down in the new Draft Treaty. They are lines which neither touch nor run parallel with the principles of the Covenant but which diverge further and further from them. Only an organic development of the Covenant can bring success—not a heterogeneous adjunct thereto. What we need is not an accumulation of treaties and agreements side by side with the Covenant but an intensification and refinement of the Covenant itself. This development cannot be achieved by opposing force to force. Illegal force will only be driven from the world by opposing it with justice whereby the force employed to meet injustice will be justified and hallowed. Forbid the forcible settlement of disputes; forbid the forcible attempt to obtain one's supposed rights altogether. Interdict all special agreements which shelve or contravene the general treaty. Remove all hindrances left by former treaties. Side by side with the Court of International Justice for purely legal disputes, create a court of arbitration for political conflicts and endow it with every guarantee for the juridical independence of its members. Decree compulsory adherence thereto as well as to the Permanent Court of International Justice. Endow both courts with the right and the duty to issue provisional injunctions *uti possidetis*, especially in reference to the ostensibly peaceful occupation of foreign territory. Appoint an organ which shall oppose the peace-breaker with the weight of the League of Nations in order to carry into effect the degrees and all other decisions of the Court of Arbitration and of the Court of International Justice. Above all, make disarmament obligatory upon all nations. Finally, see to it that the justified wishes of the population for an adjustment of frontiers be met by means of properly regulated legal procedure. Remember that development never ends, and that, unless you wish it to find vent on some violent eruption, you must not make the bootless attempt to curb and enclose it. No, we must give it free progress along the lines of right and justice. So, and only so, will it be possible to provide the premises for the vigorous efficacy of the League of Nations; so, and only so, to create the possibility of an energetic growth of its authority; so, and only so, to prepare the way for that universality of its membership without which it will never be able to fulfil its great task. Then Germany, too, would no longer need to hesitate whether she should, on condition of equality of rights, enter the community of nations united in the League and to co-operate in the maintenance of peace on the footing of justice and righteousness.

REPLY FROM THE ITALIAN GOVERNMENT

With reference to the conclusion of partial and regional agreements, the Royal Government shares the misgivings which were authoritatively expressed in the course of the preparatory work on the draft. It fears that, so far from furthering, they may jeopardise the operation of the general treaty as a means of securing peace.

As regards the provisions of Article 4 of the draft Treaty, to the effect that, in the event of hostilities, the Council of the League of Nations will determine within four days which of the High Contracting Parties is the victim of aggression and will accordingly set the machinery of the guarantee in motion against the aggressor, the Royal Government feels bound to express the opinion that in most cases it will be extremely difficult, if not impossible, for the Council to decide, within the brief period allowed, which party is the aggressor and which the victim; for it is not easy to define what either in law or in fact constitutes aggression.

Reply from the Japanese Government

The Japanese Government fully appreciates the spirit which animates the draft Treaty of Mutual Assistance. It accepts the fundamental principle that security and disarmament are interdependent. Accordingly, it has examined in the most sympathetic spirit the draft Treaty in the light of the present situation in Japan and in the world as a whole. It ventures, however, to submit a few remarks on the measures proposed.

It considers that the provisions of Article 4 form the basis for putting in motion the machinery of mutual assistance and that they are the fundamental conditions on which the possibility of attaining our common end, the reduction of armaments, depends. It is of opinion, however, that it will be difficult in practice for the Council to give a precise definition of aggression and to decide within so short a period which is the aggressor State.

It also considers that the arguments against supplementary agreements are not entirely devoid of foundation since such agreements might easily lead to the formation of opposing groups even among the Members of the League of Nations and might thus produce a result entirely different from that which we are endeavouring to secure.

Reply from the Government of the Kingdom of the Serbs, Croats and Slovenes

In the opinion of this Government, a Treaty of Assistance should be general, at least as regards Europe; further, the measures which it provides should be effective and should guarantee *absolute security* to each signatory State.

The Government is, moreover, of opinion that the general reduction of armaments is *impossible until some practical solution has been found for the problem of assistance*.

Mutual assistance should be absolute and unconditional; it should be immediately effective both as regards time and the forces employed, and it should be founded on the maintenance of the *status quo*. It should come into action automatically and rapidly as soon as the need for it is felt. Unfortunately, these requirements are not sufficiently met by the draft submitted to the Royal Government.

In cases of aggression, the draft provides for a procedure which, in the opinion of the Royal Government, could, in most cases, only be set in motion and could only produce its final result—i. e. the action taken against the aggressor (if any such action follows, for even that is not certain)—slowly and with considerable delay. As any delay would place the aggressor State in a favourable situation as compared with its victim, especially if the latter were a small Power, the effect of intervention would thus be weakened. The State assisted, whose territory would be invaded and laid waste, would have difficulty in repairing the devastation, even if it obtained reparation for the damage caused by the enemy. This has been clearly proved by the example of the *last war*.

In view of the above considerations and without going further into the details of the scheme, the Serb-Croat-Slovene Government feels that it could not entrust its safety to the guarantees provided by the draft.

ANNEX VII

TEXT OF THE PROTOCOL FOR THE PACIFIC SETTLEMENT OF INTERNATIONAL DISPUTES[1]

Animated by the firm desire to insure the maintenance of general peace and the security of nations whose existence, independence or territories may be threatened;

[1] Reprinted from World Peace Foundation Pamphlet, VII, No. 7.

Recognizing the solidarity of the members of the international community;

Asserting that a war of aggression constitutes a violation of this solidarity and an international crime;

Desirous of facilitating the complete application of the system provided in the Covenant of the League of Nations for the pacific settlement of disputes between States and of insuring the repression of international crimes; and

For the purpose of realizing, as contemplated by Article 8 of the Covenant, the reduction of national armaments to the lowest point consistent with national safety and the enforcement by common action of international obligations;

The Undersigned, duly authorized to that effect, agree as follows:

Article 1

The signatory States undertake to make every effort in their power to secure the introduction into the Covenant of amendments on the lines of the provisions contained in the following articles.

They agree that, as between themselves, these provisions shall be binding as from the coming into force of the present Protocol and that, so far as they are concerned, the Assembly and the Council of the League of Nations shall thenceforth have power to exercise all the rights and perform all the duties conferred upon them by the Protocol.

Article 2

The signatory States agree in no case to resort to war either with one another or against a State which, if the occasion arises, accepts all the obligations hereinafter set out, except in case of resistance to acts of aggression or when acting in agreement with the Council or the Assembly of the League of Nations in accordance with the provisions of the Covenant and of the present Protocol.

Article 3

The signatory States undertake to recognize as compulsory, *ipso facto* and without special agreement, the jurisdiction of the Permanent Court of International Justice in the cases covered by paragraph 2 of Article 36 of the Statute of the Court, but without prejudice to the right of any State, when acceding to the special protocol provided for in the said Article and opened for signature on December 16th, 1920, to make reservations compatible with the said clause.

Accession to this special protocol, opened for signature on December 16th, 1920, must be given within the month following the coming into force of the present Protocol.

States which accede to the present Protocol, after its coming into force, must carry out the above obligation within the month following their accession.

Article 4

With a view to render more complete the provisions of paragraphs 4, 5, 6, and 7 of Article 15 of the Covenant, the signatory States agree to comply with the following procedure:

1. If the dispute submitted to the Council is not settled by it as provided in paragraph 3 of the said Article 15, the Council shall endeavor to persuade the parties to submit the dispute to judicial settlement or arbitration.
2. (a) If the parties cannot agree to do so, there shall, at the request of at least one of the parties, be constituted a Committee of Arbitrators. The Committee shall so far as possible be constituted by agreement between the parties.

    (b) If within the period fixed by the Council the parties have failed to agree, in whole or in part, upon the number, the names and the powers of the arbitrators and upon the procedure, the Council shall settle the points remaining in suspense. It shall with the utmost possible dispatch select in consultation with the parties the arbitrators and their President from among persons who by their nationality, their personal character and their experience, appear to it to furnish the highest guarantees of competence and impartiality.

    (c) After the claims of the parties have been formulated, the Committee of Arbitrators, on the request of any party, shall through the medium of the Council request an advisory opinion upon any points of law in dispute from the Permanent Court of International Justice, which in such case shall meet with the utmost possible dispatch.

3. If none of the parties asks for arbitration, the Council shall again take the dispute under consideration. If the Council reaches a report which is unanimously agreed to by the members thereof other than the representatives of any of the parties to the dispute, the signatory States agree to comply with the recommendations therein.

4. If the Council fails to reach a report which is concurred in by all its members, other than the representatives of any of the parties to the dispute, it shall submit the dispute to arbitration. It shall itself determine the composition, the powers and the procedure of the Committee of Arbitrators and, in the choice of the arbitrators, shall bear in mind the guarantees of competence and impartiality referred to in paragraph 2 (b) above.

5. In no case may a solution, upon which there has already been a unanimous recommendation of the Council accepted by one of the parties concerned, be again called in question.

6. The signatory States undertake that they will carry out in full good faith any judicial sentence or arbitral award that may be rendered and that they will comply, as provided in paragraph 3 above, with the solutions recommended by the Council. In the event of a State failing to carry out the above undertakings, the Council shall exert all its influence to secure compliance therewith. If it fails therein, it shall propose what steps should be taken to give effect thereto, in accordance with the provision contained at the end of Article 13 of the Covenant. Should a State in disregard of the above undertakings resort to war, the sanctions provided for by Article 16 of the Covenant, interpreted in the manner indicated in the present Protocol, shall immediately become applicable to it.

7. The provisions of the present article do not apply to the settlement of disputes which arise as the result of measures of war taken by one or more signatory States in agreement with the Council or the Assembly.

Article 5

The provisions of paragraph 8 of Article 15 of the Covenant shall continue to apply in proceedings before the Council.

If in the course of an arbitration, such as is contemplated in

Article 4 above, one of the parties claims that the dispute, or part thereof, arises out of a matter which by international law is solely within the domestic jurisdiction of that party, the arbitrators shall on this point take the advice of the Permanent Court of International Justice through the medium of the Council. The opinion of the Court shall be binding upon the arbitrators, who, if the opinion is affirmative, shall confine themselves to so declaring in their award.

If the question is held by the Court or by the Council, to be a matter solely within the domestic jurisdiction of the State, this decision shall not prevent consideration of the situation by the Council or by the Assembly under Article 11 of the Covenant.

ARTICLE 6

If in accordance with paragraph 9 of Article 15 of the Covenant a dispute is referred to the Assembly, that body shall have for the settlement of the dispute all the powers conferred upon the Council as to endeavoring to reconcile the parties in the manner laid down in paragraphs 1, 2 and 3 of Article 15 of the Covenant and in paragraph 1 of Article 4 above.

Should the Assembly fail to achieve an amicable settlement:

If one of the parties asks for arbitration, the Council shall proceed to constitute the Committee of Arbitrators in the manner provided in sub-paragraphs (*a*), (*b*) and (*c*) of paragraph 2 of Article 4 above.

If no party asks for arbitration, the Assembly shall again take the dispute under consideration and shall have in this connection the same powers as the Council. Recommendations embodied in a report of the Assembly, provided that it secures the measure of support stipulated at the end of paragraph 10 of Article 15 of the Covenant, shall have the same value and effect, as regards all matters dealt with in the present Protocol, as recommendations embodied in a report of the Council adopted as provided in paragraph 3 of Article 4 above.

If the necessary majority cannot be obtained, the dispute shall be submitted to arbitration and the Council shall determine the composition, the powers and the procedure of the Committee of Arbitrators as laid down in paragraph 4 of Article 4.

Article 7

In the event of a dispute arising between two or more signatory States, these States agree that they will not, either before the dispute is submitted to proceedings for pacific settlement or during such proceedings, make any increase of their armaments or effectives which might modify the position established by the Conference for the Reduction of Armaments provided for by Article 17 of the present Protocol, nor will they take any measure of military, naval, air, industrial or economic mobilization, nor, in general, any action of a nature likely to extend the dispute or render it more acute.

It shall be the duty of the Council, in accordance with the provisions of Article 11 of the Covenant, to take under consideration any complaint as to infraction of the above undertakings which is made to it by one or more of the States parties to the dispute. Should the Council be of opinion that the complaint requires investigation, it shall, if it deems it expedient, arrange for inquiries and investigations in one or more of the countries concerned. Such inquiries and investigations shall be carried out with the utmost possible dispatch and the signatory States undertake to afford every facility for carrying them out.

The sole object of measures taken by the Council, as above provided is to facilitate the pacific settlement of disputes and they shall in no way prejudge the actual settlement.

If the result of such inquiries and investigations is to establish an infraction of the provisions of the first paragraph of the present Article, it shall be the duty of the Council to summon the State or States guilty of the infraction to put an end thereto. Should the State or States in question fail to comply with such summons, the Council shall declare them to be guilty of a violation of the Covenant or of the present Protocol, and shall decide upon the measures to be taken with a view to end as soon as possible a situation of a nature to threaten the peace of the world.

For the purposes of the present Article decisions of the Council may be taken by a two-thirds majority.

Article 8

The signatory States undertake to abstain from any act which might constitute a threat of aggression against another State.

If one of the signatory States is of opinion that another State is making preparations for war, it shall have the right to bring the matter to the notice of the Council.

The Council, if it ascertains that the facts are as alleged, shall proceed as provided in paragraphs 2, 4, and 5 of Article 7.

Article 9

The existence of demilitarized zones being calculated to prevent aggression and to facilitate a definite finding of the nature provided for in Article 10 below, the establishment of such zones between States mutually consenting thereto is recommended as a means of avoiding violations of the present Protocol.

The demilitarized zones already existing under the terms of certain treaties or conventions, or which may be established in future between States mutually consenting thereto, may at the request and at the expense of one or more of the conterminous States, be placed under a temporary or permanent system of supervision to be organized by the Council.

Article 10

Every State which resorts to war in violation of the undertakings contained in the Covenant or in the present Protocol is an aggressor. Violation of the rules laid down for a demilitarized zone shall be held equivalent to resort to war.

In the event of hostilities having broken out, any State shall be presumed to be an aggressor, unless a decision of the Council, which must be taken unanimously, shall otherwise declare:

1. If it has refused to submit the dispute to the procedure of pacific settlement provided by Articles 13 and 15 of the Covenant as amplified by the present Protocol, or to comply with a judicial sentence or arbitral award or with a unanimous recommendation of the Council, or has disregarded a unanimous report of the Council, a judicial sentence or an arbitral award recognizing that the dispute between it and the other belligerent State arises out of a matter which by international law is solely within the domestic jurisdiction of the latter State; nevertheless, in the last case the State shall only be presumed to be an aggressor if it has not previously submitted the question to the Council or the Assembly, in accordance with Article 11 of the Covenant.

2. If it has violated provisional measures enjoined by the Council for the period while the proceedings are in progress as contemplated by Article 7 of the present Protocol.

Apart from the cases dealt with in paragraphs 1 and 2 of the present Article, if the Council does not at once succeed in determining the aggressor, it shall be bound to enjoin upon the belligerents an armistice, and shall fix the terms, acting, if need be, by a two-thirds majority and shall supervise its execution.

Any belligerent which has refused to accept the armistice or has violated its terms shall be deemed an aggressor.

The Council shall call upon the signatory States to apply forthwith against the aggressor the sanctions provided by Article 11 of the present Protocol, and any signatory State thus called upon shall thereupon be entitled to exercise the rights of a belligerent.

ARTICLE 11

As soon as the Council has called upon the signatory States to apply sanctions, as provided in the last paragraph of Article 10 of the present Protocol, the obligations of the said States, in regard to the sanctions of all kinds mentioned in paragraphs 1 and 2 of Article 16 of the Covenant, will immediately become operative in order that such sanctions may forthwith be employed against the aggressor.

Those obligations shall be interpreted as obliging each of the signatory States to co-operate loyally and effectively in support of the Covenant of the League of Nations, and in resistance to any act of aggression, in the degree which its geographical position and its particular situation as regards armaments allow.

In accordance with paragraph 3 of Article 16 of the Covenant the signatory States give a joint and several undertaking to come to the assistance of the State attacked or threatened, and to give each other mutual support by means of facilities and reciprocal exchanges as regards the provision of raw materials and supplies of every kind, openings of credits, transport and transit, and for this purpose to take all measures in their power to preserve the safety of communications by land and by sea of the attacked or threatened State.

If both parties to the dispute are aggressors within the meaning of Article 10, the economic and financial sanctions shall be applied to both of them.

Article 12

In view of the complexity of the conditions in which the Council may be called upon to exercise the functions mentioned in Article 11 of the present Protocol concerning economic and financial sanctions, and in order to determine more exactly the guarantees afforded by the present Protocol to the signatory States, the Council shall forthwith invite the economic and financial organizations of the League of Nations to consider and report as to the nature of the steps to be taken to give effect to the financial and economic sanctions and measures of co-operation contemplated in Article 16 of the Covenant and in Article 11 of this Protocol.

When in possession of this information, the Council shall draw up through its competent organs:

1. Plans of action for the application of the economic and financial sanctions against an aggressor State;
2. Plans of economic and financial co-operation between a State attacked and the different States assisting it;

and shall communicate these plans to the Members of the League and to the other signatory States.

Article 13

In view of the contingent military, naval and air sanctions provided for by Article 16 of the Covenant and by Article 11 of the present Protocol, the Council shall be entitled to receive undertakings from States determining in advance the military, naval and air forces which they would be able to bring into action immediately to insure the fulfilment of the obligations in regard to sanctions which result from the Covenant and the present Protocol.

Furthermore, as soon as the Council has called upon the signatory States to apply sanctions, as provided in the last paragraph of Article 10 above, the said States may, in accordance with any agreements which they may previously have concluded, bring to the assistance of a particular State, which is the victim of aggression, their military, naval and air forces.

The agreements mentioned in the preceding paragraph shall be registered and published by the Secretariat of the League of Nations. They shall remain open to all States Members of the League which may desire to accede thereto.

Article 14

The Council shall alone be competent to declare that the application of sanctions shall cease and normal conditions be re-established.

Article 15

In conformity with the spirit of the present Protocol, the signatory States agree that the whole cost of any military, naval or air operations undertaken for the repression of an aggression under the terms of the Protocol, and reparation for all losses suffered by individuals, whether civilians or combatants, and for all material damage caused by the operations of both sides, shall be borne by the aggressor State up to the extreme limit of its capacity.

Nevertheless, in view of Article 10 of the Covenant, neither the territorial integrity nor the political independence of the aggressor State shall in any case be affected as the result of the application of the sanctions mentioned in the present Protocol.

Article 16

The signatory States agree that in the event of a dispute between one or more of them and one or more States which have not signed the present Protocol and are not Members of the League of Nations, such non-Member State shall be invited, on the conditions contemplated in Article 17 of the Covenant, to submit, for the purpose of a specific settlement, to the obligations accepted by the States signatories of the present Protocol.

If the State so invited, having refused to accept the said conditions and obligations, resorts to war against a signatory State, the provisions of Article 16 of the Covenant, as defined by the present Protocol, shall be applicable against it.

Article 17

The signatory States undertake to participate in an International Conference for the Reduction of Armaments which shall be convened by the Council and shall meet at Geneva on Monday, June 15th, 1925. All other States, whether Members of the League or not, shall be invited to this Conference.

In preparation for the convening of the Conference, the Council shall draw up with due regard to the undertakings contained in

Articles 11 and 13 of the present Protocol a general program for the reduction and limitation of armaments, which shall be laid ebfore the Conference and which shall be communicated to the Governments at the earliest possible date, and at the latest three months before the Conference meets.

If by May 1st, 1925, ratifications have not been deposited by at least a majority of the permanent Members of the Council and ten other Members of the League, the Secretary-General of the League shall immediately consult the Council as to whether he shall cancel the invitations or merely adjourn the Conference to a subsequent date to be fixed by the Council so as to permit the necessary number of ratifications to be obtained.

Article 18

Wherever mention is made in Article 10, or in any other provision of the present Protocol, of a decision of the Council, this shall be understood in the sense of Article 15 of the Covenant, namely that the votes of the representatives of the parties to the dispute shall not be counted when reckoning unanimity or the necessary majority.

Article 19

Except as expressly provided by its terms, the present Protocol shall not affect in any way the rights and obligations of Members of the League as determined by the Covenant.

Article 20

Any dispute as to the interpretation of the present Protocol shall be submitted to the Permanent Court of International Justice.

Article 21

The present Protocol, of which the French and English texts are both authentic, shall be ratified.

The deposit of ratifications shall be made at the Secretariat of the League of Nations as soon as possible.

States of which the seat of government is outside Europe will be entitled merely to inform the Secretariat of the League of Nations that their ratification has been given; in that case, they must transmit the instrument of ratification as soon as possible.

So soon as the majority of the permanent Members of the Council and ten other Members of the League have deposited or have effected their ratifications, a *procès-verbal* to that effect shall be drawn up by the Secretariat.

After the said *procès-verbal* has been drawn up, the Protocol shall come into force as soon as the plan for the reduction of armaments has been adopted by the Conference provided for in Article 17.

If within such period after the adoption of the plan for the reduction of armaments as shall be fixed by the said Conference, the plan has not been carried out, the Council shall make a declaration to that effect; this declaration shall render the present Protocol null and void.

The grounds on which the Council may declare that the plan drawn up by the International Conference for the Reduction of Armaments has not been carried out, and that in consequence the present Protocol has been rendered null and void, shall be laid down by the Conference itself.

A signatory State which, after the expiration of the period fixed by the Conference, fails to comply with the plan adopted by the Conference, shall not be admitted to benefit by the provisions of the present Protocol.

In faith whereof the Undersigned, duly authorized for this purpose, have signed the present Protocol.

DONE at Geneva, on the second day of October, nineteen hundred and twenty-four, in a single copy, which will be kept in the archives of the Secretariat of the League and registered by it on the date of its coming into force.

ANNEX VIII

EXTRACTS FROM THE OBSERVATIONS OF CERTAIN GOVERNMENTS ON THE PROTOCOL

BRITISH GOVERNMENT[1]

The declared object of the Protocol is to facilitate disarmament, and it proposes to attain this most desirable end: (1) by closing certain gaps in the scheme originally laid down in the

[1] Reprinted from *League of Nations Official Journal*, April, 1925.

Covenant for peaceably settling international disputes, and (2) by sharpening the "sanctions," especially the economic sanctions, by which, under the existing system, aggression is to be discouraged and aggressors coerced. These two portions of the scheme are intimately connected, and it may be desirable on the present occasion to consider them together.

It was, of course, well known to the framers of the Covenant that international differences might conceivably take a form for which their peace-preserving machinery provided no specific remedy; nor could they have doubted that this defect, if defect it was, could in theory be cured by insisting that every dispute should, at some stage or other, be submitted to arbitration. If, therefore, they rejected this simple method of obtaining systematic completeness, it was presumably because they felt, as so many States Members of the League have felt since, that the objections to universal and compulsory arbitration might easily outweigh its theoretical advantages. So far as the Court of International Justice is concerned, this view was taken in 1920 by the British Delegation, while the British Delegation of 1924 made a reservation in the same connection which, so far as Great Britain is concerned, greatly limits the universal application of the compulsory principle.

Into this branch of the controversy, however, His Majesty's Government do not now propose to enter. It suffices to say that, so far from their objections to compulsory arbitration being diminished by the provisions of the Protocol, they have rather been increased, owing to the weakening of those reservations in clause 15 of the Covenant, which were designed to prevent any interference by the League in matters of domestic jurisdiction.

His Majesty's Government are now more immediately concerned to enquire how far the change in the Covenant effected by the Protocol is likely to increase the responsibilities already undertaken by the States Members of the League. On this there may conceivably be two opinions. Some have held that, although in the language of the First Committee (p. 7) "there are numerous fissures in the wall of protection erected by the Covenant around the peace of the world," there is in fact but little danger that through these "fissures" any serious assaults will be attempted. The changes made by the Protocol are, in their judgment, formal rather than substantial; they aim at theoretical completeness rather than practical effect. On this view no material addition is made to responsibilities already incurred under the Covenant, nor (it must be added) is anything of importance accomplished in the cause of Peace and Disarmament. . . .

As all the world is aware, the League of Nations, in its present shape, is not the League designed by the framers of the Covenant. They no doubt contemplated, and, as far as they could, provided against, the difficulties that might arise from the non-inclusion of a certain number of States within the circle of League membership. But they never supposed that, among these States, would be found so many of the most powerful nations in the world; least of all did they foresee that one of them would be the United States of America.

It is no doubt true that there are many points of view from which these unfortunate facts have not proved to be of vital importance. The work of the League goes on, beneficent and full of promise. Though the United States remains in friendly aloofness, individual Americans have freely helped both by sympathy and service, while the generosity of the American public has greatly aided some causes in which the League is deeply interested. Could, therefore, attention be confined to the present and the past, it might be said with truth that the problems which even a weakened League has had to face have never overstrained its machinery.

The hope may be justified that this good fortune will continue. But surely it is most unwise to add to the liabilities already incurred without taking stock of the degree to which the machinery of the Covenant has been already weakened by the non-membership of certain great States. For in truth the change, especially as regards the "economic sanction," amounts to a transformation. The "economic sanction," if simultaneously directed by all the world against a State which is not itself economically self-sufficing, would be a weapon of incalculable power. This, or something not very different from this, was the weapon originally devised by the authors of the Covenant. To them it appeared to be not only bloodless, but cheap, effective and easy to use, in the most improbable event of its use being necessary. But all this is changed by the mere existence of powerful economic communities outside the limits of the League. It might force trade into unaccustomed channels, but it could hardly stop it; and, though the offending State would no doubt suffer, there is no presumption that it would be crushed or even that it would suffer most. . . .

If the particular case of aggressors who are outside the League be considered, is not the weakness of the Protocol even more manifest? The aggressors within the League are traitors in the sight of all mankind. Their moral position in the face of any opposition within their own borders will be immensely weakened, while in neutral countries they will find none to plead their cause. However low the practical importance of moral considerations such as these may be rated, the eagerness of competing propaganda in times of international crisis may convince the most cynical that a good cause counts at least for something. If so, aggressors outside the League will have a smaller load of infamy to carry than aggressors within it, and will be by so much the more formidable. How does the Protocol deal with them? It requires them to treat the situation as if they were members of the League, to accept its methods and conform to its decisions. If they refuse they are counted as aggressors, they become the common enemy, and every signatory State is bound to go to war with them. They may be in the right and have nothing to fear from impartial judges. Yet national pride, in some cases perhaps the sense of power, dislike of compulsory arbitration, distrust of the League (to which presumably they have already refused to belong)—all these motives, or any of them, may harden their objections to outside interference. If so, the Protocol, designed to ensure universal peace, may only extend the area of war—a possibility which, if realised, will not improve the chances of general disarmament. . . .

Since the general provisions of the Covenant cannot be stiffened with advantage, and since the "extreme cases" with which the League may have to deal will probably affect certain nations or groups of nations more nearly than others, His Majesty's Government conclude that the best way of dealing with the situation is, with the co-operation of the League, to supplement the Covenant by making special arrangements in order to meet special needs. That these arrangements should be purely defensive in character, that they should be framed in the spirit of the Covenant, working in close harmony with the League and under its guidance, is manifest. And, in the opinion of His Majesty's Government, these objects can best be attained by knitting together the nations most immediately concerned, and whose differences might lead to a renewal of strife, by means of treaties framed with the sole object of maintaining, as between themselves, an unbroken peace. Within its limits no quicker remedy for our present ills can easily be found or any surer safeguard against future calamities.

GOVERNMENT OF AUSTRALIA[2]

The Commonwealth Government, after having given full and most careful consideration to the Protocol for the Pacific Settlement of International Disputes, has reached the following conclusions regarding the important and far-reaching provisions that are therein contained. . . .

The aim of the Protocol, which is to further the settlement of international disputes without having recourse to war, thus ensuring to the nations of the world that measure of external security which would permit them to obtain relief from the heavy burden of armaments, is one which, in principle, must commend itself to any State anxious to see strengthened the ties that bind together the members of international communities. It is also indisputable that members of the League, recognizing as they do the relationship between military armaments and the danger of war, are bound to reduce national armaments to the lowest point consistent with national safety. The Protocol has been framed from the point of view that machinery other than that existing in the Covenant destined to provide safeguards against aggression must precede any scheme for disarmament. Relief from the burden of armaments is regarded ultimately as being dependent on the adoption of compulsory arbitration. . . .

There exist at the present time other very serious practical objections to the adoption of compulsory arbitration as a general system. To be effective, compulsory arbitration must secure the consent of all countries between which disputes may conceivably arise. To establish a general system of compulsory arbitration to which any powerful States are not parties cannot fail to be a source of danger both to the successful carrying out of the system itself and to the international organization under

[2] Reprinted from "Protocol for the Pacific Settlement of International Disputes, Correspondence Relating to the Position of the Dominions." (Great Britain, Parl. Paps., Cmd. 2458.)

which it operates. It has been a matter of grave concern always to the Commonwealth Government that certain of the foremost nations of the world have not yet become members of the League of Nations, thus accepting the international obligations which are contained in the Covenant and lending their authority for the preservation of peace, this position throwing heavier obligations on the member States than were originally contemplated when the Covenant of the League was agreed to. It is, therefore, considered that the progressive incorporation of those nations in the League should precede and not follow the assumption of greater obligations that the Protocol will impose upon member States. This reason alone is considered by the Commonwealth Government as amply sufficient to render premature any endeavour at the present time to generalize the principle of compulsory arbitration.

Articles 10 and 11 of the Protocol, which are regarded as complementary to the provisions respecting compulsory arbitration, while possessing some features that could with advantage be incorporated into the Covenant would also introduce novel, and in some respects, it is believed, undesirable, elements into the constitution of the League. These Articles accentuate very considerably the coercive provisions of the League's Charter. It is felt further that these provisions, while not actually converting the League into a super State, would tend to deflect that organization from being a powerful moral agency for the moulding of the world's opinion in the direction of peaceful and healthy international relations to being an organization for the imposition of pains and penalties. . . .

Article 10 of the Protocol defines the circumstances in which certain presumptions of aggressions arise against a State, and provides that, "in the event of hostilities having broken out, any State shall be presumed to be an aggressor unless a decision of the Council, which must be taken unanimously, shall otherwise declare (1) if it has . . . . disregarded a unanimous report of the Council, a judicial sentence or an arbitral award recognizing that the dispute between it and the other belligerent State arises out of a matter which by international law is solely within the domestic jurisdiction of the latter State, nevertheless in that last case the State shall only be presumed to be an aggressor if it has not previously submitted the question to the Council or Assembly in accordance with Article 11 of the Covenant. . . ."

It does not appear that any logical reason can be advanced to justify an award declaring that a dispute arising from a matter of domestic jurisdiction should be placed on a different footing from any other arbitral award or a unanimous decision of the Council. When a State commits an act of war against another State concerning a matter which international law declares to be one of purely domestic jurisdiction, it is obviously not in the interests of good understanding between nations that such an act of aggression, constituting, as it does, an international crime, should be covered by some special proviso. And this is particularly so as under Article 11 of the Covenant any dispute assuming the character of a war, or a threat of war, is a matter of concern to the whole League. The proviso of Article 10 (1) is, therefore, unacceptable to the Commonwealth Government. . . .

From above considerations it will be seen that the Commonwealth Government is of opinion that the Protocol contains principles and provisions which do not at present appear to be applicable to the present situation of international life. It is also believed that any endeavours to amend the Protocol so as to give effect to objections that have been raised would present but little practical utility, as these objections cut through the essential principles on which the whole reposes. But this does not imply that the prolonged efforts of which the Protocol is the outcome have been spent in vain. No serious attempt to evolve methods of preserving international peace can be considered as fruitless. The gradual strengthening of the Covenant in these directions where it reveals weakness should be, and doubtless is, the aim of all member States. Such a method seems to be preferable to that of recasting the whole principle on which the present constitution of the League is based, and the Commonwealth Government will gladly and sincerely co-operate along such lines.

GOVERNMENT OF CANADA

After careful examination of the Geneva Protocol by members of the Cabinet and by Interdepartmental Committee, our Government has come to conclusions which may be summarized as follows:

First, that we should continue to give whole-hearted support to the League of Nations and particularly to its work of conciliation, co-operation and publicity. Second, that we do not consider it in the interests of Canada, of the British Empire, or of the League itself to recommend to Parliament adherence to the Protocol and particularly to its rigid provisions for application of Economic and Military sanctions in every future war. Among the grounds for this conclusion is the consideration of the effect of non-participation of the United States upon attempt to enforce sanctions and particularly so in the case of contiguous countries like Canada. Third, that as Canada believes firmly in submission of international disputes to joint inquiry or arbitration and has shared in certain number of undertakings in this field we would be prepared to consider acceptance of compulsory jurisdiction of Permanent Court in justiciable disputes with certain reservations and co-operation in further consideration of method of supplementing the provisions of the Covenant for settlement of non-justiciable issues, including method of joint investigation reserving ultimate decision in domestic issues and without undertaking further obligations to enforce decisions in case of other States. Fourth, that we would be prepared to take part at any time in any general Conference on reduction of armaments which did not involve prior acceptance of the Protocol.

GOVERNMENT OF THE IRISH FREE STATE

Statement made in the Dail by the Minister for External Affairs

We have given earnest consideration to the Protocol for the Pacific Settlement of International Disputes, drawn up at the Fifth Assembly of the League of Nations. We have approached the subject with due advertence to the admirable intentions which animated the authors of that document, and with which we are in complete accord, namely, that a basis should be found which would enable differences arising between Nations to be adjusted without recourse to arms, and thus remove from the sphere of international relations the menace of war. . . .

In so far as the Protocol constitutes a unanimous manifestation by the States Members of the League of their genuine desire to render recourse to war impossible, we welcome the opportunity which it has afforded for the study of measures devised for the purpose, and while, on consideration of its details, we find ourselves unable to recommend its acceptance, we wish to place on record that we are by no means of opinion that the object of the framers of the Protocol is beyond the realm of achievement.

The Covenant of the League of Nations, while it marked a notable advance in the direction of international peace, cannot be regarded as an instrument capable in all circumstances of preventing war. Its machinery for dealing with disputes is somewhat unwieldy, and the preponderance on its Council of the more powerful States tends to diminish its prestige amongst the smaller nations, who have less to gain and more to suffer by international strife. But it is our opinion that the place of the League of Nation in world civilisation is not to be gauged by the suitability of its machinery to arbitrate in disputes between Nations when they arise in acute form—rather is it to be measured by the efficacy of the intercourse between States to which it has given rise in resolving differences before they become acute by harmonious interchange of ideas and by mutual appreciation of national aspirations and national difficulties.

The Covenant of the League of Nations makes provisions for certain sanctions in the case of a State which resorts to war in disregard of its obligations. It has always appeared to us that the application of these sanctions would present grave difficulties, and that the machinery for effecting them would in practice prove unworkable. It is true that sanctions could in all probability be effectively enforced against a relatively small State engaging in hostile operations for purposes of aggrandisement, where the verdict of the world-conscience would be unanimous in condemnation of the objects for which resort was had to war. But it appears equally evident that, in the case of aggressive acts by one or other of the greater Powers, and particularly where world opinion was divided as to the merits of the dispute, the sanctions could not be enforced. We are, accordingly, forced to the conclusion that, while the sanctions of the Covenant may prove a useful deterrent in the case of small and turbulent communities, they are quite powerless to prevent either the oppression by a larger Power of small States or the occurrence of a war of world magnitude. It may also be observed that the application of sanctions implies the maintenance of armaments rather than their abolition, and in this respect is scarcely compatible with one of the primary objects of the Protocol, viz., Disarmament. The portions of the Covenant, therefore, dealing with the imposition of sanctions appear to us to be the least valuable for the general purposes of the Covenant, and an extension of these provisions, such as is contemplated in the Protocol, the least profitable avenue of exploration towards improvement.

The expressed intention of the framers of the Protocol to exclude from the new system of pacific settlement any disputes which may arise regarding existing territorial divisions appears to us to detract considerably from the value of the instrument. Many existing frontiers were fixed by Treaties negotiated before the shadow of the Great War had receded and before the passions which the War aroused had subsided. The passage of years may prove these delimitations to be convenient and equitable; on the other hand, it may in time become apparent that present boundaries are in some cases unsuitable and provocative of ill-will. We realise that the stability of the Continent of Europe, and the prevention of a renewed international race in armaments must depend largely on the extent to which the existing apprehensions of nations, whether well or ill-founded, regarding possible interference with their territorial integrity can be allayed. As long, however, as some of the more powerful States refrain from participation in the League of Nations the feeling of uneasiness and distrust will continue. The continued absence of certain of these States from the Councils of the League is in some degree admittedly attributable to their unwillingness to be called upon to take active measures to maintain for all time existing frontiers even though these should prove to have been equitably drawn. We fear that the conclusion of an agreement which must to some extent appear to these Nations to partake of the nature of an alliance confined to States Members of the League emphasising by implication the immutability of these frontiers and imposing upon Members additional obligations, particularly by way of participation in disputes and in sanctions, is not calculated to induce them to accept the responsibilities of membership and is, therefore, likely to hinder rather than further the progress of world pacification and disarmament.

The Irish Free State, because of its geographical position, because its armed forces have been reduced to the minimum requisite for the maintenance of internal order, and because of its Constitution, which provides that, except in case of invasion, it can only be committed to participation war with the consent of the Oireachtas, cannot be regarded as a material factor in the enforcement of sanctions. Consequently, the foregoing observations on the Protocol are not affected by any considerations especially affecting the Irish Free State, and are dictated solely by our genuine desire that the League of Nations should realise the aspirations of its founders by uniting all nations in the common interest of world peace.

If we might express an opinion upon the measures by which these aspirations may best be realised, and naturally we do so with the utmost diffidence, we would suggest that the solution is to be found not in an endeavour to close some of the fissures in the Covenant by elaborate definition or drastic sanction, but rather in an effort to enhance the moral influence of international conscience. An extension of the principle of arbitration which serves to define and enunciate international judgment, and which relies in the last resort on the moral pressure of world opinion and not upon the application of material sanctions, appears to us to be the most effective feasible means of attaining, at least in a large measure, the objects which the Protocol has in view.

GOVERNMENT OF NEW ZEALAND

The principal objections from the point of view of New Zealand are:

1. The reference of matters to the Court of International Justice. So far Great Britain has never made a declaration under Article 36 of the Statute of the Court authorizing that Court to determine, without special submission, the matters defined in paragraphs A, B, C and D of that Article, and New Zealand never will consent to such a declaration.

But Article 3 of the Protocol binds the signatory States to accept that jurisdiction in all matters. The reference in that Article to reservations is idle and useless as the Protocol is drafted. A reservation would have absolutely no effect in limiting the jurisdiction in matters referred under the Protocol, though it might limit the jurisdiction in matters of peaceful negotiations. Where a question of international law arises in the course of arbitrations under the Protocol, that is to say, in cases where war is threatened, the Permanent Court of International Justice at the Hague is given express jurisdiction, firstly, to decide whether a claim by a nation is a claim in respect of matters within its domestic jurisdiction, and, secondly, to determine all other questions of international law, and signatories are to be bound by such decision.

New Zealand's immigration laws are framed to preserve, as far as possible, British nationality in New Zealand. No foreigner may come to New Zealand to reside without having first made written application from his country of origin. Whatever the jurists at Geneva may think, the law advisers of the Crown in New Zealand believe that there is grave danger that the International Court of Justice at the Hague, consisting mainly of foreigners, might hold that the New Zealand law is contrary to the comity of Nations, and that the New Zealand system is not a question of merely domestic jurisdiction. And our law advisers believe that, if a question arose for determination under the Protocol, the Permanent Court might decide, firstly, that the right of foreigners to reside in New Zealand was not a matter exclusively within the domestic jurisdiction of New Zealand, and, secondly, that as a matter of international law we must admit them or reduce the restrictions on their admission.

But consideration of the minor interests of New Zealand in this respect is negligible as compared with admission of the Permanent Court as the deciding factor in Great Britain's belligerent rights at sea. It seems to us idle to contend, as has been contended, that, inasmuch as such questions would only effectively arise during actual war, and as the assumption is that Great Britain will only wage war with the consent of the League, therefore the point may be waived. That seems to us idle because the question would be raised by neutrals whose vessels were stopped and searched for contraband. It is with regard to the rights of His Majesty's ships against neutrals when Great Britain is at war that difference exists between the opinions of foreign jurists and the decisions of the English Courts. And it seems obvious that the effect of adhesion to the Protocol would be deliberately to accept a foregone conclusion against the exercise of privileges in war which are essential to the defence of the Empire.

2. The Protocol, it is true, partly cuts down the rights and duties of signatory nations expressed in Article 8 of the Covenant,

but that reduction of obligation is objectionable. Provision is made in the Protocol for suspension of operations by nations about to go to war, and for non-mobilization, etc., and it authorizes defence against acts of aggression by a nation attacked. The definition of aggression in Article 10 is not, and obviously is not intended to be, exclusive, and it may be assumed that any attack on territorial integrity or political independence as mentioned in Article 10 of the Covenant would still be aggression under the Protocol, but there is absolutely no provision in the Protocol enabling or entitling a nation which is not itself attacked by aggression to come at once to the assistance of a friendly nation which is so attacked. Indeed the effect of the Protocol is to prevent such nations from entering upon war to aid another nation against actual attack on its territories, until such time (probably far too late for effect) as the Council, after the tedious procedure directed, is at liberty to authorize assistance. This may be intentional, but if it is intentional Great Britain will surely not consent to such a limitation to its rights and duties to France and Belgium as is expressed in Article 10 of the Covenant and subjected to such ludicrous limitation by the Protocol.

3. The object and effect of Articles 11 and 13 of the Protocol is to create for the Council of the League an entirely new power and authority in warfare between Signatories to the League. It is not true to say that those Articles merely define the effect of Article 16 of the Covenant. It does not appear necessary to emphasize this by quotation, the intention and the effect is apparent, and those Articles require drastic amendment.

Government of the Union of South Africa

Ministers after careful consideration of the proposed Protocol regret to have to inform British Government that they feel themselves unable to accept the same or to recommend its acceptance by Parliament. The reasons which have led Ministers to arrive at this conclusion may without going into details be stated as follows:

1. It seems generally admitted, and Ministers share that feeling, that the League of Nations as at present existing, with America, Germany and Russia standing aloof, cannot over any length of time achieve its great and primary object of ensuring

peaceable world, and must, unless these great nations become members, necessarily as time goes on assume more and more the character of political alliance. To accept Protocol, Ministers feel, would be only to make it more difficult for countries at present outside the League, notably America, to become members, and would consequently contribute very materially to making it impossible for League to attain its real object and so give an additional impulse to the diversion of its activities in the direction of an alliance having as its object the maintenance of a balance of power.

2. It is quite impossible even approximately to calculate or tell in advance what are going to be the obligations and consequences direct and indirect which may accrue from an acceptance of the Protocol or what may be the many and various international complications to which it may give rise.

3. By accepting the Protocol the character of the League will be so modified that no nation being a member of it, subject to the provisions of the Protocol, can rightly be said any longer to retain its full measure of sovereign rights. This, Ministers deem a matter of very grave concern, in view more particularly of indefinite character of the obligations which are sought to be imposed and of the practical consequences it may have for the weaker nations not possessing influence derived from power to add prestige and weight to their interpretation of the obligations thus assumed.

4. Ministers feel convinced that while public feeling in the Union may be taken as sincerely in favour of a real and genuine League of Nations, it is generally felt that the League, as it is at present, has not yet arrived at that stage, and that to have obligations of the Union under Covenant extended any further is not in the interests of this country.

5. In matters of such a grave nature as the relationship and obligations of nations over against the League professedly instituted with a view to the guardianship of the peace of the world, but under present conditions more especially the protector of the circumstances and requirements of particular nations and countries, Ministers feel they are called upon to exercise particular vigilance and to bestow particular attention upon the peculiar position and interests of South Africa, and are of the opinion that these interests demand that no international obli-

gations should be entered into which may entail a participation and interference by the Union in matters which do not, or only remotely, concern her and whereby her real and proper interests may eventually be jeopardized.

Ministers have considered question as to making suggestions which may serve as amending proposals to the provisions of the Protocol. They find, however, that, from the very nature of the circumstances which have necessitated the drafting of the Protocol, no amendment or substitute to its provisions can be expected to prove acceptable unless it carries with it an extension of obligations and responsibilities under Covenant. As already stated, Ministers are convinced that that would be against the interests of this country and contrary to the wishes of the people.

Under these circumstances Ministers must advise that they have no suggestions to offer.

ANNEX·IX

THE LOCARNO AGREEMENTS[1]

No. 1

Final Protocol of the Locarno Conference

The representatives of the German, Belgian, British, French, Italian, Polish and Czechoslovak Governments, who have met at Locarno from October 5 to 16, 1925, in order to seek by common agreement means for preserving their respective nations from the scourge of war and for providing for the peaceful settlement of disputes of every nature which might eventually arise between them.

Have given their approval to the draft treaties and conventions which respectively affect them and which, framed in the course of the present conference, are mutually interdependent:

Treaty between Germany, Belgium, France, Great Britain, and Italy.

Arbitration convention between Germany and Belgium.
Arbitration convention between Germany and France.
Arbitration treaty between Germany and Poland.
Arbitration treaty between Germany and Czechoslovakia.

[1] Reprinted from World Peace Foundation Pamphlet, IX, No. 1.

The Locarno Agreements

These instruments, hereby initialed *ne varietur*, will bear today's date, the representatives of the interested parties agreeing to meet in London on December 1 next, to proceed during the course of a single meeting to the formality of the signature of the instruments which affect them.

The Minister for Foreign Affairs of France states that as a result of the draft arbitration treaties mentioned above, France, Poland and Czechoslovakia have also concluded at Locarno draft agreements in order reciprocally to assure to themselves the benefit of the said treaties. These agreements will be duly deposited at the League of Nations, but M. Briand holds copies forthwith at the disposal of the powers represented here.

The Secretary of State for Foreign Affairs of Great Britain proposes that, in reply to certain requests for explanations concerning Art. 16 of the Covenant of the League of Nations presented by the Chancellor and the Minister for Foreign Affairs of Germany, a letter, of which the draft is similarly attached, should be addressed to them at the same time as the formality of signature of the above-mentioned instruments takes place. This proposal is agreed to.

The representatives of the Governments represented here declare their firm conviction that the entry into force of these treaties and conventions will contribute greatly to bring about a moral relaxation of the tension between nations, that it will help powerfully toward the solution of many political or economic problems in accordance with the interests and sentiments of peoples, and that, in strengthening peace and security in Europe, it will hasten on effectively the disarmament provided for in Art. 8 of the Covenant of the League of Nations.

They undertake to give their sincere cooperation to the work relating to disarmament already undertaken by the League of Nations and to seek the realization thereof in a general agreement.

Done at Locarno, October 16, 1925.

> LUTHER.
> STRESEMANN.
> EMILE VANDERVELDE.
> ARIS. BRIAND.
> AUSTEN CHAMBERLAIN.
> BENITO MUSSOLINI.
> AL. SKRZYNSKI.
> EDUARD BENEŠ.

No. 2

TREATY OF MUTUAL GUARANTEE BETWEEN GERMANY, BELGIUM, FRANCE, GREAT BRITAIN AND ITALY

The President of the German Reich, his Majesty the King of the Belgians, the President of the French Republic, and His Majesty the King of the United Kingdom of Great Britain and Ireland and of the British Dominions beyond the seas, Emperor of India, his Majesty the King of Italy;

Anxious to satisfy the desire for security and protection which animates the peoples upon whom fell the scourge of the war of 1914–18;

Taking note of the abrogation of the treaties for the neutralization of Belgium, and conscious of the necessity of insuring peace in the area which has so frequently been the scene of European conflicts;

Animated also with the sincere desire of giving to all the signatory powers concerned supplementary guaranties within the framework of the Covenant of the League of Nations and the treaties in force between them;

Have determined to conclude a treaty with these objects, and have appointed as their plenipotentiaries:

Who, having communicated their full powers, found in good and due form, have agreed as follows:

ARTICLE 1. The High Contracting Parties collectively and severally guarantee, in the manner provided in the following articles, the maintenance of the territorial *status quo* resulting from the frontiers between Germany and Belgium and between Germany and France and the inviolability of the said frontiers as fixed by or in pursuance of the treaty of peace signed at Versailles on June 28, 1919, and also the observance of the stipulations of Arts. 42 and 43 of the said treaty concerning the demilitarized zone.

ART. 2. Germany and Belgium, and also Germany and France, mutually undertake that they will in no case attack or invade each other or resort to war against each other.

This stipulation shall not, however, apply in the case of—

1. The exercise of the right of legitimate defense, that is to say, resistance to a violation of the undertaking contained in

the previous paragraph or to a flagrant breach of Arts. 42 or 43 of the said treaty of Versailles, if such breach constitutes an unprovoked act of aggression and by reason of the assembly of armed forces in the demilitarized zone immediate action is necessary.

2. Action in pursuance of Art. 16 of the Covenant of the League of Nations.

3. Action as the result of a decision taken by the Assembly or by the Council of the League of Nations or in pursuance of Art. 15, par. 7, of the Covenant of the League of Nations, provided that in this last event the action is directed against a state which was the first to attack.

ART. 3. In view of the undertakings entered into in Art. 2 of the present treaty, Germany and Belgium and Germany and France undertake to settle by peaceful means and in the manner laid down herein all questions of every kind which may arise between them and which it may not be possible to settle by the normal methods of diplomacy:

Any question with regard to which the parties are in conflict as to their respective rights shall be submitted to judicial decision, and the parties undertake to comply with such decision.

All other questions shall be submitted to a conciliation commission. If the proposals of this commission are not accepted by the two parties, the question shall be brought before the Council of the League of Nations, which will deal with it in accordance with Art. 15 of the Covenant of the League.

The detailed arrangements for effecting such peaceful settlement are the subject of special agreements signed this day.

ART. 4. (1) If one of the High Contracting Parties alleges that a violation of Art. 2 of the present treaty or a breach of Arts. 42 or 43 of the treaty of Versailles has been or is being committed, it shall bring the question at once before the Council of the League of Nations.

2. As soon as the Council of the League of Nations is satisfied that such violation or breach has been committed, it will notify its finding without delay to the powers signatory of the present treaty, who severally agree that in such case they will each of them come immediately to the assistance of the power against whom the act complained of is directed.

3. In case of a flagrant violation of Art. 2 of the present treaty or of a flagrant breach of Arts. 42 or 43 of the treaty of Versailles by one of the High Contracting Parties, each of the other Contracting Parties hereby undertakes immediately to come to the help of the party against whom such a violation or breach has been directed as soon as the said power has been able to satisfy itself that this violation constitutes an unprovoked act of aggression and that by reason either of the crossing of the frontier or of the outbreak of hostilities or of the assembly of armed forces in the demilitarized zone immediate action is necessary. Nevertheless, the Council of the League of Nations, which will be seized of the question in accordance with the first paragraph of this article, will issue its findings, and the High Contracting Parties undertake to act in accordance with the recommendations of the Council provided that they are concurred in by all the members other than the representatives of the parties which have engaged in hostilities.

ART. 5. The provisions of Art. 3 of the present treaty are placed under the guaranty of the High Contracting Parties as provided by the following stipulations:

If one of the powers referred to in Art. 3 refuses to submit a dispute to peaceful settlement or to comply with an arbitral or judicial decision and commits a violation of Art. 2 of the present treaty or a breach of Arts. 42 or 43 of the treaty of Versailles, the provisions of Art. 4 shall apply.

Where one of the powers referred to in Art. 3, without committing a violation of Art. 2 of the present treaty or a breach of Arts. 42 or 43 of the treaty of Versailles, refuses to submit a dispute to peaceful settlement or to comply with an arbitral or judicial decision, the other party shall bring the matter before the Council of the League of Nations, and the Council shall propose what steps shall be taken; the High Contracting Parties shall comply with these proposals.

ART. 6. The provisions of the present treaty do not affect the rights and obligations of the High Contracting Parties under the treaty of Versailles or under arrangements supplementary thereto, including the agreements signed in London on August 30, 1924.

ART. 7. The present treaty, which is designed to insure the

maintenance of peace and is in conformity with the Covenant of the League of Nations, shall not be interpreted as restricting the duty of the League to take whatever action may be deemed wise and effectual to safeguard the peace of the world.

ART. 8. The present treaty shall be registered at the League of Nations in accordance with the Covenant of the League. It shall remain in force until the Council, acting on a request of one or other of the High Contracting Parties notified to the other signatory powers three months in advance, and voting at least by a two-thirds majority, decides that the League of Nations insures sufficient protection to the High Contracting Parties; the treaty shall cease to have effect on the expiration of a period of one year from such decision.

ART. 9. The present treaty shall impose no obligation upon any of the British dominions, or upon India, unless the Government of such dominion, or of India, signifies its acceptance thereof.

ART. 10. The present treaty shall be ratified and the ratifications shall be deposited at Geneva in the archives of the League of Nations as soon as possible.

It shall enter into force as soon as all the ratifications have been deposited and Germany has become a Member of the League of Nations.

The present treaty, done in a single copy, will be deposited in the archives of the League of Nations, and the Secretary-General will be requested to transmit certified copies to each of the High Contracting Parties.

In faith whereof the above-mentioned Plenipotentiaries have signed the present treaty.

Done at Locarno, October 16, 1925.

> HANS LUTHER.
> GUSTAV STRESEMANN.
> EMILE VANDERVELDE.
> ARI. BRIAND.
> STANLEY BALDWIN.
> AUSTEN CHAMBERLAIN.
> B. M.
> VITTORIO SCIALOJA.

No. 3

Arbitration Convention Between Germany and Belgium

The undersigned duly authorized,

Charged by their respective Governments to determine the methods by which, as provided in Art. 3 of the Treaty concluded this day between Germany, Belgium, France, Great Britain and Italy, a peaceful solution shall be attained of all questions which can not be settled amicably between Germany and Belgium.

Have agreed as follows:

Part I.

ARTICLE 1. All disputes of every kind between Germany and Belgium with regard to which the parties are in conflict as to their respective rights, and which it may not be possible to settle amicably by the normal methods of diplomacy, shall be submitted for decision either to an arbitral tribunal or to the Permanent Court of International Justice, as laid down hereafter. It is agreed that the disputes referred to above include in particular those mentioned in Art. 13 of the Covenant of the League of Nations.

This provision does not apply to disputes arising out of events prior to the present convention and belonging to the past.

Disputes for the settlement of which a special procedure is laid down in other conventions in force between Germany and Belgium shall be settled in conformity with the provisions of those conventions.

ART. 2. Before any resort is made to arbitral procedure or to procedure before the Permanent Court of International Justice, the dispute may, by agreement between the parties, be submitted with a view to amicable settlement to a permanent international commission styled the Permanent Conciliation Commission, constituted in accordance with the present convention.

ART. 3. In the case of a dispute the occasion of which, according to the municipal law of one of the parties, falls within the competence of the national courts of such party, the matter in dispute shall not be submitted to the procedure laid down in the present convention until a judgment with final effect has been pronounced, within a reasonable time, by the competent national judicial authority.

ART. 4. The Permanent Conciliation Commission mentioned in Art. 2 shall be composed of five members who shall be appointed as follows, that is to say: the German Government and the Belgian Government shall each nominate a commissioner chosen from among their respective nationals, and shall appoint, by common agreement, the three other commissioners from among the nationals of third powers; these three commissioners must be of different nationalities and the German and Belgian Governments shall appoint the president of the commission from among them.

The commissioners are appointed for three years, and their mandate is renewable. Their appointment shall continue until their replacement, and, in any case, until the termination of the work in hand at the moment of the expiry of their mandate. Vacancies which may occur as a result of death, resignation or any other cause shall be filled within the shortest possible time in the manner fixed for the nominations.

ART. 5. The Permanent Conciliation Commission shall be constituted within three months from the entry into force of the present convention.

If the nomination of the commissioners to be appointed by common agreement should not have taken place within the said period, or, in the case of the filling of a vacancy, within three months from the time when the seat falls vacant, the President of the Swiss Confederation shall, in the absence of other agreement, be requested to make the necessary appointments.

ART. 6. The Permanent Conciliation Commission shall be informed by means of a request addressed to the president by the two parties acting in agreement or, in the absence of such agreement, by one or other of the parties.

The request, after having given a summary account of the subject of the dispute, shall contain the invitation to the commission to take all necessary measures with a view to arrive at an amicable settlement.

If the request emanates from only one of the parties, notification thereof shall be made without delay to the other party.

ART. 7. Within 15 days from the date when the German Government or the Belgian Government shall have brought a dispute before the Permanent Conciliation Commission either party may, for the examination of the particular dispute, replace its commissioner by a person possessing special competence in the matter.

The party making use of this right shall immediately inform the other party; the latter shall in that case be entitled to take similar action within 15 days from the date when the notification reaches it.

ART. 8. The task of the Permanent Conciliation Commission shall be to elucidate questions in dispute, to collect with that object all necessary information by means of inquiry or otherwise, and to endeavor to bring the parties to an agreement. It may, after the case has been examined, inform the parties of the terms of settlement which seem suitable to it, and lay down a period within which they are to make their decision.

At the close of its labors the commission shall draw up a report stating, as the case may be, either that the parties have come to an agreement and, if need arises, the terms of the agreement, or that it has been impossible to effect a settlement.

The labors of the commission must, unless the parties otherwise agree, be terminated within six months from the day on which the commission shall have been notified of the dispute.

ART. 9. Failing any special provision to the contrary, the Permanent Conciliation Commission shall lay down its own procedure, which in any case must provide for both parties being heard. In regard to inquiries, the commission, unless it decides unanimously to the contrary, shall act in accordance with the provisions of Chapt. 3 (International Commissions of Inquiry) of the Hague convention of October 18, 1907, for the pacific settlement of international disputes.

ART. 10. The Permanent Conciliation Commission shall meet, in the absence of agreement by the parties to the contrary, at a place selected by its president.

ART. 11. The labors of the Permanent Conciliation Commission are not public, except when a decision to that effect has been taken by the commission with the consent of the parties.

ART. 12. The parties shall be represented before the Permanent Conciliation Commission by agents, whose duty it shall be to act as intermediary between them and the commission; they may, moreover, be assisted by counsel and experts appointed by them for that purpose, and request that all persons whose evidence appears to them useful should be heard. The commission, on its side, shall be entitled to request oral explanations from the agents, counsel and experts of the two parties, as well as from all persons it may think useful to summon with the consent of their Government.

ART. 13. Unless otherwise provided in the present convention, the decisions of the Permanent Conciliation Commission shall be taken by a majority.

ART. 14. The German and Belgian Governments undertake to facilitate the labors of the Permanent Conciliation Commission, and particularly to supply it, to the greatest possible extent, with all relevant documents and information, as well as to use the means at their disposal to allow it to proceed in their territory and in accordance with their law to the summoning and hearing of witnesses or experts, and to visit the localities in question.

ART. 15. During the labors of the Permanent Conciliation Commission each commissioner shall receive salary, the amount of which shall be fixed by agreement between the German and Belgian Governments, each of which shall contribute an equal share.

ART. 16. In the event of no amicable agreement being reached before the Permanent Conciliation Commission the dispute shall be submitted by means of a special agreement either to the Permanent Court of International Justice under the conditions and according to the procedure laid down by its Statute or to an arbitral tribunal under the conditions and according to the procedure laid down by the Hague convention of October 18, 1907, for the pacific settlement of international disputes.

If the parties can not agree on the terms of the special agreement after a month's notice, one or other of them may bring the dispute before the Permanent Court of International Justice by means of an application.

Part II

ART. 17. All questions on which the German and Belgian Governments shall differ without being able to reach an amicable solution by means of the normal methods of diplomacy the settlement of which can not be attained by means of a judicial decision as provided in Art. 1 of the present convention, and for the settlement of which no procedure has been laid down by other conventions in force between the parties, shall be submitted to the Permanent Conciliation Commission, whose duty it shall be to propose to the parties an acceptable solution and in any case to present a report.

The procedure laid down in Arts. 6–15 of the present convention shall be applicable.

ART. 18. If the two parties have not reached an agreement within a month from the termination of the labors of the Permanent Conciliation Commission the question shall, at the request of either party, be brought before the Council of the League of Nations, which shall deal with it in accordance with Art. 15 of the Covenant of the League.

General Provisions.

ART. 19. In any case, and particularly if the question on which the parties differ arises out of acts already committed or on the point of commission, the Conciliation Commission or, if the latter has not been notified thereof, the arbitral tribunal or the Permanent Court of International Justice, acting in accordance with Art. 41 of its Statute, shall lay down within the shortest possible time the provisional measures to be adopted. It shall similarly be the duty of the Council of the League of Nations, if the question is brought before it, to insure that suitable provisional measures are taken. The German and Belgian Governments undertake respectively to accept such measures, to abstain from all measures likely to have a repercussion prejudicial to the execution of the decision or to the arrangements proposed by the Conciliation Commission or by the Council of the League of Nations, and in general to abstain from any sort of action whatsoever which may aggravate or extend the dispute.

ART. 20. The present convention continues applicable as between Germany and Belgium, even when other powers are also interested in the dispute.

ART. 21. The present convention shall be ratified. Ratifications shall be deposited at Geneva with the League of Nations at the same time as the ratifications of the treaty concluded this day between Germany, Belgium, France, Great Britain and Italy.

It shall enter into and remain in force under the same conditions as the said treaty.

The present convention, done in a single copy, shall be deposited in the archives of the League of Nations, the Secretary-General of which shall be requested to transmit certified copies to each of the two contracting Governments.

Done at Locarno, October 16, 1925.

> Str[esemann].
> E[mile] V[andervelde].

No. 4

ARBITRATION CONVENTION BETWEEN GERMANY AND FRANCE

The undersigned duly authorized,

Charged by their respective Governments to determine the methods by which, as provided in Art. 3 of the treaty concluded this day between Germany, Belgium, France, Great Britain and Italy, peaceful solution shall be attained of all questions which can not be settled amicably between Germany and France.

Have agreed as follows:

[Arts. 1–21, *mutatis mutandis*, correspond word for word with the text of the arbitration convention between Germany and Belgium.]

The present convention, done in a single copy, shall be deposited in the archives of the League of Nations, the Secretary-General of which shall be requested to transmit certified copies to each of the two contracting Governments.

Done at Locarno, October 16, 1925.

> Str[esemann].
> A. B[riand].

No. 5

ARBITRATION TREATY BETWEEN GERMANY AND POLAND.

The President of the German Empire and the President of the Polish Republic;

Equally resolved to maintain peace between Germany and Poland by assuring the peaceful settlement of differences which might arise between the two countries;

Declaring that respect for the rights established by treaty or resulting from the law of nations is obligatory for international tribunals;

Agreeing to recognize that the rights of a state can not be modified save with its consent;

And considering that sincere observance of the methods of peaceful settlement of international disputes permits of resolving without recourse to force questions which may become the cause of division between states;

Have decided to embody in a treaty their common intentions in this respect, and have named as their plenipotentiaries the following:

Who, having exchanged their full powers, found in good and due form, are agreed upon the following articles:

Part I.

Article 1. All disputes of every kind between Germany and Poland with regard to which the parties are in conflict as to their respective rights, and which it may not be possible to settle amicably by the normal methods of diplomacy, shall be submitted for decision either to an arbitral tribunal or to the Permanent Court of International Justice, as laid down hereafter. It is agreed that the disputes referred to above include in particular those mentioned in Art 13 of the Covenant of the League of Nations.

This provision does not apply to disputes arising out of events prior to the present treaty and belonging to the past.

Disputes for the settlement of which a special procedure is laid down in other conventions in force between the High Contracting Parties shall be settled in conformity with the provisions of those conventions.

Art. 2. Before any resort is made to arbitral procedure or to procedure before the Permanent Court of International Justice, the dispute may, by agreement between the parties, be submitted with a view to amicable settlement, to a permanent international commission, styled the Permanent Conciliation Commission, constituted in accordance with the present treaty.

Art. 3. In the case of a dispute the occasion of which, according to the municipal law of one of the parties, falls within the competence of the national courts of such party, the matter in dispute shall not be submitted to the procedure laid down in the present treaty until a judgment with final effect has been pronounced, within a reasonable time, by the competent national judicial authority.

ART. 4. The Permanent Conciliation Commission mentioned in Art. 2 shall be composed of five members, who shall be appointed as follows, that is to say: The High Contracting Parties shall each nominate a commissioner chosen from among their respective nationals, and shall appoint, by common agreement, the three other commissioners from among the nationals of third powers; those three commissioners must be of different nationalities, and the High Contracting Parties shall appoint the president of the commission from among them.

The commissioners are appointed for three years, and their mandate is renewable. Their appointment shall continue until their replacement, and in any case until the termination of the work in hand at the moment of the expiry of their mandate.

Vacancies which may occur as a result of death, resignation or any other cause shall be filled within the shortest possible time in the manner fixed for the nominations.

ART. 5. The Permanent Conciliation Commission shall be constituted within three months from the entry into force of the present convention.

If the nomination of the commissioners to be appointed by common agreement should not have taken place within the said period, or, in the case of the filling of a vacancy, within three months from the time when the seat falls vacant, the President of the Swiss Confederation shall, in the absence of other agreement, be requested to make the necessary appointments.

ART. 6. The Permanent Conciliation Commission shall be informed by means of a request addressed to the president by the two parties acting in agreement, or, in the absence of such agreement, by one or other of the parties.

The request, after having given a summary account of the subject of the dispute, shall contain the invitation to the commission to take all necessary measures with a view to arrive at an amicable settlement. If the request emanates from only one of the parties, notification thereof shall be made without delay to the other party.

ART. 7. Within 15 days from the date when one of the High Contracting Parties shall have brought a dispute before the Permanent Conciliation Commission, either party may, for the examination of the particular dispute, replace its commissioner by a person possessing special competence in the matter.

The party making use of this right shall immediately inform the other party; the latter shall in that case be entitled to take similar action within 15 days from the date when the notification reaches it.

ART. 8. The task of the Permanent Conciliation Commission shall be to elucidate questions in dispute, to collect with that object all necessary information by means of inquiry or otherwise, and to endeavor to bring the parties to an agreement. It may, after the case has been examined, inform the parties of the terms of settlement which seem suitable to it, and lay down a period within which they are to make their decision.

At the close of its labors the commission shall draw up a report stating, as the case may be, either that the parties have come to an agreement and, if need arises, the terms of the agreement, or that it has been impossible to effect a settlement.

The labors of the commission must, unless the parties otherwise agree, be terminated within six months from the day on which the commission shall have been notified of the dispute.

ART. 9. Failing any special provision to the contrary, the Permanent Conciliation Commission shall lay down its own procedure, which in any case must provide for both parties being heard. In regard to inquiries, the commission, unless it decides unanimously to the contrary, shall act in accordance with the provisions of Chap. 3 (International Commissions of Inquiry) of the Hague convention of October 18, 1907, for the pacific settlement of international disputes.

ART. 10. The Permanent Conciliation Commission shall meet, in the absence of agreement by the parties to the contrary, at a place selected by its president.

ART. 11. The labors of the Permanent Conciliation Commission are not public except when a decision to that effect has been taken by the commission with the consent of the parties.

ART. 12. The parties shall be represented before the Permanent Conciliation Commission by agents, whose duty it shall be to act as intermediary between them and the commission; they may, moreover, be assisted by counsel and experts appointed by them for that purpose, and request that all persons whose evidence appears to them useful should be heard. The commission on its side shall be entitled to request oral explanations from the agents, counsel and experts of the two parties, as well as from all persons it may think useful to summon with the consent of their Government.

ART. 13. Unless otherwise provided in the present treaty the decisions of the Permanent Conciliation Commission shall be taken by a majority.

ART. 14. The High Contracting Parties undertake to facilitate the labors of the Permanent Conciliation Commission, and particularly to supply it to the greatest possible extent with all relevant documents and information, as well as to use the means at their disposal to allow it to proceed in their territory and in accordance with their law to the summoning and hearing of witnesses or experts, and to visit the localities in question.

ART. 15. During the labors of the Permanent Conciliation Commission each Commissioner shall receive salary, the amount of which shall be fixed by agreement between the High Contracting Parties, each of which shall contribute an equal share.

ART. 16. In the event of no amicable agreement being reached before the Permanent Conciliation Commission, the dispute shall be submitted by means of a special agreement either to the Permanent Court of International Justice under the conditions and according to the procedure laid down by its Statute or to an arbitral tribunal under the conditions and according to the procedure laid down by the Hague convention of October 18, 1907, for the pacific settlement of international disputes.

If the parties can not agree on the terms of the special agreement after a month's notice, one or other of them may bring the dispute before the Permanent Court of International Justice by means of an application.

PART II

ART. 17. All questions on which the German and Polish Governments shall differ without being able to reach an amicable solution by means of the normal methods of diplomacy the settlement of which can not be attained by means of a judicial decision as provided in Art. 1 of the present treaty, and for the settlement of which no procedure has been laid down by other conventions in force between the parties shall be submitted to the Permanent Conciliation Commission, whose duty it shall be to propose to the parties an acceptable solution and in any case to present a report.

The procedure laid down in Arts. 6–15 of the present treaty shall be applicable.

ART. 18. If the two parties have not reached an agreement within a month from the termination of the labors of the Permanent Conciliation Commission, the question shall, at the request of either party, be brought before the Council of the League of Nations, which shall deal with it in accordance with Art. 15 of the Covenant of the League.

General Provisions

ART. 19. In any case, and particularly if the question on which the parties differ arises out of acts already committed or on the point of commission, the Conciliation Commission or, if the latter has not been notified thereof, the arbitral tribunal or the Permanent Court of International Justice, acting in accordance with Art. 41 of its Statute, shall lay down within the shortest possible time the provisional measures to be adopted. It shall similarly be the duty of the Council of the League of Nations, if the question is brought before it, to insure that suitable provisional measures are taken. The High Contracting Parties undertake respectively to accept such measures, to abstain from all measures likely to have a repercussion prejudicial to the execution of the decision or to the arrangements proposed by the Conciliation Commission or by the Council of the League of Nations, and in general to abstain from any sort of action whatsoever which may aggravate or extend the dispute.

ART. 20. The present treaty continues applicable as between the High Contracting Parties even when other powers are also interested in the dispute.

ART. 21. The present treaty, which is in conformity with the Covenant of the League of Nations, shall not in any way affect the rights and obligations of the High Contracting Parties as

Members of the League of Nations and shall not be interpreted as restricting the duty of the League to take whatever action may be deemed wise and effectual to safeguard the peace of the world.

ART. 22. The present treaty shall be ratified. Ratifications shall be deposited at Geneva with the League of Nations at the same time as the ratifications of the treaty concluded this day between Germany, Belgium, France, Great Britain and Italy.

It shall enter into and remain in force under the same conditions as the said treaty.

The present treaty, done in a single copy, shall be deposited in the archives of the League of Nations, the Secretary-General of which shall be requested to transmit certified copies to each of the High Contracting Parties.

Done at Locarno, October 16, 1925.

STR[ESEMANN].
A. S[KRZYNSKI].

No. 6

ARBITRATION TREATY BETWEEN GERMANY AND CZECHOSLOVAKIA

The President of the German Empire and the President of the Czechoslovak Republic;

Equally resolved to maintain peace between Germany and Czechoslovakia by assuring the peaceful settlement of differences which might arise between the two countries;

Declaring that respect for the rights established by treaty or resulting from the law of nations is obligatory for international tribunals;

Agreeing to recognize that the rights of a state can not be modified save with its consent;

And considering that sincere observance of the methods of peaceful settlement of international disputes permits of resolving, without recourse to force, questions which may become the cause of division between states;

Have decided to embody in a treaty their common intentions in this respect, and have named as their plenipotentiaries, the following:

Who, having exchanged their full powers, found in good and due form, are agreed upon the following articles:

[Arts. 1–22, *mutatis mutandis*, correspond word for word with the text of the arbitration convention between Germany and Poland.]

The present treaty, done in a single copy, shall be deposited in the archives of the League of Nations, the Secretary-General of which shall be requested to transmit certified copies to each of the High Contracting Parties.

Done at Locarno, October 16, 1925.

STR[ESEMANN].   DR. B[ENEŠ].

No. 7

TREATY BETWEEN FRANCE AND POLAND

The President of the French Republic and the President of the Polish Republic;

Equally desirous to see Europe spared from war by a sincere observance of the undertakings arrived at this day with a view to the maintenance of general peace;

Have resolved to guarantee their benefits to each other reciprocally by a treaty concluded within the framework of the Covenant of the League of Nations and of the treaties existing between them;

And have to this effect nominated for their plenipotentiaries:

Who, after having exchanged their full powers, found in good and due form, have agreed on the following provisions:

ART. 1. In the event of Poland or France suffering from a failure to observe the undertakings arrived at this day between them and Germany with a view to the maintenance of general peace, France, and reciprocally Poland, acting in application of Art. 16 of the Covenant of the League of Nations, undertake to lend each other immediately aid and assistance, if such a failure is accompanied by an unprovoked recourse to arms.

In the event of the Council of the League of Nations, when dealing with a question brought before it in accordance with the said undertakings, being unable to succeed in making its report accepted by all its Members other than the representatives of the parties to the dispute, and in the event of Poland or France being attacked without provocation, France, or reciprocally Poland, acting in application of Art. 15, par. 7, of the Covenant of the League of Nations, will immediately lend aid and assistance.

ART. 2. Nothing in the present treaty shall affect the rights and obligations of the High Contracting Parties as Members of the League of Nations, or shall be interpreted as restricting the duty of the League to take whatever action may be deemed wise and effectual to safeguard the peace of the world.

ART. 3. The present treaty shall be registered with the League of Nations, in accordance with the Covenant.

ART. 4. The present treaty shall be ratified. The ratifications will be deposited at Geneva with the League of Nations at the same time as the ratification of the treaty concluded this day between Germany, Belgium, France, Great Britain and Italy, and the ratification of the treaty concluded at the same time between Germany and Poland.

It will enter into force and remain in force under the same conditions as the said treaties.

The present treaty done in a single copy will be deposited in the archives of the League of Nations, and the Secretary-General of the League will be requested to transmit certified copies to each of the High Contracting Parties.

Done at Locarno, October 16, 1925.

A. B[RIAND].   AL. S[KRZYNSKI].

No. 8

TREATY BETWEEN FRANCE AND CZECHOSLOVAKIA

The President of the French Republic and the President of the Czechoslovak Republic;

Equally desirous to see Europe spared from war by a sincere observance of the undertakings arrived at this day with a view to the maintenance of general peace;

Have resolved to guarantee their benefits to each other reciprocally by a treaty concluded within the framework of the Covenant of the League of Nations and of the treaties existing between them;

And have to this effect, nominated for their plenipotentiaries:

Who, after having exchanged their full powers, found in good and due form, have agreed on the following provisions:

[Arts. 1–4, *mutatis mutandis*, correspond word for word with the text of the preceding treaty between France and Poland.]

The present treaty done in a single copy will be deposited in the archives of the League of Nations, and the Secretary-General of the League will be requested to transmit certified copies to each of the High Contracting Parties.

Done at Locarno, October 16, 1925.

A. B[RIAND].   DR. E. B[ENEŠ].

No. 9

COLLECTIVE NOTE TO GERMANY REGARDING ARTICLE 16 OF THE COVENANT OF THE LEAGUE OF NATIONS

The German delegation has requested certain explanations in regard to Article 16 of the Covenant of the League of Nations.

We are not in a position to speak in the name of the League, but in view of the discussions which have already taken place in the Assembly and in the commissions of the League of Nations, and after the explanations which have been exchanged between ourselves, we do not hesitate to inform you of the interpretation which, in so far as we are concerned, we place upon Article 16.

In accordance with that interpretation the obligations resulting from the said Article on the Members of the League must be understood to mean that each State Member of the League is bound to co-operate loyally and effectively in support of the Covenant and in resistance to any act of aggression to an extent which is compatible with its military situation and takes its geographical position into account.

INDEX

Adatci, Minéitciro, representative of Japan at Geneva, quoted, 194, 196.

Article VIII of League Covenant, recognizes relation between national safety and reduction of armaments, 153.

Aggressor State, as defined in Covenant, Draft Treaty, and Geneva Protocol, 199; determination in Draft Treaty, 175; in Protocol, 200; juridical test advocated by Lange, 162; by Ramsay MacDonald, 185; embodied in Draft Treaty by American Group, 187.

Albania, on amendment to Article X proposed by Canada, 253.

Alvarez, Alejendro, representative of Chile at Geneva, quoted, 104, 112.

American Institute of International Law, Declarations of, 8, 9.

American Journal of International Law, cited, A. J. I. L.

American Society of International Law, Root's address, 9.

Andrade, Freire de, representative of Portugal at Geneva, quoted, 99.

Arbitration, universal compulsory: attitude of Great Britain and United States, 238-240; basic principle of Geneva Protocol, 38; condition precedent to "outlawry of war," 40; essential to a genuine society of nations, 237; in Geneva Protocol, 189, 192.

Arfa-ed Dovleh, Prince, representative of Persia at Geneva, quoted, 112, 118.

Article XVI, amendment proposed at First Assembly by Norway, Sweden and Denmark, 135; amendments adopted by Second Assembly, 138-139; amendment adopted at Fifth Assembly, 141; antecedents of movement to amend, 30; as amplified by Geneva Protocol, 203-205; as interpreted in note to Germany by Powers at Locarno, 340; changes proposed by Scandinavian states at Peace Conference, 125-126; expresses principle of sanctions, 24; interpretative resolutions voted by Second Assembly, 147; report of Third Committee, Second Assembly, 137, 139, 140, 143-146; resolutions adopted by First Assembly, 133, 135. See also Sanctions of League Covenant.

Article X, amendment proposed by Canada at Third Assembly, 102-103; Cecil draft, 73; criticism by Root, 89; discussion by Second Assembly, 98-101; by Third Assembly, 103-105; by Fourth Assembly, 106-119; interpretative resolution voted by Fourth Assembly, 117; interpretative resolution proposed by League Committee on Amendments, 97; Lansing's substitute, 75; origins of, 66-75; proposal of Canada to delete, 28; recognition of claim of state to existence and security, 23; Report of League Commission of Jurists, 93-95; and of Committee on Amendments, 95-97; reservations of United States Senate, 78-83; sets up legal obligation for League Members, 24, 85; Wilson's interpretation, 76; his original draft, 72. See also Woodrow Wilson.

Australia, observations on Geneva Protocol, 310.

Index

Babinski, L., representative of Poland at Geneva, quoted, 104.

Baker, Philip, cited, 66, 190, 191; quoted, 74.

Baker, Ray Stannard, cited, 67, 73, 122, 125, 236; quoted, 66, 71.

Barthélemy, Joseph, representative of France at Geneva, quoted, 103, 111, 114, 118.

Belgium, invasion by Germany focused attention on security problem, 64; observations on Resolution XIV, 166, 266; on amendment to Article X proposed by Canada, 254; supports Draft Treaty, 181.

Benes, Edouard, representative of Czechoslovakia at Geneva, quoted, 132, 183.

Borah, Senator William E., discussion with President Wilson on obligations of Article X, 77.

Borden, Sir Robert, opposes Article X at Peace Conference, 88.

Branting, Hjalmar, representative of Sweden at Geneva, quoted, 180.

Briand, Aristide, 211.

Brierly, J. L., quoted, 6, 242.

British, attitude toward universal compulsory arbitration, 208, 238-239; guarantee of arbitration conventions between Germany and Western neighbors, 214; observations on Draft Treaty, 34, 285; on Geneva Protocol, 38, 40, 207-210, 306; oppose French plan for sanctions of Covenant, 124; reservation on jurisdiction of Permanent Court under Geneva Protocol, 190; seizure of Danish fleet, 56.

Brown, P. M., quoted, 47.

Bryce, Viscount, quoted, 1.

Bulgaria, on amendment to Article X proposed by Canada, 257.

Canada, amendment to Article X proposed at Third Assembly, 102, 103; observations on Draft Treaty, 35, 289; on Geneva Protocol, 312; on Resolution XIV, 268; opposes Article X at Peace Conference, 88; proposal to delete Article X, 91.

Cecil, Lord Robert, draft of Article X, 73; on obligation of League Members under Article XVI, 127; resolutions on disarmament and security, 33, 154; quoted, 131.

Chamberlain, Sir Austen, reports opinion of British Government on Geneva Protocol, 38, 40, 207-210.

China, on amendment to Article X proposed by Canada, 257.

Cohn, Georg, cited, 26.

Czechoslovakia, observations on Draft Treaty, 290; on Resolution XIV, 268.

Davis, Arthur Kyle, Jr., acknowledgement to, x.

Denmark, amendment to Article XVI at First Assembly, 135; observations on Resolution XIV, 167, 169, 269; on sanctions of the Covenant, 125, 126.

Dickinson, Sir Willoughby, representative of Great Britain at Geneva, quoted, 114.

Dickinson, E. D., cited, 44.

Disarmament, associated with security problem in Resolution XIV, 163; Cecil Resolutions, 33, 160, 161.

Dissesco, M., representative of Roumania at Geneva, quoted, 103.

Doctrine of Necessity, applied by England, 56; and Germany, 59; by Japan, 58; and the United States, 60.

Doherty, C. J., representative of Canada at Geneva, quoted, 100, 102; submitted memorandum at Peace Conference opposing Article X, 88.

INDEX

Domestic Questions, as a source of international disputes, 242; authority of League Council to discuss, 197; British attitude, 208, 239; exempted from settlement by League Council, 192; Japanese proposals at Fifth Assembly, 194; need of international jurisdiction for, 243; under Geneva Protocol, 192-197.

Draft Treaty of Mutual Assistance, embodied principles of Resolution XIV, 33; extracts from report of Third Committee, Fourth Assembly, 173-174; general provisions, 175-177; reasons for rejection, 36, 181.

Erich, R. W., representative of Finland at Geneva, quoted, 111.

Existence, right to of state to; declaration by American Institute of International Law, 9; not a protected interest, 10; stated as a fundamental principle of international law, 10; under what conditions forfeited, 61; recognized through Article X of Covenant, 24.

Fenwick, C. G., quoted, 43, 50.
Fielding, W. S., representative of Canada at Geneva, quoted, 158.
Finch, George A., cited, 81.
Fisher, H. A. L., representative of Great Britain at Geneva, quoted, 131, 157.
Fock, M., representative of Holland at Geneva, quoted, 131, 133.
France, alliance with Czechoslovakia and Poland, 225; observations on Resolution XIV, 165, 166, 271; on amendment to Article X proposed by Canada, 257; opposition to Canadian proposal to delete Article X, 29; plan for sanctions of Covenant, 122-124; rejection of amendment to Article XVI, 141; reply to German proposal for Rhineland Pact, 215; support of Geneva Protocol, 211.

Garner, J. W., quoted, 5.
Geneva Protocol, amendments proposed by Japanese delegation, 194; basic principle of, 38; definition of aggressor state, 198; domestic questions, 192; duty of League Council on domestic questions, 196; general features of, 188; jurisdiction of Permanent Court of Justice, 189-191; methods for identifying aggressor state, 199-201; objections offered by British Government, 207-210; peaceful procedure, 192; sanctions, 203; states signatory to, 206; underlying principles essential to genuine society of nations, 237.

Germany, invasion of Belgium, 8, 57-59; memorandum to France on Rhineland Pact, 211-212; observations on Draft Treaty, 292.
Gouin, Sir Lomer, representative of Canada to Geneva, cited, 106.
Greece, on amendment to Article X proposed by Canada, 259.
Grey, Sir Edward, defense of British and French military and naval plans prior to 1914, 157.

Hall, W. E., quoted, 10, 11, 17, 19, 52, 55, 57.
Hays, Will H., letter from Elihu Root on Article X, 89.
Herriot, Edouard, representative of France at Geneva, quoted, 185.
Hershey, A. S., quoted, 46, 58.
Hill, David Jayne, quoted, 18, 20.
Hitchcock, Senator Gilbert M., reservation on Article X, 81; letter from President Wilson, quoted, 68.
House, Colonel E. M., draft of Covenant, 71; on origins of Article X, 69.

Hudson, Manley, O., cited, 30.
Hungary, on amendment to Article X proposed by Canada, 260.
Hurst, Sir Cecil, member League Commission of Jurist for interpretation of Article X, 92; quoted, 197.
Hurst-Miller Draft of Covenant, 72, 74.
Hyde, C. C., quoted, 15, 23, 61-62.

Institute of Politics, Williamstown, Bryce lectures, 1.
International Blockade Committee, report of, 136, 145.
International Law, defects, 5, 9; demands for reconstruction, 6, 22; effects of League Covenant on, 22, 23, 27, 120; recognizes right of state to resort to war, 17; sanctions, 12, 13; weakness in affording security to the state, 60.
Irish Free State, observations on Geneva Protocol, 313.
Italy, observations on Draft Treaty, 293; on proposal of Canada to amend Article X, 260.

Japan, amendments to Geneva Protocol, 194; observations on Draft Treaty, 294; on application of League procedure to domestic questions, 194; violation of Korean neutrality, 58.
Jaurès, Jean, proposed juridical test for designation of aggressor state, 162.
Jugoslavia, observations on Draft Treaty, 294.

Komarnicki, Titus, cited, 66.
Krabbe, H., quoted, 61-62.

Lange, C. L., representative of Norway at Geneva, quoted, 13, 21, 122, 159, 162, 179, 235.
Lansing, Robert, differs from President Wilson over form of territorial guarantee, 74, 75; proposed self-denying covenant, 75; quoted, 73, 75.

Lapointe, Ernest, representative of Canada at Geneva, 102.
Latané, John H., acknowledgment to, ix.
Lawrence, T. J., quoted, 46.
League of Nations Covenant, antecedents of, 13; breach of, 31, 139, 148; methods of peaceful procedure, 26; relation of provisions to principles of international law, 22, 120; results of evolution, 28; response of states to, 26, 42, 228.
League to Enforce Peace, Wilson's address, 21.
Lebrun, A. F., representative of France at Geneva, quoted, 171.
Limburg, J., representative of Netherlands, at Geneva, quoted, 116.
Locarno Agreements, antecedents in Covenant, Draft Treaty, and Geneva Protocol, 226; application in Eastern Europe, 224; arbitration conventions, 222, 224; correspondence preceding, 211-219; essential principles, 219, 226; French alliance with Poland and Czechoslovakia, 225, 226; Permanent Conciliation Commissions, 223, 224; Permanent Court of Justice, 223; territorial guarantee, 219; Treaty of Mutual Guarantee, 219-221.
Lodge, Senator Henry Cabot, attitude toward Article X, 82, 84; reservation on Article X, 83.
Loudon, J., representative of Netherlands at Geneva, quoted, 192.

MacDonald, Ramsay, quoted, 183, 184.
Manolesco-Ramniceano, representative of Roumania at Geneva, quoted, 111.
Miller, David Hunter, 74.
Miller-Auchincloss, memorandum on affirmative guarantee in Covenant, 74; proposed self-denying covenant, 75.

INDEX

Moch, Gaston, proposed juridical test to designate aggressor state, 162.

Motta, Guiseppe, representative of Switzerland at Geneva, quoted, 105.

Munch, P., cited, 31; quoted, 127.

Negulesco, Demetre, representative of Roumania at Geneva, quoted, 133.

Netherlands, observations on Resolution XIV, 167, 168, 272; on amendment to Article X proposed by Canada, 261.

Neutrality, ethical justification of, 14; modified by Article XVI of Covenant, 25; precepts of natural law writers, 16; under League Covenant, 25.

Nippold, Otfried, quoted, 16.

New Zealand, observations on Geneva Protocol, 316; on Permanent Court and domestic questions, 39.

Norway, observations on Resolution XIV, 169, 274; submits amendment to Article XVI at First Assembly, 135.

Oldenburg, Andreas, representative of Denmark at Geneva, quoted, 159.

Oppenheim, L., quoted, 3, 41, 48, 49.

Panama, opposition to amendment to Article X, 118.

Peaslee, A. J., quoted, 10.

Permanent Advisory Commission, composition of, 154.

Permanent Court of International Justice, British attitude toward compulsory jurisdiction, 39; jurisdiction under Geneva Protocol, 189, 190; under Locarno treaties, 223.

Persia, on amendment to Article X proposed by Canada, 261.

Phillimore, G. G., quoted, 14.

Phillimore, Lord, draft of Covenant, 71.

Phillipson, Coleman, quoted, 19.

Poland, observations on Resolution XIV, 275; on amendment to Article X proposed by Canada, 262.

Politis, Nicholas, representative of Greece at Geneva, quoted, 188, 201, 202.

Portugal, on amendment to Article X proposed by Canada, 264.

Pound, Roscoe, quoted, 27; cited, 44.

Rappard, William E., quoted, 37, 165.

Reeves, J. S., quoted, 6.

Réquin, Colonel, plan for mutual assistance, 170.

Resolution XIV of Third Assembly, expresses interdependence of disarmament and security, 33; summary of opinions of Government on, 172; text of, 163.

Reynald, M., representative of France at Geneva, quoted, 141.

Rivas-Vicuna, M., representative of Chile at Geneva, quoted, 160.

Rivier, quoted, 45.

Roosevelt, Theodore, advocates guarantee for safety of small states, 65; opinion on German invasion of Belgium, 60.

Root, Elihu, address before American Society of International Law, 9, 12; letter to Will H. Hays proposing amendment to Article X, 89.

Rolin, H., representative of Belgium at Geneva, cited, 110; quoted, 99, 104, 109, 151.

Roumania, on proposal of Canada to amend Article X, 265.

Roxburg, R. S., cited, 12.

Sanctions of League Covenant, advocated in unofficial programs for a League, 13; attitude of Scandinavian states at Peace Conference, 30, 125; conflict of Anglo-Saxon and Continental viewpoints at Peace Conference, 124; derived from British draft of

Covenant, 125; embodied in Article XVI, 24; French plan, 123-124; memorandum of Secretary-General of League, 128; report of International Blockade Committee, 136; utility of, 230, 234. See also Article XVI.

Schanzer, Carlo, representative of Italy at Geneva, quoted, 131, 133, 146.

Scialoja, Vittorio, representative of Italy at Geneva, quoted, 113.

Scott, J. B., cited, 8, 58, 59.

Self-Preservation, right of state to: doctrine as stated by natural law writers, 45; by Hall, 52; by Hershey, 46; by Lawrence, 46; by Oppenheim, 48, 49; by Rivier, 45; by Westlake, 54; by Wheaton, 45.

Senate, United States, reservations on Article X, 80-83.

Shotwell, James T., cited, 170.

Spain, on amendment to Article X proposed by Canada, 265.

States, absolute rights of, 44, 45, 47, 48.

State of Nature, nations in condition of, 1, 2.

Struycken, A. A. H., cited, 88.

Temperley, H. W. V., History of Peace Conference at Paris, cited, 66, 91; quoted, 64, 67, 124.

Temporary Mixed Commission, composition, 154; adopts Cecil proposals, 154.

Toynbee, A. J., cited, 35, quoted, 181, 185, 189.

Unden, Oesten, representative of Sweden at Geneva, quoted, 159.

Underwood, Senator Oscar A., resolution for ratification of Versailles treaty rejected, 81.

Union of South Africa, observations on Geneva Protocol, 318.

Urrutia, F. J., representative of Columbia at Geneva, 101.

Vattel, E., cited, 44; quoted, 2.

Venezuela, observations on Resolution XIV, 275.

War, outlawry of, 40; purpose of Geneva Protocol to annihilate, 38; right of state to resort to, 17; restraints on introduced by Covenant, 26.

Westlake, J., quoted, 16, 47, 54, 56.

Wheaton, H., quoted, 45.

Winiarski, B., representative of Poland at Geneva, quoted, 115.

Willoughby, W. W., acknowledgment to, ix; quoted, 2, 4, 17, 86.

Wilson, Woodrow, accepts Hitchcock reservation on Article X, 82; address before Pan-American Scientific Congress, 68; and League to Enforce Peace, 70; United States Senate, January, 1917, 71; advocates guarantee of territorial integrity and independence for states of Western Hemisphere, 69; conference with Senate Foreign Relations Committee, 75-77; declares support of United States for an association of nations, 21; defends Article X on Western tour, 79; divergence of judgment from advisers at Paris on form of territorial guarantee, 74-75; drew inspiration for Article X from American documents, 66; first draft of Article X contained provision for future territorial changes, 72; interpretation of Article X before Senate Foreign Relations Committee, 76; opposes French plan for international army, 125; primarily responsible for Article X, 67; regards Article X as essence of Americanism, 67; text of letter to Senator Hitchcock on Article X, 249-253.

Wuertemberg, Marks von, representative of Sweden at Geneva, quoted, 116.